LAW AND NEURODIVERSITY

LAW AND NEURODIVERSITY
Youth with Autism and the Juvenile Justice Systems in Canada and the United States

Dana Lee Baker, Laurie A. Drapela,
and Whitney Littlefield

UBCPress · Vancouver · Toronto

© UBC Press 2020

All rights reserved. No part of this publication may be reproduced, stored in a retrieval system, or transmitted, in any form or by any means, without prior written permission of the publisher, or, in Canada, in the case of photocopying or other reprographic copying, a licence from Access Copyright, www.accesscopyright.ca.

29 28 27 26 25 24 23 22 21 20   5 4 3 2 1

Printed in Canada on FSC-certified ancient-forest-free paper (100% post-consumer recycled) that is processed chlorine- and acid-free.

Library and Archives Canada Cataloguing in Publication

Title: Law and neurodiversity : youth with Autism and the juvenile justice systems in Canada and the United States / Dana Lee Baker, Laurie A. Drapela, and Whitney Littlefield.
Names: Baker, Dana Lee, author. | Drapela, Laurie A., author. | Littlefield, Whitney, author.
Description: Includes bibliographical references and index.
Identifiers: Canadiana (print) 20200196804 | Canadiana (ebook) 20200196847 | ISBN 9780774861366 (hardcover) | ISBN 9780774861380 (PDF) | ISBN 9780774861397 (EPUB) | ISBN 9780774861403 (Kindle)
Subjects: LCSH: Autistic youth — Legal status, laws, etc. — United States. | LCSH: Autistic youth — Legal status, laws, etc. — Canada. | LCSH: Juvenile justice, Administration of — United States. | LCSH: Juvenile justice, Administration of — Canada. | LCSH: Autism — Government policy — United States. | LCSH: Autism — Government policy — Canada.
Classification: LCC KF480.5.A94 B35 2020 | DDC 346.7301/30874 — dc23

Canadä

UBC Press gratefully acknowledges the financial support for our publishing program of the Government of Canada (through the Canada Book Fund), and the British Columbia Arts Council.

Printed and bound in Canada by Friesens
Set in Warnock Pro and Futura by Apex CoVantage, LLC
Copy editor: Judy Phillips
Proofreader: Sophie Pouyanne
Cover designer: Gabi Proctor

UBC Press
The University of British Columbia
2029 West Mall
Vancouver, BC V6T 1Z2
www.ubcpress.ca

For Mary Ellen Harvey Baker and Donald Arthur Baker, for their commitment to autistic people and because the story of this book began in no small part the day they met at the University of British Columbia more than fifty years ago ... and for all who live, work, and interact with the juvenile justice systems in North America who go too often forgotten or ignored. We hope the pages that follow honour and, ultimately, improve your lived experiences.

Contents

List of Figures and Table / ix

Acknowledgments / xi

1 Autism, Disability Policy, and the Juvenile Justice System in Canada and the United States / 3

2 Autism, Delinquency, and Juvenile Rights / 18

3 Autism on Trial / 46

4 This Kid Is Different: Health Care Management and Developing Empathy / 75

5 Zero Tolerance for Difference: The Role of the Education System in Defining Delinquency / 102

6 The Social World of Juvenile Custody / 130

7 Transitioning beyond Juvenile Justice Systems / 153

8 Looking Forward: Conclusions, Recommendations, and Next Steps / 176

Glossary / 189

Caselaw and Legislation / 197

References / 199

Index / 227

Figures and Table

Figures
1 Chapter 2 summary / 45
2 Chapter 3 summary / 74
3 Chapter 4 summary / 101
4 Chapter 5 summary / 129
5 Chapter 6 summary / 152
6 Chapter 7 summary / 175

Table
1 Case process terminology in criminal and juvenile systems / 27

Acknowledgments

The authors of this book thank first and foremost all who work in the juvenile justice system on a day-to-day basis. This work lies beyond the comprehension and attention of far too many in our societies. Maintaining not only a daily commitment but a focus on hope, justice, and progress involves tremendous challenges, often Herculean effort, and truly astonishing amounts of emotional labour. Our youth, our communities, and our societies benefit every day from your work in the juvenile justice system. We salute you.

Dana Lee Baker is eternally grateful to her family, including friends who are family. An abundance of blessings precludes listing all names of my beloveds. My parents, Don and Mary Baker, set and maintained high expectations for their children while also teaching us humour in the face of both daily life and adversity. This particular (and sometimes peculiar) parenting gave us each the opportunity to develop resilience. Both Don and Mary learned much about this approach to life from their own parents (Winona and Art Baker, and Helenita and Bob Harvey). My siblings, Alan, Brian, and Cate, are dearest companions, even in their always regretted absences, however long that might be. I am also lucky to have a diverse collection of cousins dear to my heart and unfailingly supportive of my work – especially Carmen Seki (whose strength and intelligence are ever-astonishing), Michelle Wardle (a fraternal twin cousin), and Scot Smith (who just gets me, no matter what). Of course, these cousins were all born of amazing aunts and uncles: John Smith, Val Smith, Doug Baker, Pamela Edwards, Helen Baker, and Steven Baker. The ones wearing my heart on their sleeves – my children Kalai Harvey Baker and Dawn Mary Catherine Baker – are the reason for everything and the motivation for much of my work. Mama loves you no matter what, as much as space and time all combined. My opportunity to learn about love, laughter, and light have come from thus far seventeen foster children – regardless of for how short or long a time they were in my home. During the writing of this book, Kameron (aka "The Cuttlefish") spent the most time in my home and delighted me and many of my friends with his beautiful brilliance. Finally, I am grateful for the wide circle of students, colleagues, team members, fellow parents, and other friends populating my little corner of the world. Thank you for making life inordinately sublime.

Laurie A. Drapela feels lucky to have people in her life supporting and encouraging her efforts to be a mother, wife, daughter, sister, friend, scholar, mentor, and teacher. It is impossible for me to complete any labour such as this manuscript without the love and succour of my husband, Nick McRee, and daughter Margot Sophia McRee (Maggie). They are there for me when I am glorious and when I am ... not. Their unrelenting love and encouragement quite simply allow me to breathe and keep moving forward. My mother and father, AJ and Allie Drapela, taught me how to be strong, smart, and resilient by showing up in my early life every day, loving me, and providing shining examples of how family strength is sown and grows over time. My sister, Susan Drapela, showed me unconditional love and the beauty of a genuine Texas juke joint. Phil McRee and Donna Baron gave me the beauty of beach walks, glorious summer evening meals, and the blessing of being in their family. Mark C. Stafford showed me how to believe in myself as an intellectual simply by never questioning my ability to complete any endeavour to which I put my mind. Many women fight the shade of their self-doubts; finding a mentor in early adulthood who taught me to have pride in my intelligence and ideals greatly enhanced my quality of life. Faith Lutze picked up the baton and has been a mentor, friend, and fundamentally important force in helping me become a better human being. Finally, I express gratitude for all of the colleagues, students, and support staff in the Washington State University system who helped me transform from a fledgling faculty member to a seasoned street-level bureaucrat in academe. So many thanks must be shared to my community of women friends from all walks of life. I am gifted by your friendship and proud to be part of the positivity that keeps all of us keepin' on.

Acknowledgments xiii

Whitney Littlefield appreciates the unconditional support from her husband, Dylan. Writing this book on top of working two jobs cut into our free time to spend together and with our loved ones. Thank you for always understanding and being kind toward my career goals. I would also like to thank my parents, David and Mavis Hafer, for their positive example of how to juggle a million things at once and for encouraging me to set unprecedented goals for myself. It is with extreme fortune that I have two best friends, my brothers Nickolas Hafer and Samuel Hafer. I depend on you both so much for your humour, encouragement, and support, especially when I am acting as my own worst enemy. I could never forget my co-workers and bosses who have helped mentor, train, and guide me in my many different roles in juvenile justice. I especially want to thank Steve Jones and Steve Hogg for leading by example and believing in the people who work for you. It has been a privilege to be taken under your wings. Lastly, I want to thank every youth who I have the privilege to serve as a juvenile probation counsellor. Each and every one of you is special and has much to offer this world.

This book teems with insights derived from student effort and engagement with its creation. In particular we recognize the work of Yolanda Barragan and Adriana Huerta, two extremely promising students at California State University Channel Islands, who contributed to the post-peer review edits of the text and brought new perspectives to enrich the work. We are also very grateful to have worked with student collaborators engaged in the project as a result of faculty-directed research courses or course assignments (and in some cases both). We thank Isabella Acevedo, Katherine Almquist, Alicia Andring, Justin Aspon, Julian Avalos, Nikayla Banks, Ashlie Beed, Cody Bender, Michael Berry, Austin Bissel, Anna Boneski, Emily Boyd, Jennifer Brockmoller, Larry Burnham, Eveling Cabello Ramirez, Casey Chase, Steven Cooper, Silvia Czafit, Tyler Davis, Michael DeManti, Robert Doyle, Anthony Edmundson, Eric Gilcrease, Wendy Goolsby, Kevin Gordon, Andrea Grande, Naomi Grande, Travis Guernsey, Isabella Guetter, Connor Haggerty, Josh Hansen, Nicholas Hansen, Madison Harden, Billy Henry, Sydney Hickey, Dan Higgins Jr., Jessica Higgs, Amandrea Horton, Trent Hungate, Brady Jackman, Kazim Jafri Jackie Jones, Patricia Juan, Shaun Kent, David Kinsman, Tiffany Kolar, Derek Kyker, Mikayla LaFontaine, Thomas Loren, Tawny Maruhn, Cathleen McCormick, Grace McKnight, Julie Mercado, Maresa Miranda, Alexandra Moore, Ian Muck, Tonya Oyala, Chris Parker, Michael Perez, Justus Phelps, Ashmi Prasad Prakash, Radhika Raj, Chadd Reel, Nick Robbins, Jose Scott, Citlalli Silva-Rodriguez, Drew Sizemore, Hailey Smith, Lauren Smith, Bryan Stebbins, David Stevens,

Cathan Tautfest, Connor Thun, Max Vasilyev, Heather Williams, Michael Williams, Justin Wood, Michael Worman, and Liliya Zhukova for their passion, efforts, and energy. Watching how these students, many of whom are in or hope to pursue careers in the justice system, responded to and thought about the topics of this text both inspired and assisted tremendously with this project. Knowing that students such as these intend to enter criminal justice and related fields provide hope for us all.

The authors would like to thank our colleagues at California State University Channel Islands (CSUCI), Washington State University (WSU), and the many venues, ranging from the British Museum to the library of beers (McMenamins), which supported and played host to our work in progress. We are especially grateful for the financial support of the project provided by both CSUCI and WSU Vancouver. At CSUCI, Dana thanks especially Theresa Avila, Raquel Baker, Geoffrey Chase, Michelle Dean, Cynthia Flores, John Griffin, Andrea Grove, Tiina Itkonen, Sean Kelly, Vandana Kohli, Matthew Mendez, Jim Meriwether, Robin Mitchell, Kara Naidoo, and Jacqueline Reynoso. At WSU, we are especially grateful for those serving the School of Politics, Philosophy, and Public Affairs and the Department of Criminal Justice and Criminology on the Vancouver campus. At the time of this writing, our colleagues included Kathryn Dubois, Susan Finley, Jerry Goodstein, Katrina Leupp, Carolyn Long, Anthony Lopez, Alair MacLean, Clayton Mosher, Mark Stephan, Paul Thiers, and Tom Tripp. Additional WSU colleagues who were especially supportive of the project include Craig Hemmens, Faith Lutze, Karen Schmaling, and Mary Stohr.

Last, but far from least, this project would never have been completed without the support of Randy Schmidt, senior acquisitions editor at UBC Press. The road was long. The work was hard. We are so lucky to have had you by our side.

LAW AND NEURODIVERSITY

1

Autism, Disability Policy, and the Juvenile Justice System in Canada and the United States

Disability engages all aspects of human existence. Even so, the act of how disabilities interact with juvenile justice systems remains incompletely understood. People commonly lack awareness of the richness of disability history and of the complexities of disability politics. Too often, concern about disability in the juvenile justice systems proves to be minimal at best. Yet such circumstances are out of keeping with modern rights-based understandings of disability. They also fail to effectively advance juvenile justice policies and practices beyond punishment and revenge. *Law and Neurodiversity: Youth with Autism and the Juvenile Justice System in Canada and the United States* discusses both the nature of these policy gaps and approaches to interactions between juvenile justice systems and autism more in keeping with rights-based disability policy than in the past. Four primary questions guide the inquiry that follows: 1) Why consider autism in the context of juvenile justice? 2) How do juvenile justice systems particularly affect youth with autism and autistic youth? (The distinctions and commonalities between "youth with autism" and "autistic youth" are discussed later in this text. Essentially it depends on personal identity preferences within neurotypes and the degree to which autism is considered the primary identity characteristic in a given context.) 3) How can circumstances be improved for youth with autism, autistic youth, and the personnel who interact with them in juvenile justice settings? And, most importantly, 4) What does rights-based disability policy look like in the context of the rehabilitation of children with autism and autistic children involved with juvenile justice systems?

Two primary reasons motivated the selection of autism as a case study exploring the intersections of rights, accountability, identity, and diversity in the context of disability in juvenile justice systems. First, over the past few decades, the clinically recorded prevalence of autism rose dramatically in both Canada and the United States. While the degree to which this increase represents a genuine change, neurodiversity in the population remains debated – the recorded increase has implications for public programs serving youth. The politics of neurodiversity remain under-recognized in both Canada and the United States. For example, in a study of English-language Canadian media attention to autism, Gregor Wolbring and Katie Mosig (2017) found only four articles including the word "neurodiversity," and two of those articles referenced the neurodiversity movement only in passing. As they explain, "that these four articles are the only ones using the term 'neurodiversity' in the 300 Canadian newspapers surveyed reveals a clear deficit of coverage of the neurodiversity narrative ... in general, the newspaper coverage is biased toward a medical and negative framing of autism" (Baker 2017, 68). In the context of juvenile justice, implications of increased neurodiversity include heightened demand for a multitude of services but also gaps in expertise regarding disability as an element of diversity in public programs. Second, increased public awareness of autism motivates autistics and people with autism to exercise their rights by seeking accommodations in the juvenile justice system. Using these rights as a mechanism for better inclusion can help youth with autism and autistic youth reduce their interactions with justice systems. Juvenile justice institutions benefit from stakeholder awareness of how systems are designed around expectations of neurotypicality and from a singular definition of human worth and success rooted in the preferences and capacities of people considered neurologically typical. As a result of this awareness, scholars and stakeholders can better understand how to create more neuroethical justice systems.

The paradigm of neurotypicality has long dominated human pursuits. Ableism remains more broadly accepted than do other forms of discrimination. Social construction of "the normal" developed alongside democratic policy subsystems founded on principles of human and civil rights. Discerning which elements of disability policy subsystems are misconstructed and which elements are features essential for policy designed to affect the behaviour of human beings proves challenging at best. A comparative case study of two closely related but distinct democracies illuminates how differences in federalist systems, institutional infrastructures, policy design, and practice manifest distinctions in the successes and failures in work with youth with autism and autistic youth.

Disability studies explores disability as a positive element of identity. Throughout much of the twentieth century, disability studies focused on two primary concepts. First, disability came to be understood as a social construct. This conception of disability exists in the intersection of embodied characteristics and inflexible social, political, economic, legal, cultural, and physical infrastructures (O'Donovan 2010). Where participation across capacity differences exists, disability vanishes. Second, disability studies aims to reveal and resist ableism. By focusing on the history of people with disabilities and disabled people and on contemporary factors limiting expression of disability as diversity, disability studies expands understanding of discrimination rooted in a preference for capacities considered typical.

Early scholarship in disability rights focused on how social activism and legal litigation on behalf of persons with disabilities and disabled people afforded them opportunities to satisfy their basic human needs. While some areas of disability studies have arguably moved beyond a rights-based approach, how rights are established and protected in the context of juvenile justice remains insufficiently explored in current literature. As such, the intention in engaging the rights basis of public policy in this book is not to negatively essentialize disability or to ignore the fundamental interdependency of the human superorganism. Rather, we aim to highlight how rights can be better actualized in an environment where rights are both purposively restricted and of paramount, daily importance. Consideration of justice-involved youth with autism and autistic youth as an issue of rights provides an opportunity to understand how policy and practice can be strengthened for all stakeholders.

A Note on Language

Writing about disability can be tricky. This reality is not new. Each society uniquely and variously constructs disability. Designation of disability historically connotes systemic power differentials. Choice of words used to describe differences in capacity identified as relevant in a given society communicates many layers of meaning. Sometimes these layers have been intentionally selected by the author, sometimes not. Always the words chosen will fall short of the ideal for at least some readers.

In the twenty-first century, no universally preferred language form exists in either Canada or the United States. During the final decades of the twentieth century, efforts to create consensus on the use of person-first language gained salience across North America, including in Mexico (Baker and Leonard 2017). Appropriate writing about disability in this language form requires first mentioning that the person or people described are people and then providing either a specific diagnosis or a more general term. For example, person-first language would refer to "a juvenile with autism" rather than to "an autistic juvenile."

Person-first language encumbers benefits. Human beings have a long history of othering individuals or groups considered decisively different. All too often, this othering harmed or oppressed persons and groups so identified. Responsible progression into the future of juvenile justice systems requires perennial remembrance of the fact that the differences called "disability" have been historically understood as crimes in and of themselves (Trent 2016). Detection of disability has been understood as reason enough to relieve individuals of their rights and to apply the harshest punishments imaginable, including death, torture, or lifelong incarceration (Baker 2011; Trent 2016). Given that much-forgotten history and the ongoing ableism in Western societies, use of person-first language appears prudent in much discourse about disability.

Furthermore, human identity is complex. Particularly in contemporary democracies, each individual belongs to various groups and embodies numerous characteristics considered relevant. Respect for lived experience and human agency requires allowing each individual the opportunity to decide which element of their own identity holds primary importance in a given context. For example, a diagnosis of autism may or may not mean that the individual prefers to lead with that element of his or her identity at school. Some students might form a club proudly designated as being for autistics and their allies, whereas others might prefer to spend time partaking in some other activity, such as the math club or playing basketball. As long as the choice of identity is freely made and, ideally, without a sense of shame surrounding the other components of the individual's unique combination of identity characteristics, articulated individual preference prevails. Given that, in the absence of known preferences, person-first language remains (at least potentially) the most appropriate and correct use of language.

In any wicked problem, well-informed and honest stakeholders should frequently disagree. Absence of disagreement signals danger both in the practice of science and in the development of public policy. In the context of the politics of autism in early twenty-first-century North America, strident disagreement with the preferred use of person-first language exists. Sources of opposition cluster on two ends of the continuum of comprehension of disability as an element of diversity (Pitney 2015). One attitudinal tribe is composed of those supporting the (less-than-completely-justly-labelled) proponents of the medical model of disability. Although diversity exists within this group of individuals who have yet to accept disability as an element of diversity, the primary characteristic of those who *still* use disability-first language is ignorance of the disability rights movement and the history of disability culture, particularly events of recent decades. Reasons for this stance vary from outright bigotry, to intellectual immaturity, to cultural differences, to belief in eugenics, to concerns that some of the more radical claims of the disability rights movement dismiss the very real pain and suffering associated with certain physical or mental conditions.

The other attitudinal tribe currently employing disability-first language includes those who have most actively engaged in the disability rights and identity movements. Of course, this diversity-language phenomenon is not unique to disability (Dolmage 2014). Reclaiming language can play a leading role in restoring or creating a positive version of an element of human identity (Rand 2014). In some circumstances, language reclaiming involves articulating by whom once exclusively derogatory terms or language forms can be justly used. For example, racial and ethnic minority group members have reclaimed terms, with the proviso that the language can be appropriately used only by members of the historically oppressed group. This use of language can promote positive in-group identity formation. In other circumstances, language reclaiming aims at changing the use and meaning of the term for the population at large. For example, the word "queer," though once unequivocally derogatory, is being reclaimed by the communities at which it was aimed and its general use is encouraged by many activists and advocates, at least as part of the LGBTQIA+ acronym (ibid.).

Disability-first language has been reclaimed in both ways. Members of disability communities sometimes use once-derogatory terms within their groups as a way of building insular group identity. Proponents of disability-first language also tend to promote its general use by all stakeholders. In recent decades, advocates of disability-first language from this attitudinal tribe are often autistic (Silberman 2016). One reason voiced for this preference is that the experience of disability is too fundamental to the autistic way of being to be distinguishable from the person in question.

Given this, this language type is referred to as identity-first, rather than simply disability-first. As Lydia Brown explains in an article posted on the Autistic Self Advocacy Network's website on the topic of identity-first language, "it is impossible to affirm the value and worth of an Autistic person without recognizing his or her identity as an Autistic person ... Referring to me as 'a person with autism,' or 'an individual with ASD' [autism spectrum disorder] demeans who I am because it denies who I am" (Brown, n.d., n.p.). Individuals and groups that consider autism a core element of their identity are appropriately described with their select identity first.

A shared way of being does not necessarily produce shared identity preferences. Furthermore, dynamic, varied, and passionate composition of individual identity preferences can be especially important to, and for, adolescents. There are individuals who dislike having autism either due to their lived experience or ongoing environmental factors associated with the condition or both (Silberman 2016). Others choose not to lead with neurological difference in describing personal identity because of the relative importance of other identity characteristics, such as nationality, gender, profession, religion, race, sexuality, political philosophy, or other disability. Furthermore, there are people with autism and autistic people who do not realize (or who have only just begun to realize) that they are autistic or are a person with autism. As a result, mandating identity composition through the use of disability- or identity-first language creates dissonance or discomfort for such individuals that can also be demeaning.

The language used in this book never aims to demean neurological difference. While we understand that intentions incompletely protect against harm, writing requires compromise. In salient political issues with rapidly evolving (or even punctuating) public policy, language becomes more poignantly compromised. In this book, both person-first and identity-first language are used simultaneously and, generally, together. When the language preference of the individuals or groups referenced is well established, language use reflects that preference. In direct quotes of policies, scholarly works, or other materials, the language used in the original text is maintained. Finally, when discussing infants, young children, or other people not yet able to communicate preferences with regard to rank order of elements of identity, person-first language is employed. To the extent that books are intended to facilitate back-and-forth communication, dynamic consideration of the language choices – including instances where the reader believes a more accurate or appropriate language choice exists than the ones made by the authors of this book – serves to enhance understanding of disability for all scholars and stakeholders. Readers wishing to communicate or discuss this with the authors are encouraged to be in touch and, importantly, to avoid making the perfect enemy of the good in the examination of the interactions between autism and the juvenile justice systems of twenty-first-century North America.

A Note on Autism

Autism was first described as a distinct condition in the first half of the twentieth century. Ongoing debate surrounds the exact origin of the diagnosis. While a full detailing of this history is beyond the scope of this book, current interpretation of this history has been documented recently in works such as *Neurotribes* (2016) by Steve Silberman and *In a Different Key* (2016) by John Donvan and Caren Zucker. No doubt this history will continue to be revised and enhanced as human understanding of neurology increases as a result of our expanding ability to observe the functioning of living brains and as awareness of disability history grows.

Some arcs of history are particularly relevant to the topics explored in this book. First, as mentioned, the numbers and proportion of individuals understood as being autistic or having autism increased dramatically in recent decades. Second, autism is not usefully understood as a new human experience. When recorded incidence and prevalence of autism rose, one response was to search for a causal explanation for a novel human experience. Among the most influential of the hypotheses was that childhood vaccines or specific components of vaccines – in particular thimerosal, a mercury-based additive – caused autism (Baker and Stokes 2007; Silberman 2016). Sustained study demonstrated no such link (Taylor, Swerdfeger, and Eslick 2014). More importantly from the perspective of autism history, however, vaccine avoidance showed how – for some proportion of the population at least – parents proved more willing to risk the death of their child and others' than have a child with a neurological difference. This choice reflects ongoing bias and discrimination against individuals with neurological differences and the neurodivergent.

The history of formal recognition of autism is also relevant to the topics explored in this book. Practitioners began using autism to describe a handful of people during the first decades of the twentieth century. As a formal diagnosis in North America, autism is defined by the American Psychological Association's *Diagnostic and Statistical Manual of Mental Disorders* (DSM). This manual was first published in 1952, after several years of work by a committee. The DSM-1 was not the first formal effort to classify the neurology of humans. After all, the World Health Organization added information about mental disorders to the sixth edition of its *International Statistical Classification of Diseases*, published in 1949. Even so, the DSM became the leading source of information about mental disorders, and, by extension, neurological differences, used by diagnosticians, educators, service providers, and other stakeholders in North America.

The content of the DSM has changed over time, both to reflect advances of scientific understandings of human beings and in response to changing social mores. Most famously, homosexuality was removed as a disorder in 1973 in response to evolving understandings of normal human sexuality. Autism has been specifically included as a standalone condition in the DSM since 1980, at which point it was officially distinguished from childhood schizophrenia. First called "infantile autism," the name of the condition in the nomenclature was revised by the DSM to "autism disorder" in 1987 and then came to include "Asperger's syndrome" in 1994. In DSM-5, released in 2013, the diagnostic categories connected to autism were collectively reclassified as "autism spectrum disorder." In DSM-5, the diagnostic criteria for autism include "persistent deficits in social communication and social interaction across multiple contexts" and "restricted, repetitive patterns of behaviour, interests, or activities which manifest in childhood, [and] exist to a degree that is considered clinically significant and cannot be better explained by an intellectual disability" (Autism Speaks, n.d.[b]). The text also includes specific examples of behaviours fitting the diagnostic criteria, intended to be useful in identifying the condition.

From the perspective of juvenile justice and autism, it is important to understand that autism is a behaviour-based diagnosis rooted in observation of social interactions. It is also important to understand that while autism diagnoses may be a point of consensus among many professionals, said diagnoses can nevertheless become politicized or operationalized to serve various motives. For example, a family in the United States might pursue a diagnosis of autism on behalf of their child with a neurological difference that includes only a few of the diagnostic criteria because they or their attorney believe that it will facilitate access to desired special education services in a public school. On the other hand, another set of parents might reject the diagnosis for a neurologically similar child because of their bias against individuals with autism and autistic individuals or for fear that their child will face discrimination resulting from the label that he or she might otherwise avoid. Finally, although less prevalent a problem now than in the past, a child in North America with a racial or ethnic background originating outside of Europe might not be diagnosed with autism as a result of a discriminatory belief that autism affects only white people (Silberman 2016).

No biomedical test for autism exists, meaning that diagnosis always takes place in a social context. Importantly, autism is not in any sense of the word contagious, despite the tendency of some authors and other stakeholders to refer to "an autism epidemic." The intention behind the description of autism as a spectrum disorder is to illustrate the essential diversity of the condition itself. Of course, all experiences of human minds, bodies, and spirits are unique, and the construction of the norm constitutes an artificial human invention. This reality is augmented in experiences understood as different from the norm (or the ideal). For example, everyone who experiences asthma or diabetes will experience these conditions and their adverse effects slightly differently. Similarly, everyone who experiences human differences more or less universally understood as positive, such as extraordinary physical attractiveness or strength, will experience these conditions and their positive effects slightly differently. Organizing differences into taxonomies remains useful, since grouping around shared characteristics is one way for humans to manage large-scale projects of any kind. As long as the description is understood as general rather than definitive, a neuroethical approach to neurodiversity can be maintained.

Objections to the removal of Asperger's syndrome from the DSM continue, in part because of connections between neurological difference and identity that are just beginning to be understood (Silberman 2016). Owing to the habitual characterization of individuals with Asperger's as high functioning, some have raised objections to their (perceived) dominant role in defining and communicating first-person experience of autism to the general public. Responses to this objection include that such characterizations originate in a misunderstanding of autism as ranging from low functioning to high functioning and a failure to fully respect the lived experiences of neurodivergence. A core aspect of the experience of young people with autism and young autistics involves the formation of identity. When it comes to autism in contemporary North America, this identity formation exists in tensions between essentialist and constructivist elements of disability. Ken Gobbo and Solvegi Shmulsky explain:

> As diagnoses increase, more adolescents and emerging adults may be forming identities amidst two movements that disagree on the best way to

understand autism. The autism acceptance movement, which stems from a disability studies perspective, maintains that autism is a normal human variation that should be accommodated by an informed mainstream. Efforts associated with autism acceptance include the neurodiversity movement, autistic self-advocacy, and autism rights. The medical model perspective, from which a great deal of scientific and educational research has emerged, views autism as a pathology in need of a cure. (Lim 2016, 2)

How to best negotiate these understandings in the contexts of increased comprehension of human neurology, postmodern identity construction, and expanding understanding of disability as an element of diversity represents an ongoing challenge for contemporary democracies. In the meantime, effective and ethical public management of juvenile justice programs involves maintaining a high level of awareness of the politics of autistic identity and the necessity of understanding autism not simply as a disease. It is also important for scholars and practitioners of juvenile justice to understand that experiences of autism and responses to those experiences will vary greatly within and among individuals. One especially important concern involves avoiding the assumption that intellectual capacity is correlated with the ability to speak, as recent research establishes no such relationship (Nader et al. 2016). Maintaining a dynamic and evolving understanding of neurological difference rests at the centre of appropriate approaches to the design and implementation of juvenile justice programs in neurodiverse societies.

A Note on Age-Based Terminology

This book focuses largely on a specific population of young people involved with the juvenile justice system. Throughout the book, we refer to people under the age of majority using various words, including "juveniles," "youth," and "children," with preference for the terms appropriate for a given topic. Even so, there are no universal definitions of "juvenile," "youth," "child," or for that matter, "childhood" (Ansell 2016). At times, juvenile justice practitioners informally use the terms "juveniles," "youth," and "children" interchangeably. More formally, however, practitioners select the language depending on the context, often in regard to the terms used in relevant legislation or administrative policy.

The term "juvenile" commonly refers to any person under the age of eighteen years. In the United States, each state has the power to choose the age at which a juvenile reaches the age of jurisdiction to enter the juvenile system (18 U.S.C. § 5031). For example, in Washington State, the age of jurisdiction is between eight and seventeen years. In comparison, age seven is the minimum age of jurisdiction in the state of New York. In Canada, the Young Offenders Act of 1984 eliminated the province-to-province variation for the age of criminal responsibility based on the position that such interprovincial variation is unconstitutional. Canada recognizes criminal law as federal jurisdiction and therefore sets the age of jurisdiction for the nation as a whole between twelve and seventeen years (Hoge 2008). In Canadian practice, the terms "juvenile," as well as "offender" and "delinquent," are used to refer to this age group in all criminal and judiciary matters.

The term "child" as used in this book refers primarily to a person below the age of puberty. Sometimes it is used more generally to refer to someone under the age of majority, especially when a reminder of the essential lack of maturity of teenagers is important to the topic at hand. Of course, in the context of disability, "child" represents an especially contested term given, for example, the long history of infantilization of people with disabilities and disabled people. The ongoing tendency to employ phrases such as "adult children" to refer to disabled adults and adults with disabilities and the disabled, either economically or otherwise dependent on their parents or guardians, further intensifies the precariousness of this term. In juvenile justice systems, practitioners also use the term "child" in specific circumstances, such as to describe a person who is a dependent, meaning, through no fault of their own, which they find themselves being removed from their home by the state because of abuse or neglect.

The term "youth" refers to a person under the age of eighteen years. Broader use of "youth" exists in juvenile justice contexts than do the other terms referring to minors. Practitioners use the terms "youth" or "client" in regular communication with service providers, as it is perceived as less stigmatizing than "juvenile" or "offender." Language can affect how youth perceive themselves and whether they believe that the juvenile system, and its services, will indeed help them. In this book, the authors use the specific language that refers to the person or population as appropriate to the formal context of the language described above.

A Note on Intersectionality

Modern identity is inherently complex. Furthermore, the movement away from defining individuals on the basis of a preselected, single characteristic constitutes a foundational design element of democracy. As discussed above, individuals in modern democracies are understood as being free to construct their identity by highlighting whatever elements of identity they prefer. Even so, in the consideration of public policy and administration, particularly in areas as complex as juvenile justice, combinations of some sets of characteristics tend to result in more systematically differentiated experiences than others. This book focuses primarily on a single identity characteristic. Even so, at least some consideration of intersectionality of identity is crucial to the consideration of autism and the juvenile justice systems in Canada and the United States.

Particularly in the United States, writing about identity in the context of criminal justice requires specific consideration of intersection with racial and ethnic background. During the second decade of the twenty-first century, the plight of racial minorities, especially males, in interactions with some members of the police became more public, largely as a result of smart-phone technology enabling the rapid distribution of videos through social media. Differential experiences of racial minorities with justice systems in the United States have a long, tragic history. For example, as Booth et al. (2016, 87) explain, "public discourse is replete with details publicizing the dire straits of African American boys and men in comparison with other members of society." In both Canada and the United States, intersectionality involving Native populations also holds tremendous relevance owing to past and ongoing social and economic injustices, in addition to the differential legal status of Indigenous peoples. Not only are people of colour more likely to be arrested, they are also more likely to have more stringent sentences assigned to their crimes (Alexander 2012). In the United States, such disparities were exacerbated by the implementation strategies employed as part of the War on Drugs (ibid.; Wagner and Rabuy 2017). Canada also waged a war on drugs, but to a lesser degree than in the United States and involving fewer complications resulting from the economic incentives related to privatization. While some of the policies created during the time of Stephen Harper's administration seemed to be veering toward more punishing approaches, under Prime Minister Justin Trudeau, this pattern has been reversed. Nevertheless, in both Canada and the United States, the drug policy design of the late twentieth century has resulted in increased incarceration of youth, and has had pronounced effects on youth from racial and ethnic minority backgrounds (Omura et al. 2014; Wagner and Rabuy 2017). Finally, in the United States, policies targeting those seeking asylum in the United States and without documentation allowing for legal long-term residence have not only horrified the general public but also augmented the fears of many who are (or might be believed to be) recent immigrants.

Gender also constitutes an important intersectional characteristic within juvenile justice systems. Women and girls have historically been under-represented in juvenile justice systems (Epstein, Blake, and González 2017; Gaarder, Rodriguez, and Zatz 2004). While there may be less difference in underlying tendencies and actions than was once considered to be true, the crimes for which young people are detained also differ along gender lines (Epstein, Blake, and González 2017). Beyond separating youth from adults, many juvenile justice systems segregate boys from girls, often according to traditional binary gender, as well. Contemporary conceptions of gender, including divisions along gender lines, create new opportunities and complications for all spaces and organizations. In both Canada and the United States, awareness of gender as a continuum rather than as a binary has increased. Importantly, this observation of more than two genders has existed in other cultural contexts for extended periods (Hollimon 2015). Despite these precedents, in Western democracies, public conceptions of gender that have been historically understood as being exclusively male and female persist. Until very recently, strong socio-cultural reinforcement of restrictive gender roles connected to gender was observed at the moment of birth, which therefore constrained human identity. Resistance to gender diversity rooted in a sense of connection to these traditions persists across North America.

Finally, both juvenile justice systems and the history of autism intersect with socio-economic status. Children and youth from families of lower or middle socio-economic status are more likely to be incarcerated than are children from families of high socio-economic status for same offence (Annamma 2014; Barker et al. 2015). In the United States, costs of public defenders and fees resulting from involvement with the juvenile justice system create extreme economic burdens for youth and their families of origin. Furthermore, failure to pay fees can extend time under supervision for no other reason than that of youths or their families cannot afford to pay fees levied by juvenile justice systems. While such extension typically means more time on probation at the first pass, being on probation increases the likelihood that a youth will spend time in detention for behaviours in which young people commonly engage, such as underage drinking or verbal arguments at school (Humes 2015). Finally, whereas children from wealthy families can afford to pay for private attorneys and interventions courts might consider programs or services in lieu of detention (for instance, attendance at a drug treatment facility), these options are beyond the economic reach of most families. These realities can become especially punishing for families of children with special needs, since the costs of education, medical care, child care, and other interventions tend to be greater for children with special needs than for those without (Sharpe and Baker 2011). Given such program and policy designs, attention to intersectionalities of socio-economic status is crucial to the understanding of autism and the juvenile justice systems in Canada and the United States.

A Note on Theory

This book includes insights drawn from the areas of disability studies, sociology, criminology, juvenile justice, political science, public administration, and public policy, with the intent of helping close the gap between contemporary knowledge of autism, disability rights, and the theory and practice of criminal justice directed at young people in North America. The aforementioned academic disciplines include a multitude of theories into which scholars situate their work.

However, because this book focuses on the juvenile justice system of two nations, the text that follows primarily highlights theories drawn from comparative public policy analysis. Readers of this book need not have substantial prior experience with comparative policy theory. In his book *Explaining Politics*, Oliver Woshinsky (2008, 88) describes how most people "are not interested in politics most of the time" because of lack of time and resources. Even so, both crime and disability have historically polarized communities, stakeholders, and political parties. Autism and the juvenile justice systems of Canada and the United States intersect broadly with the interests, hopes, goals, fears, and expectations of too many communities and stakeholders to be safely ignored.

Furthermore, comparing social policy is not necessarily an automatic instinct in public policy, in part because of the influence of social, history, and cultural contexts on policy design (Baker and Steuernagel 2009). Frequency of such comparisons is further reduced by American exceptionalism, rooted in a belief that the United States holds a special and unique position in the world. However, previous works have demonstrated the potential for learning across North America. Despite their geographic proximity and substantial shared history, Canada and the United States have not taken fully congruent paths in the development of juvenile justice or disability policy.

The next six chapters of this book each briefly summarize an aspect of relevant policy and administrative history in Canada and the United States. The comparative policy analysis herein is a blended theoretical framework drawing from regime theory, institutional frameworks, punctuated equilibrium, punishment theories, and conceptualizations rooted in the intersectionalities of gender, ethnicity or race, and socio-economic status. In each chapter, one or two of these theoretical frameworks serves as a backbone for the discussion of that topic. This framing does not imply that those aspects of autism and juvenile justice situate only in that particular theoretical perspective, however. Readers of this text are encouraged to build on the practices, recommendations, and suggestions presented and to think broadly about adapting them to enhanced neurodiversity in juvenile justice.

2

Autism, Delinquency, and Juvenile Rights

Modern disability politics and juvenile justice systems both value rights. Juvenile justice inherently involves state action. Much of state action in this policy subsystem necessarily focuses on negative rights. The state holds legal authority to deprive of their liberty those juveniles found to have violated the law, by confining them to custody or requiring compliance with community-based supervision protocols. In either situation, the state restricts and regulates the juvenile's freedom as public functions of government intended to protect the rights of the population as a whole (Gilmour and Jensen 1998; Malatesta and Carboni 2015). When such actions involve youth with disabilities and disabled youth, balancing the rights of the youth with the rights of others has historically proven challenging at best.

History of Rights and Juvenile Justice in Canada

The evolution of rights in Canada shapes and reflects its national histories, especially as compared with those of United States. Recorded European invasion of the lands that later became Canada began, as it did in the United States, at the end of the fifteenth century. The Indigenous population included many societies, all of which suffered tremendous losses of population, territory, and culture during the subsequent centuries. France and Great Britain led colonization of the lands that later became Canada. After the conclusion of the Seven Years War, Great Britain dominated in all but Quebec.

The Dominion of Canada was established in 1867, creating limited independence for Canada as part of the British Empire. At first, Canada enjoyed incomplete control over its laws, policies, and public programs. However, in subsequent decades, Canada, like other Dominion countries, witnessed increased desire for autonomy and a rising sense of national pride on the part of the resident population, especially following the First World War. In 1931, the Parliament of the United Kingdom sought to better articulate powers held by the Canadian Parliament (and those other Commonwealth nations) vis-à-vis those of the British Government. According to Historica Canada, "it granted these former colonies full legal freedom except in those areas where they chose to remain subordinate to Britain" (Hillmer and Foot 2015, n.p.). Over the next several decades, Canada gradually gained control of its own affairs. Canadian citizenship was formalized as fully distinct from British nationality in the Canadian Citizenship Act of 1946. In 1982, the Constitution Act patriated the Canadian constitution and created the Charter of Rights and Freedoms (Historica Canada 2013).

Understanding the gradual unfolding of Canadian independence is the key to comparing its policy subsystems with that of the United States. In addition, Canadian policy systems reflect the ever-evolving relationship between French and English Canada, as well as with First Nations and other Indigenous peoples. The question of sovereignty for Quebec has long been a salient issue. The history of the issue includes public referendums on the issue. While both times the sovereigntists lost, these referendums and a sense of cultural, political, and historical distinction of Quebec have shaped the history of all policy subsystems in Canada.

Aboriginal populations experienced relentless oppression in the centuries following initial European occupation. The 1982 Charter of Rights and Freedoms defines three categories of Aboriginal peoples: First Nations, Métis, and Inuit. The Inuit and First Nations people have a right to self-government, the 1982 Canadian Charter of Rights and Freedoms recognizing "the rights of Inuit and First Nations people to make decisions about matters internal to their communities, integral to their unique cultures, traditions and languages, and connected with their relationship to the land and resources." Some individuals from such ethnic heritages may choose to register under the Indian Act (first passed in 1876). Others are not members of a group that signed treaties with the Crown. Jurisdictional cloudiness remains and these negotiations continue alongside contemporary efforts to redress historical wrongs as fairly and proactively as possible.

Doli incapax addressed delinquent and neglected youth in the British Empire until 1857. Derived from English common law, this legal construct was incorporated into Canada's criminal code in 1892 to provide age-graded guidelines on when children became old enough to be held responsible by the state for law-violating behaviour. The code considered children younger than seven years as incapable of forming criminal intent and did not generally hold them legally accountable for delinquency. Furthermore, immunity from criminal conviction extended to youth aged seven to fourteen years. Exceptions to this rule depended on evidence that a specific youth could discriminate right from wrong (Anand 1999).

During this era, governments created reformatories for juveniles found to have violated the law. Youth under age twenty-one went to these facilities rather than (or as well as) penitentiaries. Physical sites of these facilities varied. For example, one site had been army barracks during the War of 1812, exemplifying the human tendency to repurpose institutional sites). As was the case in the United States, reformatories were chronically under-resourced, leaving them less than well equipped to provide adequate services for the youth (Department of Justice Canada 2004).

The Juvenile Delinquents Act of 1908 elaborated on the doli incapax. The act states that "every juvenile delinquent shall be treated, not as a criminal, but as a misdirected and misguided child" (Department of Justice Canada 2004, 21). This policy required separate housing for children and adults, with rare exceptions tied to the severity of the crime. This formalization of doli incapax sought to provide welfare rather than punishment to youth. Despite this act, the services provided under the umbrella of this act remained less than exclusively rehabilitative (Bala 2004).

Between the Industrial Era and the Progressive Era, Canada and the United States experienced rapid industrialization, immigration, and the proliferation of abandoned or orphaned children (Department of Justice Canada 2004; Anand 1999; Rothman 1980). Social movements of the early twentieth century compelled North American governments to progressively expand social policy infrastructures. Child-saving movements arose, pressuring governments to provide meaningful care for children who violate the law. These child savers were generally private, external-issue stakeholders (Knupfer 2001; Platt 2009). Even so, their vision for what society could achieve for vulnerable children depended heavily on state actors' actions.

The latter part of the twentieth century restricted the scope of governmental power in responding to law-violating behaviour by juveniles. In Canada, the Young Offenders Act (YOA) of 1984 extended Canadian youth rights by providing some rights once reserved for adults, such as legal counsel and the right of appeal for convictions (Department of Justice Canada 2004). The YOA covered youth between the ages of twelve and seventeen. This law treated children under twelve more benignly than the Juvenile Delinquent Act of 1908. Any youth sentenced in the juvenile court under the YOA could receive no more than two years of detention unless the standard sentence for the crime normally resulted in a life sentence. Rare transfers to adult court resulted in a maximum sentence of three years for juveniles.

In 2003, the Canadian government enacted the Youth Criminal Justice Act (YCJA). The desire to limit use of the formal criminal justice system and increase reintegration protocols for all youth drove the creation of this legislation (Department of Justice Canada 2004). This act enhances the accountability aspect of the Youth Offenders Act of 1984, turning to more alternative, community-based responses in lieu of detention (Hoge 2008). The YCJA also allows for community volunteers to participate in the court process by attending meetings, conferences, or boards to help young people understand the impacts of behaviours.

History of the Rights and Juvenile Justice in the United States

As with Canada, the examination of the history of rights in the United States as such begins with the arrival of European explorers and colonizers. The size of the population and number of cultures present when the continent was invaded remains debated. What is known is that after the initial arrival of explorers, the population of Native Americans declined rapidly. The conception of the United States as a distinct, unified nation was initiated with the American Revolution, declared in 1776. The revolution ended in 1783, at which point the original thirteen colonies became independent from Great Britain. Over the next centuries, states and territories were added to the United States. At the time of writing, Hawaii and Alaska stand as the most recently added states, having gained admission in 1959.

Rights flow from the United States Constitution. The first constitutional convention convened in 1787, as many believed that the original Articles of Confederation insufficiently framed the national government and the federal system. In the view of most, the Constitution of the United States is a living document including amendment protocols and provisions. Currently, the Constitution has twenty-seven amendments; the most recent, addressing pay increases for Congress, was ratified only in 1992, despite having been proposed in 1789.

Each state maintains its own constitution. State constitutions cannot contradict or limit rights provided by the United States Constitution. However, additional rights can be created above and beyond those provided by the national constitution. During the middle of the nineteenth century, the United States suffered a crisis of its federation centred on the states' rights. Specifically, political movements emerged challenging ownership of human slaves. This crisis culminated in the American Civil War, in which eleven states attempted to separate from the union in order to preserve slavery. The Civil War lasted from 1861 to 1865 and resulted in the return of the seceding states to the United States and the abolition of slavery across the nation. Tensions surrounding the balance of authority between states and the national government continue to this day. A legacy of racial tension and strong differences of opinion regarding the role of slavery in the Civil War and other national political movements also persist.

The history of juvenile justice in the United States includes both cooperation and rancour. During the children's rights movement of the Progressive Era (1890–1920), several child welfare agencies welcomed the idea of a state actor bearing legal responsibility for neglected, abandoned, and delinquent children. Historically, private or religious child charity organizations incompletely served needy or delinquent children given parental permission or absence.

The doctrine under which government works with youth in juvenile justice derives from *parens patriae*, or literally, the state as parent (Vito and Kunselman 2011). This construct establishes government responsibility for holding juveniles accountable for violating legal codes. It also takes on additional responsibility of protecting juveniles from further harm (ibid.). With the advent of the juvenile court and parens patriae in 1899, these organizations gained authority to work directly with the court to provide services to these youth (Rothman 1980; Mays and Winfree 2006). The court was empowered to order services for children under its authority. Resulting interagency interactions involved distinctions between the child as private client of the welfare agency and as ward of the juvenile court. As with many well-intentioned Progressive Era policy designs, the moral authority of the court to manifest social change ideals faced daunting levels of community need, coupled with inconsistently monitored community partnerships unevenly attending to the child's well-being (Rothman 1980).

Over subsequent decades, Supreme Court decisions limited state authority over juveniles under parens patriae. Starting in the 1960s, a series of decisions required jurisdictions to provide legal counsel for juvenile defendants upon transfers to adult court (*Kent v United States*) or, for dispositions where juveniles could face confinement, formal charges and presence of counsel (*In re Gault*); to use the standard of proof for juvenile proceedings as for adult proceedings (*In re Winship*); and to honour double-jeopardy protections (*Breed v Jones*). Later cases also prohibited capital punishment for juveniles (*Roper v Simmons*) and sentencing youth to life imprisonment without the possibility of parole (*Graham v Florida; Miller v Alabama*). These and still later cases inserted procedural due process into juvenile court, thereby diluting the power of parens patriae.

Efforts to improve juvenile justice systems and better protect the rights of youth in custody continue to this day. For example, in 2007, Joseph Galloway reported sexual abuse by detention officers in a juvenile detention centre in Texas where he served time. He also reported that the facility aggressively extended original sentences for rule violations during incarceration. These claims resulted in a review of the cases of over a thousand youth to locate unjust extensions of sentence and allegations of sexual abuse (Moreno 2007). Then, in 2011, the discovery of two Pennsylvania juvenile court judges bribed by local businesspeople to sentence juveniles to privately owned detention centres who otherwise would have had community-based sanctions illustrated ongoing gaps in the safeguarding of juveniles from predatory private entities. Detection of this criminal activity resulted in the overturning of thousands of juvenile convictions and tightening of contract oversight procedures (Ecenbarger 2012).

Private facilities have also hosted corruption and abuse. In 2016, the Inspector General of the Justice Department audited a sample of the private prisons and found that privatizing prisons and detention centres costs more, increases security risks, and proves less effective than government-operated facilities (Burnett 2016). President Barack Obama directed the Justice Department to begin phasing out private detention centres and prisons used to incarcerate approximately thirty-five thousand people. Although this executive order focused on the federally controlled prisons and detentions, its goals included leading by example to influence individual state decisions on privately ran facilities. During the Trump administration, progress toward reducing the exploitation of the privatization of government programs stalled.

Despite instances of well-documented abuses in the child welfare and juvenile justice systems dating back to the Progressive Era, parens patriae solidified state actor sovereignty over the lives of delinquent, neglected, and abandoned youth in the United States. Julian W. Mack (1909 107), then a circuit court judge for Cook County in Chicago, asked: "Why is it not just and proper to treat these juvenile offenders, as we deal with the neglected children, as a wise and merciful father handles his own child whose wrongs are not discovered by the authorities?" The majority of states now use the Juvenile Detention Alternatives Initiative (JDAI) model, a project funded by the Annie E. Casey Foundation. This program aims to reduce detention populations by using alternative sanctions for youth deemed through a risk assessment screening as unlikely to commit another offence or pose a risk to community safety. Alternative sanctions include programs such as restorative community service, community accountability boards, victim impact units, and specific therapy programs. Juvenile justice systems aim to protect the rights of youth not only through principles and laws but also through the sentences handed down by judges. In making decisions, judges seek to balance the best interests and needs of the youth with the protection of the public (Bala 2004). Importantly, evaluation of these complicated decisions, especially when considered in hindsight, can also turn on changing attitudes toward youth, disability, and crime.

Constitutions and Justice

When considering juvenile justice systems' responses to delinquent or criminal behaviour of youth with autism and autistic youth, procedural justice arises as immediately concerning. After all, autism remains a behaviour-based diagnosis, and society's infrastructures privilege neurotypical behaviours. Furthermore, articulation of disability rights complicates long-held understandings of social norms and public responsibilities. The Constitution of the United States establishes procedural justice through the due process clauses applied to those whose life, liberty, and pursuit of happiness become constrained following formal criminal accusation. The Fifth, Sixth, Eighth, and Fourteenth Amendments forge procedural due process guarantees applied to criminal proceedings. Section 7 of the Canadian Charter of Rights and Freedoms sets forth similar guarantees of the right to life, liberty, and security of the person.

The Supreme Court of the United States articulated the bulk of due process rights of juveniles through four landmark cases. *Kent v United States* (1966) established minimal rights and formed specific criteria before the waiving of juvenile rights. Juvenile justice practitioners use *Kent* standards to determine appropriateness of case transfer to adult court. Even so, in the United States, transfer of youth to adult court became easier over time. Since 1992, forty-five states have amended their laws regarding transfer of juveniles to adult court (Wald and Losen 2003). In general, eight factors determine transfer protocols, including the seriousness of the offence; the manner in which the offence was committed; whether the offence was against a person or property; the merits of the complaint; if there are adult co-suspects; sophistication and maturity of the juvenile; juvenile offence history and police contacts; and the prospect of whether the juvenile can be rehabilitated (*United States v Kent* 1965). Changes to state and local policies drove an increase in the number and type of transfer cases from the juvenile to adult systems (Hockenberry and Puzzanchera 2015). In 2013, 4,000 of the 1,058,500 juvenile cases transferred to adult court, not including cases subject to automatic adult jurisdiction. About 1 in 6 of the cases transferred to adult court involved non-violent crimes (Wald and Losen 2003). During the first decade of the twenty-first century, one out of every ten juveniles incarcerated in the United States was held in an adult facility (Eggleston 2007).

Nevertheless, significant social pressure to avoid transfer of juveniles to the adult system exists. In part, this reflects improved understanding of human brain development after age eighteen. It also mirrors new social norms reflected in policies such as the US Patient Protection and Affordable Care Act provisions allowing children to stay on the parents' health insurance until age twenty-six regardless of whether they remain in school (Goldstein 2016). The Marshall Project published an article in October 2016 entitled "Who's a Kid?" which examines the blurred lines of the social and cultural transition from adolescent to adult. In it, the author, Dana Goldstein (2017, 3), quotes Terrie Moffitt, professor of psychology and neuroscience at Duke University, as saying, "as long as you make a cut point based on age, you are treating both groups the same." In other words, determining juvenile court jurisdiction based solely on chronological age runs the risk of treating children as adults. Of course, basing this determination on a construction other than chronological age raises the spectre of lifelong child status once routinely assigned to individuals with disabilities, people of colour, and women, for example.

In 1967, *In re Gault* extended the following rights and privileges: right to a notice of charges, right to counsel and appointment of counsel if the family cannot afford one, protection against self-incrimination, and right to cross-examine witnesses. Not all justices were convinced the decision was in the best interest of juveniles. In a dissent of the majority opinion, Justice Stewart criticized the decision as a step backward for juveniles, saying that the "answer does not lie in the Court's opinion in this case, which serves to convert a juvenile proceeding into a criminal prosecution" (*In re Gault* 1967, n.p.). Some contemporary stakeholders agreed with Justice Stewart on the grounds that the juvenile system mimicked the adult system, contradictory to the foundational principles of the juvenile justice system (Sickmund, Sladky, and Kang, 2017). Focus on rehabilitation means that cases involving juveniles required more rigorous proof than adults (*In re Winship* 1970; Sickmund, Sladky, and Kang, 2017). Juveniles, on the other hand, do not have the right to a jury trial in juvenile proceedings, hardly surprising given the additional complications surrounding convening a jury of a youth's peers. As Justice Blackmun made clear, the juvenile system differs from the criminal system in *McKeiver v Pennsylvania* (1971) "despite disappointments, failures, and shortcomings in the juvenile court procedure" (Justice Blackmun in *McKeiver v Pennsylvania* 1971).

The evolution of due process rights in the juvenile courts of both Canada and United States rebalances youths' protective rights with liberating rights (Stafford 1995; Ritzer 2004). A protective right exemplifies a positive right, or a claim to other persons' efforts, forcing someone to take concrete action to provide for the right in question (ibid.; Baker 2011). Responsibilities of juvenile courts under protective rights include providing food, shelter, education, medical care, and safety from abuse and neglect. Negative rights also expanded over time, given that the state could no longer make decisions against the juveniles' interests. Ultimately, juvenile courts in Canada and the United States share the same three underlying missions: to protect the community of jurisdiction; to hold the offender accountable for their crime; and to confront the issues that led to the criminal activity. The third mission also shapes the role of the probation officer and other support staff in the juvenile justice system working with the youth.

The Juvenile in Justice

As discussed above, juvenile justice systems in both Canada and the United States evolved distinctly from adult criminal systems. Even so, much about the underlying conceptions of what constitutes fair and appropriate process for determining guilt and consequences coincides. In particular, juvenile courts implement the same steps as the criminal systems with different terminology for each step of the process.

Differentiated language aims to reduce adverse effects of labelling of youth. During the 1960s, Howard Becker, a professor of sociology at Northwestern University, found that labelling a person a deviant, criminal, or

Table 1 Case process terminology in criminal and juvenile systems

Criminal systems	Juvenile systems
Jail/prison	Detention/institution
Criminal	Delinquent, juvenile, youth
Inmate	Resident
Trial	Adjudication hearing
Sentence	Disposition
Complaint/indictment	Petition
Parole	Probation/aftercare

delinquent promotes the internalizing of that negative identity, prompting people to behave in a way that reflects the characterization and its associated behaviours (Mays and Winfree 2006). Describing juveniles as a criminal and treating them as such augments their risk of perceiving themselves as criminal. This increases the risk of recidivism.

Even so, questions about real implications of language differences persist. Differences in nomenclature can create an illusion of greater differences than those that exist in the practice of justice. The systems follow similar legal logic and procedural paths. For example, an adjudicatory hearing examines a juvenile's behaviour to determine delinquency and violation of laws. Likewise, a trial of an adult involves examining evidence to determine innocence or guilt in a criminal proceeding. Nevertheless, the belief that juveniles should not endure the same punishments as adults remains. Ultimately, the effects of the differences in nomenclature are unclear.

Many typical youth traits, such as being influenced be peer pressure, impulsivity, deficiencies in thinking ahead or future thinking, and impaired risk analysis render juveniles less culpable than adults. Thus, the juvenile system having too much similarity with the adult system constitutes cruel and unusual punishment (*Roper v Simmons* 2005; Scott and Steinberg 2008). Differences in treatment of young people also connect to their ability to understand their actions. Younger people do not necessarily understand cause, effect, and consequences in the same way older people should. Determining *mens rea*, or criminal intent, includes culpability as one of the three core elements needed to prove guilt for a criminal act. In determining culpability, juveniles in the United States have the right to a competency hearing to examine whether there is "reasonable cause to believe that the defendant may presently be suffering from a mental disease or defect rendering him mentally incompetent to the extent that he is unable to understand the nature and consequences of the proceedings against him or to assist properly in his defense" (*Pate v Robinson* 1966).

Competency hearings follow a request from an attorney or other juvenile justice employee as a result of this formal recognition of the relevant difference in the youth. Before a competency hearing, the juvenile participates in psychiatric evaluations to establish whether they can stand trial (have an adjudication hearing). A determination of competence involves evaluating whether the juvenile understands their rights and has a basic understanding and recognition of implications of legal proceedings (Mayes 2003). Without competency, the court cannot prove criminal intent (mens rea), and charges are either diverted or dismissed. Unfortunately, given factors such as the expectation of neutrality, the potential for resource constraints in competency evaluation procedures, and a focus on a deficit model of disability inherent in this question of competency, this process holds the potential for traumatizing or stigmatizing interactions between the youth, their family, and professionals.

In Canada, common law traditions tied back to the British Empire and France criminal law jointly contributed to the foundation of determinations of competency. Although many traditions surrounding competency sprang from British common law, Canada was one of several countries that "passed acts making the accused competent before England finally took that step … [and] before the conquest of Quebec in 1759, the criminal law of New France was contained in the ordinance promulgated by Louis IX in 1670" (Noble 1970, 266). As Noble notes, such laws favoured conviction. Contemporary British law held individuals' as incompetent witnesses about crimes for which they stood accused. However, over the course of the first half of the nineteenth century, much debate regarding adult competency drove a series of changes to the laws defining competency.

At the beginning of the twenty-first century, Prime Minister Harper (in office from February 2006 to November 2015) set a tone of toughness on crime. Changes in policy during this era included the amendment of section 672.1 of the Criminal Code, on mental disorder. According to Yanick Charette and co-authors (2015, 128, emphasis in original), "people are found NCRMD (*not criminally responsible on account of mental disorder*) if they committed a criminal offence while suffering from a mental disorder that caused them to be incapable of knowing that the offence was wrong (mens rea) or that prevented them from controlling their behaviour (*actus reus*)." Under new amendments to policy, a new status of high risk "suggests they have a higher probability of reoffending than people found NCRMD who did not commit a serious personal injury offence, and (or) commit more serious violence if they do reoffend" (ibid.).

Tough-on-crime stances render people with autism and autistic people more vulnerable to contact with justice systems. Having autism can present challenges in understanding consequences of an action or how an action negatively impacts another person (O'Sullivan 2017). Moreover, determining the core requirements of criminal behaviour – mens rea and actus reus – can involve difficulties from both a clinical and a legal perspective with any person who cannot understand or articulate their motives, drives, and a particular action regarded as criminal by the state (Freckelton 2013). Because legal systems do not rapidly incorporate current research on autism into justice practice (O'Sullivan 2017; Salseda et al. 2011), the risk of ableist justice has a distinct salience for persons with autism and autistic individuals, especially during childhood and youth.

The case of Andrew, an eleven-year-old with autism charged with having sexually molested a minor, serves as an example of how autism might compromise understanding of legal stipulations. Andrew and a neighbour child were charged with sexually molesting Andrew's sister over a period of two years. Andrew's parents previously sanctioned him for attempting to take illicit photos of his sister on a mobile device. They implemented these rules: 1) he was not allowed to take pictures of his sister, 2) he was not allowed to be alone with her in a room, and 3) the neighbour could not come to Andrew's house (Thompson and Morris 2016). After Andrew was apprehended for the sexual abuse of his sister, he was upset that he was being punished even though he had obeyed the rules: he did not take pictures of his sister (he engaged in sexual contact behaviour); he was not alone with her in a room (the neighbour was with Andrew); and the neighbour was not at Andrew's house (all abuse incidents took place at the neighbour's house) (ibid.). Andrew's attorney struggled to get him to understand the seriousness of the charges against him, not an unusual difficulty with very young defendants. She stated that while intelligent, Andrew did not interact with her very well, further challenging rapport with him and making it more difficult to learn about his state of mind during the abuse episodes (ibid.).

In addition to a competency proceeding, youth with disabilities and disabled youth may have to enter a capacity hearing. Capacity hearings are for juveniles age twelve and under who are accused of committing a crime. Capacity considers whether the youth knows that the act is wrong. In the United States, the majority of states recognize juveniles under the age of eight as not held legaly responsible for their acts because they are too young to know right from wrong. Therefore, the state cannot prove whether the juvenile "intentionally, knowingly, purposefully, maliciously, recklessly, or negligently" committed a crime, leaving no ability to prove mens rea (Mayes 2003, 94). The prosecutor can overcome the capacity hearing by presenting evidence in an evidentiary hearing that demonstrates the youth knew the act was wrong at the time they committed the crime. In Canada, however, capacity hearings parallel competency hearings in the United States. Determination of capacity in the Canadian juvenile courts aims to discern whether the juvenile is fit to stand trial and if they are criminally responsible for their actions. Doli incapax – intent to commit the crime – still must be found; that is, that at the time of the act, the juvenile knew their actions were wrong, even if their current state renders them unfit to stand trial.

Who commits a crime influences how the public feels about the incident (Cullen, Fisher, and Applegate 2000; Roberts 2004). For example, a general sense of appropriate sentencing for murder tends to depend on perpetrator characteristics, referred to as aggravating or mitigating circumstances. As previously described, adolescents generally appear less blameworthy than adults, and presence of a disability or illness may further reduce perceived responsibility (Scott and Steinberg 2008). "Diminished capacity" recognizes the mental state or disability of the offender, and is taken into consideration in determining whether they should be held criminally liable for committing the crime. "Proportionality" refers to criminal sentences that consider the culpability of the person accused of the offence, meaning that two people may commit the same offence but have different sentences (ibid.).

A young person charged with an offence must be found to have broken the law. Legal definitions of certain crimes require some recognition of the mental state during the time of the crime. The act of killing another human, depending on the perpetrator's intention, can result in a different charge or degree of charge altogether, for instance murder, homicide, or manslaughter. After a charge is made, the judge or jury attempts to assess the juvenile's mental state at the time of the crime in order to determine whether the crime was committed intentionally, knowingly, recklessly, and grossly (Mayes 2003). Both the existence and judgment of mens rea becomes less supportable when an individual's autism includes difficulty with abstract thought and understanding consequences of actions.

These due process protections enhance rights during legal proceedings. The due process revolution in juvenile justice came about through a series of Supreme Court cases starting in the early 1960s (Feld 2003). Taken together, they delineate legal independence for persons under the age of majority processed by the juvenile court, representing a significant setback to the legal authority of parens patriae. These cases prohibited juvenile courts from adjudicating youth outside the presence of legal counsel, processing them in the absence of witnesses who could prove their innocence in court, and sentencing them to confinement or other state supervision for indefinite periods (Vito and Kunselman 2011). Such cases forced juvenile courts to recognize due process of law as a human right as much as a legal right.

In Canada, the Young Offenders Act mandated due process for youth adjudicated through the juvenile court. This federal law required juveniles to have legal counsel and provided a right for them to appeal a conviction. This normative shift in Canada's legal authority to process cases was both a reaction to and furtherance of the due process revolution in the United States (Anand 1999). In 1965, the Canadian government published the *Report of the Department of Justice Committee on Juvenile Delinquency*, documenting the problems around rights and other issues in the juvenile justice systems and suggested reforms. During the late 1960s, Canada's new act sought to balance juveniles' due process rights and society's need to hold them accountable for law-violating behaviour, while still providing the juvenile court the legal capacity to meet juveniles' unique needs (Department of Justice Canada 2004).

During the due process revolution, the disability rights movement contemporaneously grew out of its nascent stage (Anand 1999; Pitney 2015). The United Nations' Universal Declaration of Human Rights of 1948 included consideration of disability and capacity differences. Article 25 states: "Everyone has the right to a standard of living adequate for the health and well-being of himself and his family ... and the right to security in the event of unemployment, sickness, disability, widowhood, old age, and other lack of livelihood in circumstances beyond his control" (United Nations General Assembly 1949, art. 25, 4). Disability activists across North America strove for the expansion of rights using philosophies (and tactics) similar to those underlying the due process revolution.

Original juvenile justice systems pursued individual justice in order to achieve specific services, with an overall goal of reducing recidivism. However, immense political pressure to be tough on crime continues to advance punitive approaches to it. Restorative justice aims to balance these pressures with progress. Restorative justice scholar and advocate Tony Marshall states that "restorative justice is a process whereby all the parties with a stake in a particular offense come together to resolve collectively how to deal with the aftermath of the offense and its implications for the future"

(Van Ness, Maxwell, and Morris 2003, 5). Juvenile facilities adopting the restorative justice model seek to address community safety, accountability, and development of the youth. Juvenile justice practitioners work with the youth to help them understand how their behaviour has impacted the community, and provide them with ways to restore the damaged caused by their delinquent behaviour. This philosophy holds them accountable by requiring specific tasks in the restoration process to mend the harm caused, these tasks building skills and competency. Both nations' ongoing reforms of their juvenile justice systems demonstrate how changes in state actor behaviour influence normative changes regarding rights, sovereignty, self-determination, and the scope of legal authority. The overarching challenge involves balancing maintenance of order with the rights and freedoms of the populace.

Disability Rights Revisited

The Universal Declaration of Human Rights articulates the right of persons with disabilities and disabled people to enjoy the same rights as other human beings. It inspired national governments and various societies to begin thinking of disabled persons and people with disabilities as part of the continuum of individuals for whom rights are articulated in international law (Rioux and Carbert 2003). Early disability rights statements and policies nevertheless placed said persons on par with other vulnerable humans: the ill, financially insecure, and elderly. This approach became less universally acceptable with fuller actualization of rights of individuals with disabilities and disabled people. After all, groups allowed to fully participate in society generally grow less comfortable with presumed status vulnerability over time. In particular, young people newly surviving disabilities acquired during combat service became less and less willing to accept presumptions of vulnerability on their return from service in the wars of the twentieth century (Baker and Leonard 2017). As state actor theory suggests, patriotic reactions to veterans and their service lent additional legitimacy to disability rights as fundamental human rights. This perspective also helps explain the defence and provision of these rights as an appropriate use of public resources.

During the second half of the twentieth century, the United Nations articulated a stance on disability rights. Specifically, in 1975, the United Nations issued the Declaration on the Rights of Disabled Persons. This declaration called on member nations to enumerate in their legal codes full civil and political rights for persons with disabilities and disabled people, and to enact measures allowing every person to become self-reliant (Galer 2015). Moreover, this declaration urged member nations to take into account the needs of disabled persons and persons with disabilities in all stages of economic and social planning, the provision of legal aid to secure their rights, and consultation of disability organizations by governing bodies when engaging in matters related to disability rights (United Nations 1949). Also, the United Nations declared 1981 the International Year of Disabled Persons, with the goal of raising awareness and encouraging action to establish and enhance disability rights. Two years later, in 1993, the United Nations launched the World Programme of Action Concerning Disabled Persons and named 1983–92 the United Nations Decade of Disabled Persons (Rioux and Prince 2002; Stienstra 2003).

As is the case with many social movements, the disability rights movement occurred in waves (Stienstra 2003). The first wave took place in the late nineteenth century, as part of the Progressive Era. The belief that persons with disabilities and disabled people could have their lives positively changed by new treatments and educational techniques captured the public imagination throughout North America. Such a perspective contrasted with earlier historical perceptions of persons with disabilities and disabled people as part of the worthy poor – individuals who through no fault of their own could not provide for themselves. Such distinctions in Canadian society derived from English Poor Laws, which separated the deserving from the non-deserving based on their physical capacity to perform labour (Rioux and Prince 2002). These socio-legal norms permeated Canadian disability policy by providing disability benefits to those who were stereotyped as unemployable. Members of society perceived these benefits as charity for the needy, reinforcing the individual pathology model of disability (ibid.).

The Progressive Era in Canada included the creation of various schools and homes for children with specific capacity differences, such as schools for children with physical and developmental disabilities and homes for those who were blind or hearing impaired. Despite the largely good intentions characterizing this era, these advocacy services and organizations kept persons with disabilities and disabled people within institutional settings, segregating them from society at large and their families and, often, embraced racism (Shapiro 1994; Trent 2016). Too frequently, such institutions deteriorated into simple warehousing of persons with disabilities and disabled people (Stienstra 2003).

The second wave of the disability rights movement began shortly after the end of the Second World War. The war accelerated development of technology, education, and advanced industries. The military industrial complex's increased demands for educated workers persisted after the war, facilitating expanded participation in higher education. In addition, the Allied victory over Axis Powers – Nazi Germany in particular – increased awareness of how critical human rights are to building and sustaining just societies (Adams and Balfour 2009). The government of Saskatchewan was one of the first to use state action to articulate social democratic principles in its legal charters, and it was through this charter that mental health advocates obtained better hospital conditions for their patients (Neufeldt in Stienstra 2003).

Other disability advocacy organizations also emerged. Disabled veterans advocated for themselves, claiming rehabilitation to be a human right to full and equal participation in society. Parents lobbied for their children with intellectual disabilities and created the Canadian Association for Community Living (CACL), an inclusion advocacy organization for persons with intellectual disabilities and their families. Activists played a leading role in obtaining new services for persons with intellectual disabilities and disabled people as well as in developing other organizations that served as a research repository for assisting persons and their families (Stienstra 2003).

The third wave of disability rights started in the 1970s. By this time, four major disability organizations represented the interests of many people with disabilities: CACL, Canadian Mental Health Association, Canadian National Institute for the Blind, and Canadian Rehabilitation Council for the Disabled. At this time, clinicians with select training displaced individuals with disabilities or their families in decision making regarding the lives of individuals with disabilities and disabled individuals. As the gulf between individual agency and service provision grew over time, disability advocates formed their own organizations, such as the Council of Canadians with Disabilities. Disability advocates resisted the notion of persons with disabilities and disabled people as weak, sick, or inferior. Activists pushed for acknowledgment of their rights to receive not only services but full legal protection from discrimination, including codified recognition of their fundamental humanity. Disability became understood as a social construction subject to elimination through social action, education, cultural shifts, and policy change. First and foremost, activists sought to distinguish between impairment and disability, with the former referring to difference in capacity and the latter referring to selective state exclusion from everyday society because of public infrastructures assuming typical human capacities (Winter 2003; Ben-Moshe 2011). Social construction of disability marginalized the excluded persons and created the stigma underlying much of society's perceptions and infrastructures. These constructions reinforced otherness and kept disability out of mainstream society (Winter 2003). Notably, many efforts targeting the elimination of barriers neglected full consideration of neurological differences as disabilities.

The disability rights movement continues to this day (Pielke 2007). Elimination of marginalization based on disability is at the core of the movement (Shapiro 1994; Reid 2017). Barriers to inclusion vary alongside the impressive diversity of both disability and infrastructures (Shapiro 1994; Pitney 2015). For persons with physical differences, the elimination of barriers involves redesigning physical environments through elements such as ramps and signage in Braille. For neurological differences, broadened policies increase the participation of individuals with all ranges of cognitive capacities and limit unnecessary exclusions on the basis of irrelevant capacity differences in society. For example, alternative locations for standardized testing allow for better completion by those with sensory differences such as those frequently associated with autism. Such changes empower persons with disabilities and disabled people to shape both their lives and their societies (Winter 2003; Pitney 2015).

Very few (if any) changes driven by the disability rights movement would have succeeded in the absence of state action providing both positive and negative rights to individuals with disabilities and disabled individuals. While the United Nations' proclamations for its member nations matter, only sovereign state actors have the power to implement policy and practise responses to disability rights activists' concerns. In Canada, the United Nations decrees created a global charge by which federal and provincial governments could craft disability policy with these broader changes in mind. After the 1981 International Year of Disabled Persons, the Canadian government formed the Special Committee on the Disabled and the Handicapped to study issues related to persons with disabilities and disabled people (Stienstra 2003). This committee travelled throughout Canada seeking input from the public about disability-related obstacles faced in pursuit of the rights outlined in the UN Declaration of 1975.

While these meetings resulted in a lengthy report entitled *Obstacles*, disability activists critiqued the process as having limited accommodations for persons with disabilities or disabled individuals to access these meetings (Stienstra 2003). Despite these limitations, each province and territory in Canada established advisory councils to study and formulate responses to discriminatory practices against persons with disabilities and disabled people in Canada before the end of the UN's Decade of Disabled Persons (ibid.). Known as collaborative federalism, these self-governing provinces partner with the federal government in addition to municipalities and community organizations to design and implement disability policy in Canada (Prince 2002). In 1982, Canada passed the Charter of Rights and Freedoms, which recognizes persons with disabilities and disabled people with full rights and equal protection under the Canadian constitution (Orsini and Smith 2010). This expanded disability rights by serving as the sovereign authority for federal statutes. For example, the Council of Canadians with Disabilities petitioned the Canadian federal court to merge the Canada Elections Act with the charter to ensure persons with restricted mobility could enjoy full voting rights (Stienstra 2003). In 1996, the Federal Task Force on Disability Issues, known as the Scott Task Force further incorporated organizations of people with disabilities and disabled people by creating a Reference Group charged with advising the committee on how to design legislation modifying civil infrastructure, employment practice, taxing practices, and other matters to include the interests of disabled citizens (ibid.).

Since that time, Canadian disability organizations increased in number and broadened their range of constituencies and services (Prince 2009). This intensified the disability policy discourse and direct advocacy with state actors. Growth of this sector also deepened participation in policy networks serving "as structural bridges between the disability community and the disability state" (ibid., 118). Policy networks facilitated interaction between specific disability organizations and state actors on issues such as disability benefits, child care, school testing and inclusion, employment assistance, and transportation. Disability organizations represent diversified interests and an expanded disability community. Some organizations are composed of persons with disabilities and disabled people, some are made up of families or other allies of persons with disabilities, some are dominated by professionals, and others are a combination of stakeholders (Prince 2009).

Drawbacks of this complexity include the dilution of the messages of diverse advocates and complicate the capacity of the community to collectively strategize advocacy tactics in the policy-making process (Baker 2011). On the state actor side, there are at least thirty federal agencies providing services and guidance programs to persons with disabilities and disabled people. Each of these programs and services include eligibility rules and requirements that have the potential to further divide disability communities. High-quality policy discourse depends on well-articulated, shared missions and clear policy-making apparatuses (Prince 2009). As with most policy processes, efficacious ways to fully bring public input into multifaceted disability policy changes remain elusive (Davidson and Orsini 2013).

In the United States, less direct acknowledgment of United Nations' actions regarding integration of disability into human rights legislation occurred than in Canada (Charlton 1998). However, one watershed moment of disability policy in the United States occurred with the reauthorization of Rehabilitation Act of 1973, which prohibited discrimination on the basis of disability by federal agencies, programs, or activities administered by the federal government, or any entity receiving federal funds (Scotch 2001). This legislation also expanded rehabilitation assistance and increased funds for research and training programs. These changes impacted state and local programs, as many disability organizations were receiving federal funds to operate (Charlton 1998).

Discourse around the social meaning of disability and the ability of disabled individuals to define and meet their own needs remained a largely a grassroots endeavour connected to contemporary social movements (Shapiro 1994). Local advocacy and program centres such as the Berkeley Center for Independent Living and Access Living of Metropolitan Chicago provided living laboratories on how successful differentially abled persons could live (Charlton 1998; Scotch 2001). In 1984, the National Council on Disability was created as an independent federal agency, charged with informing the president and Congress about disability rights and accommodations in health, work, and education. This body recommended the enactment of a sweeping disability rights bill that would incorporate more rights for persons with disabilities and disabled people and provide more oversight of the enactment of the law. Such efforts culminated in the passage of the Americans with Disabilities Act (1990).

As well as policies more focused on adults, the incorporating of disability rights into education policy began in the last few decades of the twentieth century. In Canada, state authority for inclusive education resides with the provincial and territorial governments. Provincial and territorial governments define disability, operationalize what constitutes inclusive education policies, and provide funding to schools for policy implementation. As such, inclusion can vary widely (Towle 2015). Nevertheless, the Supreme Court of Canada retains final say on whether provincial and territorial governments achieved educational inclusivity consistent with the Charter of Rights and Freedoms. Two Supreme Court cases provided a check on provincial government power to define inclusion and provide appropriate education for children with disabilities and disabled children: *Eaton v Brant County Board of Education* [1995] and *Moore v British Columbia* (2012).

In the *Eaton* case, the court affirmed the sovereignty of the school board to define inclusion. Specifically, the court affirmed the school board's decision to move a special education student, Emily Eaton, to a segregated special education classroom. Emily's parents objected, as it would mean removing their daughter from their neighbourhood school to one in a different community. They argued that inclusion involves maintaining connection to the community of origin, as particularly symbolized by neighbourhood schools for children. The Supreme Court cited a different dilemma, in which the relative harm or benefit of inclusion or segregation is highly variable and relativistic in nature. The court ruled for the school board. However, the court underscored that fixed variables cannot design a policy of segregation of children who have disabilities and disabled children. Individual factors must prevail to assure equality of access for education of youth with disabilities and disabled youth.

In the *Moore* case, the Supreme Court of Canada affirmed special education services as a public right, not a supplemental service subject to elimination in fiscal shortfall (Philpott and Fiedorowicz 2012). In this case, Jeffrey Moore received accommodations connected to dyslexia in his public elementary school until the school district cancelled these services, citing budget cuts. His parents enrolled him in a private school and filed a discrimination lawsuit against the school district, alleging that termination of services resulted from a perspective that special education as a luxury service, not a right. The parents also alleged discrimination in remuneration by the school district to cover educational expenses. The Supreme Court's ruling affirmed that the provision of special education constitutes a non-negotiable legal obligation of school districts (Philpott 2012).

Autism-related policy decisions have also been specifically reviewed by the Supreme Court of Canada. *Auton v British Columbia* (2004) addressed the issue of autism through a health rights lens, rather than that of educational rights. The parents of Connor Auton sued the Government of British Columbia for refusing to fully fund Lovaas therapy, an intensive therapeutic treatment for autism. Auton's parents claimed British Columbia's interpretation of the Medicare Protection Act discriminated against children with autism and autistic children. Lovaas therapy, a type of formal behavioural intervention, fell outside core health care services provided by the government. As such, the government limited services for children with autism even while it provided more comprehensive services to other children (Ontario Justice Education Network 2009). Connor's parents sued for redress under the Charter of Rights and Freedoms. The Supreme Court ruled that the Medicare Protection Act did not create a legal obligation on the province's part to provide specific or comprehensive medical treatment for any condition, let alone a controversial treatment (Ontario Justice Education Network 2009). As such, the provincial government's creation of a formulary of covered services was determined not to violate Auton's right to health care, since the right to insist on a specific treatment never existed for any child in the court's opinion.

Also in 2004, parents of children with autism filed a class-action lawsuit against the Ontario provincial government for failing to comprehensively fund autism services in public schools. The parents claimed therapies such as applied behavioural analysis (ABA) and intensive behavioural intervention did not receive similar amounts of funding relative to interventions for other disabilities. The Ontario Court of Appeal struck down a portion of their claims related to age discrimination, since schools do not provide autism services after the age of six. In 2008, the Supreme Court refused to hear the case (Tyler 2008).

Generally, schools in Canada pursue inclusion through individualized instruction plans. Such plans aim to ensure full, equal access to education through instruction delivery specific to needs. Canada's signatory status on two statements from the United Nations – Convention on the Rights of the Child, and Convention on the Rights of Persons with Disabilities – mandates increased accountability for state action at both the federal and provincial levels for implementing special education with maximum fidelity (Pesco et al. 2016; Towle 2015). Parental involvement in program planning constitutes a core design feature of individualized plans. School principals retain primary responsibility for faithful program delivery (Zitomer 2016). Insufficient funding of special education undermines capacities to achieve true integration of students with disabilities and disabled students. Such restrictions can constrain the imagination of professionals. For example, Towle (2015) reviewed definitions of inclusion and funding allocations for districts in New Brunswick and found limited scope in definitions of inclusion.

In the United States, as in Canada, specialized education for many children with disabilities and disabled children involves individualized plans and accommodations. Even though federal funds constitute a small proportion of school funding, the overlap of policy systems and political pressure inherent in the federalist system creates substantial pressure to comply with federal law in education. Furthermore, the creation of a rights basis of special education has increased legal risk for school systems found in violation of federal laws. In 1975, Congress enacted the Education for All Handicapped Children Act, requiring any educational entity accepting federal funds for the purposes of teaching children to provide equal access to education for children with disabilities and disabled children (Hulett 2009). This mandate required schools to assess children and design plans for access to education equivalent to children without disabilities (Leiter 2004). Acknowledging families of disabled children and children with disabilities as natural ecologies for youth with a physical or neurological difference, under Educational for All Handicapped Children, parents gained the authority to review accommodation plans, request changes if parents felt it necessary, and contest the substance of the plan in a court of law (Hulett 2009; Leiter 2004).

The US Congress reenacted this legislation in 1990, renaming it the Individuals with Disabilities Education Act (IDEA). The legislation includes six areas of emphasis: education plans tailored to the individual needs of children with disabilities and disabled children (Individualized Education Program, or IEP); appropriate education provided free of charge to students and their families (free and public education, or FAPE); integration of children with disabilities into classrooms with children who do not have disabilities (least restrictive environment, or LRE); parents as partners with teachers in implementing education plans; mandatory assessments of children to determine the best approach for educating them; and procedural safeguards protecting these rights (Hulett 2009).

As in Canada, special education court proceedings refined policy designs. In 1989, a US circuit court defined two dimensions of a free and appropriate education for children with disabilities and disabled children (*Daniel R.R. v State Board of Education* in Hulett 2009). The first dimension considers whether the child is receiving satisfactory education in a regular classroom with supplemental aides and services. The second asks whether the school integrated the child with a disability into a regular classroom to the maximum extent appropriate. If the answer to the first question is no, then least restrictive environment has not been satisfied and the district must revise its approach with the youth in question. If the answer is yes to both questions, the district is in compliance.

In 1994, a US district court decision expanded the criteria for least restrictive environment. School districts' compliance with least restrictive environment involves four dimensions: 1) whether the benefit to the child of a more restrictive environment significantly outweighs the use of additional services and aides inside a regular classroom; 2) whether the social and emotional needs of the child factor in assessing a less restrictive environment versus a more restrictive environment; 3) whether the presence of a student with a disability presents an adverse impact on the regular education classroom environment; and 4) whether the cost of placing the child with a disability in a regular classroom is exceedingly expensive to the school district (*Sacramento City Unified School District v Rachel H.;* Hulett 2009). In 1998, the US Fourth Circuit Court of Appeals used these four criteria to determine that the social and emotional benefits of mainstreaming a child with autism did not outweigh the students' academic needs. Absence of academic progress supported placement in a more restrictive environment and did not violate IDEA (*Hartmann v Loudoun County Board of Education* 1997; Hulett 2009).

In a similar trajectory to the *Auton* case in Canada, US courts set the parameters for the types of services schools offered families of children with autism and autistic children. As state actor theory anticipates, work on these parameters occurred in the education as opposed to the health policy subsystem given the differences in definition of rights. In a foundational case for school funding of special education services, the US Supreme Court ruled in 1982 that students receiving an adequate education under a disability accommodation plan is consistent with the free and appropriate requirement of IDEA (*Board of Education of Hendrick Hudson Central School District v Rowley* 1982). In essence, the Supreme Court of the United States established a pedagogical or fiscal floor in funding special education services and declined to create a ceiling, though it had the opportunity to do so.

In the case regarding this standard, Amy Rowley's family requested a sign-language interpreter so she could maximize her understanding of the classroom teacher. Amy read lips well but understood less than half of spoken language. Nevertheless, she performed at grade level equal to or better than her classroom peers and was promoted to the next grade each year. Her parents sued the school district, arguing that the lack of a classroom sign-language interpreter resulted in the failure to fulfill a free and appropriate standard because relying on lip-reading did not provide a fully inclusive educational environment.

The Rowley decision clarified one dimension of free and public education under IDEA. US lower courts went on to articulate specific services satisfying the floor of appropriateness. Courts have also deferred to school districts when determining which specific services and interventions to provide to students with disabilities and disabled students (Hulett 2009). However, limits to such discretion exist. In 2004, the US Sixth Circuit Court of Appeal ruled that predetermining appropriate services by school systems for students with autism and autistic students to the exclusion of other therapies violated IDEA (*Deal v Hamilton County Board of Education* 2004).

IDEA requires juvenile justice agencies to provide special education services to youth with disabilities and disabled youth under its care. Several barriers impede full implementation. Comprehensive assessment of system compliance proves difficult given the evolving state of the research on compliance (Mears and Aron 2003). Leading causes for this include insufficient fiscal commitment on the part of legislators for funding IDEA, especially in juvenile justice agencies; restricted or weak communication and information sharing among schools, juvenile justice agencies, and child welfare agencies; limited information about disabilities and the rights of children with disabilities and disabled children among juvenile justice practitioners; and limited data about the prevalence of youth with disabilities in the juvenile justice system (Osborne and Russo 2014). In addition to these barriers, frequent transitions within or between facilities in a given juvenile justice system interrupt the continuity of education (Mears and Aron 2003). Finally, the ongoing punitive organizational focus impedes progress to fully implementing IDEA in many juvenile justice facilities. Even today, youth with autism and autistic youth under juvenile court authority retain the risk of being underserved, due to the weak state of the research on how to substantively connect with these young people, especially in complex public programs (Silberman 2016) such as those pursuing restorative justice.

Public policy can achieve only so much in the absence of a consensus on goals. As discussed above, a focus on crime control grew throughout the juvenile justice policy subsystem in the late twentieth century, reducing the therapeutic intent of the juvenile court (Vito and Kunselman 2011). Nevertheless, commitment to rehabilitative approaches survives. One promising state action involves federal grant programs similar in structure to the national Second Chance Act of 2007. This legislation funds re-entry programs for inmates returning to their communities from prisons. These grants require jurisdictions to submit plans where justice agencies and community non-profits partner to serve these individuals. Agencies and partners hold responsibility for resource sharing, information sharing, and conducting process and outcome evaluations of their programming (Espinoza and Warner 2015). In a parallel structure, school districts and juvenile justice agencies submit grants to a federal funding source providing for information sharing, resource sharing, community partners, and research as part of the activities funded under the grant. Such fiscal federalist programs could help alleviate barriers to the full implementation of IDEA.

Conclusion

When first created, juvenile justice systems emphasized children as innocents vulnerable to vice and predatory adult behaviours, worthy of being saved by the paternalism embodied in the courts' parens patriae and doli incapax legal charters. Courts collaborated with private or religious non-profits serving children under their authority, but often did so in institutional settings, shuttering the children from public view. Early wards of the court who had disabilities were thrice hidden by the intersections of poverty, institutional rehabilitation, and disability. Since these early days, North American societies have transformed their courts in the face of social movements such as the Civil Rights movement and the due process revolution, and the deinstitutionalization of both juveniles under court supervision and persons with disabilities and disabled people.

Persons with disabilities and disabled people rejected ableism by exercising their rights under Canadian and US law to gain equal access to housing, jobs, education, and appropriate treatment in their communities (Stienstra 2003; Winter 2003). Activists advanced the social model of disability, which holds that social conditions create disability from impairment. State actions are cause, consequence, and catalyst for disability rights movements in Canada and the United States. Both societies implemented disability policy that met resistance among individuals with disabilities and disabled individuals who were ostensibly the beneficiaries of these services (ibid.). Public programs once delivered rehabilitative services to persons with disabilities and disabled persons in institutional settings away from public view, depriving the general public of the opportunity to perceive them as human beings. This social distance also promoted abuses and neglect of these persons by their caregivers' because of a habitually weak regulatory oversight by the state (Rothman 1980; Blevins, Cullen, and Sundt 2007). Institutional care also promoted the medical model of disability, which understands physical and intellectual differences as the result of disease and impairment, rather than the result of punitive social policies toward persons with disabilities and disabled persons (Winter 2003).

Following state action to eliminate barriers to inclusion, people with disabilities and disabled people experienced daily life in Canada and the United

States as never before. Deinstitutionalization aimed to restore justice in the context of disability (Prince 2009; Winter 2003), but this effort has had unanticipated consequences. People with disabilities and disabled people in Canada and the United States live in poverty at nearly twice the rate of those without identified disability (Prince 2009; Erickson, Lee, and von Schrader 2014). In both nations, experiencing poverty increases risk of involvement with justice systems. While the right to live in communities remains central to disability rights, the paucity of community-based programs in the decades after deinstitutionalization resulted in an overall decrease in the standard of living for many people (Shapiro 1994; Baker and Leonard 2017). Until poverty disconnects from disability, true (juvenile) justice will remain elusive.

Juvenile justice systems in both Canada and the United States adjudicate youths apart from adults to reduce the stigma of criminal behaviour and to maximize juveniles' rehabilitative potential. Both countries also provide special education services and therapeutic services for youth in need under their care as a matter of compliance with education law. When practitioners suspect or understand that a youth has a neurological difference, both systems require legal hearings to determine the soundness of the juvenile's mind, to ensure that the individual in question knowingly and willingly violated the law. The aforementioned services and proceedings exemplify the power of state action to require that public agencies care for juveniles' legal, social, and educational needs while under state authority.

Youth with disabilities and disabled youth processed by juvenile justice systems depend on a second set of rights – those of due process. Legal due process rights for juveniles under state authority emerged in the latter part of the twentieth century to guarantee civil rights for youth. Since that time, both nations' struggles with observing juveniles' legal rights, fulfilling their disability rights, and protecting public safety characterize public dialogues and justice policy implementation in Canada and the United States. The intersection of these three parameters fuels modern dilemmas on how best to ascertain youths' culpabilities, hold them legally accountable for their actions, and incorporate disability research and acceptance into rehabilitative strategies to support growth of whole human beings.

Chapter 2 summary

1. **Why consider autism in the context of juvenile justice?**
   - Juvenile justice agencies are required to provide special education services to youth with disabilities under their care.
   - Juvenile justice practitioners, attorneys, and judges need to consider an autism diagnosis to ensure proportionality in sentencing, which takes into consideration the culpability of the juvenile in the context of the crime.

2. **How does the juvenile justice system particularly affect youth with autism and autistic youth?**
   - Treating a youth like a criminal can have long-term adverse effects, including influencing the youth to self-identify as a criminal, and therefore behave like a criminal.
   - Whether a youth with autism is culpable of certain crimes is a competency question that considers whether that behaviour is a manifestation of their disability. Culpability should be taken into consideration at every point in the court process to ensure procedural due process.

3. **How can circumstances be improved for youth with autism, autistic youth, and the personnel who interact with them in juvenile justice settings?**
   - The court system is confusing! To ensure that actors in the system do not become complacent, assume that every youth should be handled differently, to support the especially vulnerable in getting the consideration they need to understand the process before them.
   - Courts should adopt the restorative justice model, with a focus on community safety, accountability, and skill development of youth. This model promotes individualized and appropriate responses based on the juvenile, the crime, and the community.

4. **What does rights-based disability policy look like in the context of rehabilitation of youth with autism and autistic youth who have become involved with the juvenile justice system?**
   - The concept of culpability can directly challenge the rights of those with disabilities with regard to whether they understand the consequences of their behaviour and that the criminal system is put in place to hold them responsible.
   - Involving a disability advocate throughout the court process could improve the interactions between youth with autism and autistic youth and the juvenile justice practitioners. These advocates are usually available through nonprofits and some state or provincial departments.

Figure 1 Chapter 2 summary

3 Autism on Trial

Crime exists in deliberate behaviours considered sufficiently antisocial to warrant state-administered consequences. Defining crime proves to be less straightforward than often assumed. Laws evolve continuously in response to changing norms, public pressure, and elite preferences (Kingdon 2010). As a result, criminalized behaviours vary between cultures and change over time (Michalowski 2016). Furthermore, potentially illegal behaviour does not always constitute a crime. In modern democracies, assessments of behaviour and intent combine to determine the existence and degree of a crime. For example, removing items from another's home with permission violates no laws. However, the same act becomes criminal if consent was illegally forced or the items were taken without permission.

Like with all groups of people, some individuals with autism and autistic individuals commit crimes (Brewer and Young 2015). However, in both Canada and the United States, some behaviours signalling potential crime overlap with behaviours typical of autism and causing no substantial injury to others. As Jerrod Brown et al. (2016, 2) describe, "individuals with ASD [autism spectrum disorder] may display non-traditional social skills that persons other than their caregivers may not understand." Interpretation of these behaviours as being connected to malicious intent can inspire fear. Juveniles with autism and autistic juveniles get accused of committing crimes resulting from behaviours associated with difficulties with adapting to environmental change, conversational give and take, and other challenges with social interactions (Rava et al. 2017). For example, a juvenile with autism may experience emotional dysregulation and respond atypically to social cues such as requests to calm down. They may begin violently pounding on walls when frustrated, leave the school grounds when startled, or follow others in a crowd more closely than typical. Given this, they could be charged with offences such as property damage, harassment, or stalking as a result of the intentions others assume from observed behaviours.

All youth run this risk. However, autism can compromise capacities for learning from experiences and making accurate judgments about dynamic social norms when it comes to the letter of the law. Autism in contemporary societies establishes differential susceptibility, since the neurological difference plays a definitive, but often invisible, role in interactions (Mallett 2013). Importantly, differential susceptibility can occur whether the autism exists in the youth, law enforcement personnel, (alleged) victim, or bystanders. Neuro-intersectionality also enhances complexities in the power and oppression dynamics echoed in interactions between individuals with various differences co-involved in stressful situations. Furthermore, as seen in recent viral videos of 911 calls regarding (at most) hardly criminal behaviours, those embodying historical privilege sometimes vastly overestimate the harm experienced from the public conduct of others. Practising intersectional diversity involves moderating one's reactions to others' differences when no genuine threat to physical safety exists. Radical acceptance of the fact that "persons with the disorder [sic] are not *freaks of nature* but everyday citizens who experience difficulties in certain areas" (Brewer and Young 2015, 9, emphasis in original) rests at the core of useful work with autism in juvenile justice systems. Even so, law enforcement personnel can have difficulty recognizing autism, sometimes because of the exposure to a large population of juveniles with similar behaviours but with more criminal intent. As a result, public displays of autism can result in an augmented risk of arrest with presumed intent relative to non-autistic youth.

Juvenile justice systems teem with formal processes and procedures. In many jurisdictions, the volume of proceedings leads to an institutional culture favouring efficiency at the cost of effectiveness and, sometimes, basic justice (Humes 2015; Perlin and Lynch 2017). When resources are scarce, little room for balancing the individual needs of the youth with the legal and procedural requirements of the system exists. In such contexts, organizations face a diversity-efficiency dilemma (Waslander 2007; Barman and Canizares 2015). This chapter explores how diffferential susceptibility and the diversity-effciency dilemma affect the experience of due process in juvenile justice systems for autistics and individuals with autism.

Due Process, Crime, and Difference

Understanding relationships between susceptibility, diversity, and efficiency starts with knowing that disability and crime share a long, storied history. Past understandings of disability ranged from disability as a crime in and of itself to the equally discriminatory belief that disability renders people incapable of committing a crime (Berger 2013). People with disabilities and disabled people were considered so predisposed toward the commission of a crime or so likely to become victims of crime so as to present an ongoing danger to others or themselves (Brewer and Young 2015). Autism as perceived by the public has archtypically existed in children, exacerbating existing social tendencies to infantilize on the basis of disability. After all, the condition first appeared in the third edition of the *Diagnostic and Statistical Manual of Mental Disorders* in 1980 as, exclusively, infantile autism. Whether uniformly vilified or infantilized out of culpability, one-dimensional responses to disability dominated historical thinking about disability and crime. Ironically, both stereotypical notions led proponents to advocate removing people with disabilities from society, either through incarceration or a lifelong commitment to an institution (Shapiro 1994; Berger 2013). Autism proved no exception to standardized responses to disability, in either Canada or the United States.

As discussed in Chapter 2, polite attitudes toward disability have now shifted toward acceptance in North America and much of the world (Berger 2013; Baker 2004). In particular, the notion that disability automatically implies individual or family deviance has fallen out of favour. Casual acceptance of ableism also decreased, especially since the turn of the twentieth century (Baker 2011; Berger 2013; Pitney 2015). Even so, echoes of bias persist. Habitual dependence on disability as crime narratives surfaces in response to stress or crisis. For example, one mechanism of rationalization of public atrocity involves armchair, *ex post facto* diagnosis of autism in the perpetrator. As Neil Brewer and Robin L. Young (2015, 7–8) point out:

> The application of the *on the spectrum* tag has not ... been restricted to the off-the-cuff labelling of high-profile achievers ... it has also been applied to individuals such as Nicky Reilly, Robert Napper, William Cottrell, Jeffrey Dahmer, Ted Kaczynski, Adam Lanza, Martin Bryant, and Anders Breivik – all men who have committed brutal crimes such as rape, arson, and mass murder.

Given this ableist reflex, fair treatment of individuals with disabilities and the disabled requires consideration of how legacies of a harmful history continue to affect professionals, policies, and procedures.

In the context of autism and juvenile justice, distinctions between prosecution and persecution remain murky. According to *Merriam-Webster* online, ethnocentrism is "characterized by or based on the attitude that one's own group is superior." Presumptions of neurotypical superiority pervade contemporary societies. For example, some treatments for autism focus training away from the expression of autistic personality traits (Gobbo and Shmulsky 2016). Gobbo and Shmulsky (2016, 4) argue, "according to the autism acceptance perspective, ableism is the central difficulty for neurodiverse individuals." For many autistics, the goal of passing as neurotypical augments existing cultural ethnocentrism. Comparing the experiences of people with autism and autistic people in two nations requires considering these processes with attention to the role of ethnocentrism from the perspectives of both national and neurotypical cultures.

Due process distinguishes democratic systems from other forms of governance. While far from perfectly implemented, Canadian and American justice systems attend to this fundamental goal. The degree to which due process manifests in the day-to-day practice of criminal justice marks success in the protection of disability-related rights. In the discussion that follows, comparative policy frameworks of punctuated equilibriums and ethnocentrism shape the consideration of this intersection of autism and juvenile justice. These theories connect to the diversity-efficiency dilemma and differential susceptibility through the role of policy entrepreneurs in manifesting changes in public policy design (Baumgartner and Jones 2010). Policy entrepreneurs shape nationally specific definitions of public problems and urge the adoption of preferred solutions in response to a given social phenomenon, thereby directing the flow of resources and privileged understanding of complex situations (Baker and Steuernagel 2009). While key to a national narrative of social progress, successful policy entrepreneurship can also tread close to ethnocentrism through the competition for best-practice status among favoured policy designs and the degree to which the sacrifices of practice of intersectional diversity occurs in the name of public sector efficiency.

Initiations: Arrest and Crime Rates

Initiation into the juvenile justice system involves suspicion of law violation, potentially followed by arrest. In 2017, 809,700 juvenile arrests were made in the United States, down from 1,470,000 in 2011 (OJJDP 2013). In Canada,

101,000 youth were accused of breaking the law in 2014, representing 48 percent of the total arrests in the nation that year (Allen and Superle 2016). Arrests of youth most frequently involved misdemeanour thefts, assault, possession of marijuana, and mischief-related behaviour (ibid.).

Crime occurs less routinely than in the past (Pinker 2012). Between 2001 and 2014, Canada observed a 42 percent drop in crime rates (Allen and Superle 2016). This drop continues a trend from the 1990s, when, for example, homicide rates dropped by 33 percent (Mishra and Lalumière 2009). Juvenile crime rates also decreased in Canada toward the end of the twentieth century. For example, between 1993 and 2001, property crime charges against twelve- to seventeen-year-olds declined 66 percent (Bunge, Johnson, and Baldé 2005, 12). This trend continued into the new century as the number of youths charged by Canadian police decreased 25 percent between 2011 and 2015 (Miladinovic 2016). In the United States, overall crime rates similarly dropped between 1990 and 2001, with homicide rates declining 45 percent, other violent crime decreasing 35 percent, and property crime down 32 percent (Mishra and Lalumière 2009). According to the Office of Juvenile Justice and Delinquency Prevention (OJJDP 2018, n.p.), in the United States, "the juvenile arrest rate for all offences reached its highest level in the last two decades in 1996, and then declined 72% by 2017." In Canada and the United States, people are much safer than in the past, despite augmenting fears of juveniles among the general population (Skenazy 2010).

Debate remains as to why crime rates declined. Furthermore, no consensus exists as to why certain youth are caught committing crimes. Charging children with crimes seems strange. In idealized images of childhood, children engage in misbehaviour and, in the worst-case scenario, become a neighbourhood scamp expected to mature into prosocial behaviour. Of course, another stereotypical image shadows this mirage, that of a corrupted childhood originating in discrimination against "othered," economically disadvantaged communities. Magical thinking about parenting fuel this prejudice, as demonstrated by the frequent assertion that straightforward application of a favoured disciplinary technique would prevent juvenile crime (Skenazy 2010). Even a cursory review of social media posts on a given crime provides a sure opportunity to read confident assertions of prevention of crime through best parenting. Ethnocentrism, historical bias, and a public impulse to rush to judgment perennially render interpretation of juvenile crime especially thorny.

In reality, children and youth sometimes commit crimes or engage in non-criminal activities with devastating consequences. To determine juvenile crime, extensive processes conducted within complex institutions follow the discovery of a concerning behaviour or proposed consequence of a youth's actions. Accurate and fair contemplation of juvenile justice remembers that statistics reflect the population at large rather than the prescriptive expectations of any particular child or youth. As discussed in earlier chapters, both observed and reported criminal behaviour distribute unevenly across populations. Reported crime concentrates geographically. Furthermore, certain schools elevate the risk of police involvement for contemporary youth. Because of resource constraints, expanded record-keeping expectations for teachers, and the more frequent presence of school resource officers assigned to patrol campuses, school personnel have become more inclined to call law enforcement to handle students' behaviour. Chapter 5 explores how this change in climate increased the number of referrals made by law enforcement to prosecutors for behaviours once handled in-house by school officials, particularly in the United States. No consensus exists as to whether this concentration reflects behaviour, systemic bias, institutional resources, or other factors, including the disturbing possibility that both the diversity-efficiency dilemma and ethnocentrism make the concentration of effort an appealing tool for managing complexity.

In keeping with responses to all wicked problems in mature democratic systems, "institutional complexity is not a hypothesis – it is a fact and reality of governance" (Lubell 2013, 537). Separate systems require a collective choice to attend to diversity over efficiency as stakeholders grasp fundamental differences between adults and youth. Even so, articulating the boundary between the two systems can tip daily management of the diversity-efficiency dilemma toward efficiency when the placing of an individual case in one system or the other follows straightforward chronological age or rushed formal processes. In both Canada and the United States, the juvenile crime rate peaks at age seventeen for boys (Allen et al. 2014; Sickmund and Puzzanchera 2014; Hockenberry and Puzzanchera 2015). In the United States, detention rates for girls, who represent only 15 percent of the population in detention, peak at age sixteen (Hockenberry 2016). Across North America, seventeen is tantalizingly close to the age of majority, meaning that "transitioning youth may experience more independence and community participation as they enter adulthood; however, these overall positive changes may be accompanied by increased levels of risk" (Puzzanchera and Hockenberry 2017, 340). The peak age also pulls systems and processes toward the needs, abilities, and capacities of older youth. To the degree that older youth are perceived as not quite children as a result of disability or intersectionality, neurotypical and cultural ethnocentrism can reduce enthusiasm for investment in truly distinct juvenile justice systems.

Youth with disabilities experience more contact with law enforcement than typically developing youth, whether or not they engage in criminal activity. This observation is not new. In the United States, the FBI reported in 2001 that those with developmental disabilities are seven times more likely to come into contact with law enforcement than are people without a disability (Debbaudt 2001; Debbaudt and Rothman 2001). Disability increases the chance of arrest by age twenty-eight by 13 percent (McCauley 2017). Similarly, the Centre for Addiction and Mental Health, in Canada, reports that 40 percent of people diagnosed with mental disorders experience arrest at least once (CAMH 2013). According to Rava et al. (2017, 340), "by age 21, approximately 20% of youth with autism and autistic youth had been stopped and questioned by policy and nearly 5% had been arrested." Furthermore, in recent years, one in four people shot and killed by police in the United States had a mental illness or developmental disability (Roth 2018).

Prosecution for a crime after arrest appears potentially less likely for autistic youth and youth with autism since prosecutors may choose not to press charges even if an arrest occurs (Cheely et al. 2012). This reflects divergent circumstances of arrests in situations involving autism. Law enforcement personnel often respond to calls from parents, caregivers, and educators who are requesting assistance with worrisome or dangerous behaviours sometimes associated with autism. These calls are regularly handled well. For example, 63 percent of Canadian parents report being satisfied with the unfolding of a police contact with their child with autism (Tint et al. 2017). The combination of declining crime rates, peaked rates nearly coincident with the age of majority, and the disproportional involvement with law enforcement of youth with disabilities creates an urgent need to reform juvenile justice policies and practices to better fit contemporary understandings of disability. The creation of separate systems deliberately augmented instutional complexity during a punctuation of policy design focused on childhood during the Progressive Era (approximately 1890–1920). Over time, resource-constrained systems gravitate toward choosing efficiency over diversity. Raised awareness of disability as diversity, neurotypical and cultural ethnocentrism, and intersectionality points toward a likely upcoming punctuation of juvenile justice policy.

Punctuating Rights

Punctuated equilibrium describes how biological species evolve. As a biological theory, punctuated equilibrium suggests that whereas species usually develop through tiny changes, occasional punctuations occur when a change of larger magnitude fundamentally alters a given species. In the context of public policy, punctuated equilibrium posits that public policy changes usually occur incrementally. However, as with biological species, occasionally tremendous changes in policy or political systems occur, up to and including national revolutions. Such punctuations can, but do not have to, focus on diversity and inclusion. In some political systems or policy environments, pointing to replicable successes in other nations facilitates punctuation, even in national contexts tending toward ethnocentrism during normal periods of policy making.

During the late twentieth century, a punctuation in disability policy occurred in democratic systems around the globe (Baker 2011). Section 504 of the Rehabilitation Act of 1973 punctuated disability policy in the United States (Scotch 1984). According to Scotch (1984), the inclusion of disability on the list of characteristics of proscribed discrimination in federal programs surprised many and happened with little, if any, direct discourse by Congress and with little reference to practices in other nations. Section 504 reads:

> No otherwise qualified individual with a disability in the United States, as defined in section 705(20) of this title, shall, solely by reason of her or his disability, be excluded from the participation in, be denied the benefits of, or be subjected to discrimination under any program or activity receiving federal financial assistance or under any program or activity conducted by any Executive agency or by the United States Postal Service. (29 U.S. Code §794)

The identity of the author of this text remains a mystery (Scotch 1984). Although drawn from a primordial soup of nascent policy proposals, this legislation passed without public discussion of its implications (Baker and Leonard 2017; Kingdon 2010; Scotch 2001).

Section 504 involved reframing disability as a rights-based issue on par with the politics of race, ethnicity, age, religion, sexuality and gender (Scotch

2001). Earlier disability policy focused on disability as suffering that could be alleviated by treatment or care. While this aspect of disability policy persists, after the creation of section 504, in the United States the question of rights – or disability as a cause – defined disability policy innovation (Baker 2011). In Canada, this rights-based punctuation became most dramatically evident through the inclusion of disability rights in the Charter of Rights and Freedoms, making Canada the first country in the world to constitutionally prohibit disability-based discrimination. Implementation of rights-based disability policies remains uneven. While some consider disability rights already sufficiently articulated to argue for a post-rights approach to disability, scholars and stakeholders more commonly find that current policies and programs insufficiently address lived experiences of ableism and intersectionality.

As discussed in Chapter 2, protecting the rights of youth with autism and autistics proves especially challenging from the moment of initial law enforcement contact through to the end of involvement with the juvenile justice system (and beyond). Youth on the autism spectrum face expectations of neurotypical behaviour in court, which can unnecessarily truncate the protection of their rights. For example, the Clark County Juvenile Court in Washington State published a guide to assist youth in court appearances that recommends making eye contact with the judge to demonstrate respect. Autism can involve pain when making eye contact with others, meaning that forcing eye contact creates suffering alongside supposed respect. Furthermore, the guide fails to imagine the possibility of a judge's neurological difference, rendering eye contact uncomfortable for some court personnel. Even minor instances of ethnocentric neurotypical preference contribute to a divergent experience as a youth proceeds through the juvenile justice system. Although the disability policy has punctuated into a rights-based subsystem, ableist ethnocentrism stymies expression of rights in the context of juvenile justice systems. Without deliberate attention to the politics of neurodiversity led by committed policy entrepreneurs, policies and programs shaping entry into juvenile justice programs stand to contribute to oppression rather than to justice.

Becoming Involved: An Overview of Entry into Juvenile Justice Systems

Involvement with the juvenile court takes place in phases, each step involving distinct challenges to and opportunities for expression of disability rights. In both Canada and the United States, entry into the juvenile justice system begins with an official suspicion of law-violating behaviour. Given substantial evidence that a crime has occurred, law enforcement initiates responses to the situation. In the absence of substantial evidence that a crime has been committed, a youth may be let go with a warning. In 2014, the arrest rate was 65 percent for all juvenile offences in the United States (OJJDP 2015b). In both nations, arrest on observation of delinquent or otherwise illegal behaviour varies regularly in correlation with perceived immutable characteristics. In some circumstances not involving an indictment or arrest, an officer completed a report in case it proved useful for a later arrest. In Canada, about 45 percent of police contact resulted in no further action (Tint et al. 2017, 2643). Importantly, the vast majority of interactions with law enforcement appear non-injurious to participants. Not every police encounter results in a physical altercation or arrest.

Law enforcement employs professional discretion in deciding how to respond to reported or observed violations, often including the choice to arrest or not. Decisions can turn on ableist, ethnocentric assumptions, especially if autistic responses to social cues deviate from those reflexively and culturally understood as respectful (Debbaudt 2002). Importantly, calling out ethnocentrism as ableist does not afford the individual with autism or autistic individual a right to injure others or commit crimes without consequence, especially in the presence of law enforcement officials. Over-accommodation of harmful behaviour is also discrimination, as such paternalism depends on understanding disability as making a person less human (Baker and Leonard 2017). Instead, a critique of divergent arrest experiences based on disability means law enforcement runs the same risk of misunderstanding cues and contributing to escalation as any individual operating exclusively from neurotypical assumptions. In Canada, such discrimination potentially violates the Charter of Rights and Freedoms. In the United States, however, such actions do not violate the Constitution in the absence of other civil rights violations.

Police officers provide first-responder services and serve as gatekeepers, at times recommending initial services for the youth, transporting youth for medical intervention, or, in some cases, serving in a public-guardian function to de-escalate fraught situations (Roth 2018). Presently, limited field resources exist for officers focused on working with people with autism and autistic people in crisis throughout North America. Detaining youth with disabilities can be a high-risk situation for law enforcement and youth alike. Arrest can be especially dangerous in neurodiverse contexts, since participants in the event are known to process information differently from other neurotypes. High-profile cases of tragic miscommunication between individuals on the spectrum and law enforcement have regularly occurred in recent years. In one Canadian case, eighteen-year-old Dane Spurrell endured arrest and detention by a police officer with the Royal Newfoundland Constabulary. The officer presumed that the young man's gait, lack of eye contact, and terse responses to verbal inquiries indicated intoxication. Moreover, the policing agency refused the young man's requests to call his mother. Spurrell was released only after his mother independently contacted the police and explained his autism to agency personnel (Payette 2015).

Similarly, in August 2015, police officers in St. Paul, Minnesota, observed seventeen-year-old Marcus Abrams behaving in a manner that raised suspicions he was under the influence of illegal drugs. When communication attempts faltered, the officers assaulted Marcus (Autistic Self-Advocacy Network 2015). During the interaction, Marcus suffered a seizure, resulting in a hospital visit. Similarly, in June 2016, an officer in South Florida shot an African American man working with an autistic adult while the man was lying on the ground with his arms up. The officer stated afterward that he did not know why he fired his weapon. Confusion about the unfolding situation and behaviour of the adult with autism overtook police likely also succumbing to racial bias. After the shooting, the officer handcuffed and took the autistic man into custody for no discernible reason. The officer involved was subsequently charged with attempted manslaughter and sued by the autistic man's family (CBS Miami 2017). In 2018, personnel at Guiding Hands School killed an autistic teenager by illegally restraining him face down for more than an hour after he kicked a wall (Schuknecht 2018).

Responding to potentially criminal (or otherwise unsafe) behaviours includes instances of restraint in contemporary juvenile justice practices. However, substantial expansion and improvement of field-level resources are necessary to prevent further injustices when autism mixes with juvenile justice. In addition to the fundamental concerns of justice and public safety, such interactions increase potential cost of lawsuits for the misuse of force, especially in the United States. Furthermore, body cameras worn by law enforcement personnel and widespread use of cell phones able to take and post videos to social media allow for unprecedented public access to police contacts. When it comes to interactions between law enforcement and people on the autism spectrum, research indicates "conflicting views on the quality of interaction" (Rava et al. 2017, 344). Strained resources represent a reason *for* widespread investment in understanding neurodiversity among personnel, rather than an add-on investment justifiably sacrificed in the name of efficiency.

Preliminary efforts to equip first responders to work effectively with youth with autism and autistic youth date back decades. In 2001, the FBI released a bulletin entitled *Contact with Individuals with Autism: Effective Resolutions* (Debbaudt and Rothman 2001). This bulletin aimed to educate law enforcement personnel about autism in order to protect the community and reduce agency liability. Diffusion of information about working with autism in criminal justice operations remains incomplete and has been partially thwarted by "tough on crime" attitudes popular during the 1990s and early 2000s (Baker and Leonard 2017). For example, communicating with law enforcement in a command-follow style falls outside the skill set of many autistics and youth with autism, whereas many law enforcement personnel consider reliance on such protocols key to long-term survival given the dangers inherent in law enforcement (Roth 2018). While searchable databases of law enforcement interactions exist, such tools may provide little insight into a youth's specific ecology. Programs designed to better manage information relating to special needs, such as the Crisis Intervention Team Model (CIT), exist and have achieved some notable local successes. CIT training aims to equip police officers to work with mental health crises, including those involving people on the autism spectrum. Diffusion of such public guardian–oriented programs exists but remains incomplete (Compton et al. 2014). Even proponents of such programs express concern that not all law enforcement personnel have temperaments appropriate for the associated protocols (Roth 2018). Furthermore, implementing disability-tailored approaches runs the risk of their turning into disability profiling, a concern as thorny as racial or ethnic profiling. Local policy entrepreneurs committed to public guardian–criminal justice design and with first-person law enforcement experience appear fundamental to a thriving CIT program.

Realizing a policy punctuation in contexts of ethnocentrism and entrenched professional cultures involves building success through local experiments. In both countries, street-level law enforcement agencies and autism advocacy organizations are highly decentralized, providing opportunities for ever-expanding collaborations or tailored experimentation. National, state, and provincial governments can nurture, support, and facilitate interactions between and among local policy entrepreneurs in order to raise the profile of best practices and allow for global learning from well-intentioned policy failures.

Current efforts range from ad-hoc to more formally implemented curriculums. For example, RCMP working in Nova Scotia noticed an increase in calls for service involving autistic people and people with autism. Officers voiced concerns about their ability to engage these calls productively and requested training on autism (Burke 2014). The RCMP collaborated with Autism Nova Scotia to educate officers in autism-friendly de-escalation techniques such as giving the autistic person additional time and space to initiate calming, and using short declarative sentences (ibid.). This program also sought to avoid classifying autistics and individuals with autism as emotionally disturbed persons (EDPs), since persons labelled as EDP are overrepresented in police shootings and other situations involving extreme use of force (CAMH 2013). Although avoidance of one diagnosis of neurological difference as a prevention strategy for adverse outcomes hardly constitutes complete practice of neurodiversity, such experiments take tentative first steps toward realizing the essential responsibility of law enforcement to protect rights across the diversity of the human population.

In another example of local experimentation, the Coral Gables, Florida, police department, the non-profit organization Disability Independence Group, and the University of Miami–Nova Southeastern University Center for Autism and Related Disabilities collaborate on resources and call-response strategies. The Coral Gables police department website provides a training video that includes information for people on the spectrum on how to interact with law enforcement. The partnership also developed a wallet card, a free personalized identification card to help communicate disability information to law enforcement (City of Coral Gables, n.d.). Details provided on the card include a disability diagnosis if the person is non-verbal, emergency contacts, and other customized information (Disability Independence Group, n.d.). Kelly Denham, policy entrepreneur for the wallet card, states that "someone who has a cognitive issue could be portrayed as somebody who is not following police commands, or might appear to be under the influence of drugs or alcohol when it is not the case ... The wallet card will help ease that communication and help officers understand more" (Maden 2015, n.p.).

As the wallet-card protocol exemplifies, practice of diversity requires awareness. When a referral occurs, law enforcement and juvenile justice practitioners do not automatically receive diagnosis information. Information gaps can form even when, for example, referring school personnel is well aware of a student's diagnosis, owing to the student's participation in special education programs. In contemporary Canada, 56 percent of autism diagnoses occur by age six, and 90 percent by age twelve (Public Health Agency of Canada 2018). Even so, when law enforcement responds to a call, no formal system for notification exists between bureaucratic systems. Separation of records exists to protect privacy. In Canada, federal laws such as the Privacy Act (1983) and the Personal Information Protection and Electronic Documents Act (2000) set privacy protections standards for public sector agencies and private organizations (Privacy Laws in Canada, n.d.). Provincial articulation of these standards varies but uniformly limits real-time communication of diagnosis information (Austin 2006 "PIPEDA in Brief" 2019). In the United States, policies such as the Health Insurance Portability and Accountability Act (1996) and Family Educational Rights and Privacy Act (1974) create national standards for the protection of the privacy of records. Furthermore, on the ground, interpretation of these policies tends to augment restrictions on sharing information beyond the letter of the law in both nations. Local systems and databases used by police officers in the field do not have a standard or universal flagging protocol for disabilities. Understanding disability as a private rather than public experience dates back to care-based conceptions of disability and connects to ongoing ableism.

The goal of immediate communication of a diagnosis presents challenges for any public sector effort relying on individual identification of disability. Terrible enthusiasm for eugenics during the late nineteenth and early twentieth century inspires extreme caution about disability registries. Success in interactions between law enforcement and those with neurological differences relies on familiarity with neurodiversity to overcome the effects of ableist ethnocentrism and the exclusive dependence on the awareness of an individual's diagnosis. After all, as mentioned, autism increases the likelihood of encounters with law enforcement (Mayes 2003). Recent Canadian research shows that one in six youth with autism and autistic youth experienced at least one police contact over the past year (Tint et al. 2017). Increased disability literacy habitually brought into in every encounter with youth by law enforcement serves to reduce the augmentation of risk in these interactions.

Novel technology also helps communication with law enforcement and other first responders. Smart911 collects information about resident characteristics, such as property information, household information, and medical conditions and disabilities. A profile automatically appears to dispatch centres when a 911 call is made (Smart911 2018). Smart911 gives law enforcement or first responders time to prepare before arriving and to get a better understanding of the needs at the scene. This profile travels with individuals, so during an emergency outside the community of residence, the central dispatch of the current location will also receive the profile, if on the system, if an emergency call comes in (Pieper 2012). Although this service exists throughout the nation, local law enforcement agencies must elect to install the technology. Smart911 is quite successful in the areas that have adopted it (ibid.).

Select police departments in Canada and the United States also actively seek out positive ways to influence their standing with the public and signal their commitment to neurodiversity (O'Connor 2017). For example, the New Rochelle Police Department in New York began using an "autism awareness police patch" for their police vehicles, as part of its Autism Patch Challenge. The patch covers their agency association logo for April, in recognition of National Autism Awareness month. The police bureau official stated that this was "a way to educate both the public and his officers about dealing with special needs individuals" (Reiner 2017, n.p.). The New Rochelle Police Department explains that the use of the patch, which has the iconic colourful puzzle background used by many autism-related organizations, demonstrates interest in working proactively with a disability as diversity. While such symbolic policy can appear inconsequential at first glance, affirmative commitment to symbols associated with a policy punctuation communicates the expected trajectory of public policy, especially when combined with ongoing efforts to implement change.

After Arrest: Autism Comes to Court

How the court system processes juveniles depends on the structure of the jurisdiction (Sickmund, Sladky, and Kang, n.d.). When a youth is arrested and detained, they will likely be held in a detention facility until they appear before a judge for a detention hearing. In many cases, this period of initial detention lasts at least overnight. Youth detained overnight may not be given any opportunity to communicate directly with their parents or guardians, despite pop culture portrayals of the right to make a call after arrest. Parents may or may not have the opportunity to deliver supplies, including medications, for the youth, even those detained overnight. These challenges intensify if arrest occurs outside standard business hours. If a youth is arrested on a Friday night, medication and guardian contact may not be permitted until the youth appears in court the following Monday. During the detention hearing, the judge determines whether probable cause exists to justify holding the juvenile. If the judge finds probable cause, an attorney is appointed and a court date set. In the United States, in one in every five cases, the juvenile is detained from the time of the crime disposition of their case (Sickmund, Sladky, and Kang, n.d.). If the judge does not find probable cause, the youth will be released to the community. Disagreement exists among scholars, policy makers, and other stakeholders about whether detaining youth with disabilities and disabled youth reflects discrimination in and of itself. Whether justified by circumstances or discrimination, disability increases likelihood of detention (Tulman 2003).

When a youth is in detention, contact with others can be restricted to particular hours on given days, can exclude direct contact, and can be limited to selected people. Contact with youth in county detention can be less intensive than for adults held in state prison for more serious crimes. For example, in Clark County, Washington, youth detained in county facilities experience less opportunity for direct contact than do youth in state facilities with maximum security or adults in county facilities, since at the juvenile facility the contact takes place using a phone system with a window between participants and visiting hours are relatively limited. Additional stressors on the family include per-day fees for juvenile detention and other assorted court fees.

Non-juvenile justice professionals involved with the youth such as therapists, physicians, teachers, religious leaders, mentors, and tutors cannot continue serving the youth while in detention without having specific, case-by-case permission granted by the facility or court. Furthermore, little, if any, information about working with the particular youth is collected from such personnel, especially if the period of detention is expected to last only a matter of days or weeks. For example, restricting the delivery of educational resources is common, and communication between schools and education programs in detention minimal. Even if a youth with autism or autistic youth has an individual education plan or a 504 plan for accommodations in school, no routine communication of information about such plans occurs between these providers of (public) education. As a result, even short periods of detention can disrupt articulated special education programs. Especially the first time a youth is arrested, transitions between systems can be jarring (and potentially traumatizing) for the youth and family members. When the youth is on the autism spectrum, potential for harm from transitions rises.

If a youth is released after arrest, law enforcement sends a police report to the juvenile prosecutor, and the youth waits in the community for the case processing. According to 2011 statistics collected for the OJJDP report *Juveniles in Residential Placement,* 79 percent of juveniles are not detained while their case is pending (OJJDP 2014). The juvenile might also be booked and released if the officer needs additional time to conduct an investigation. In the United States, this happens frequently, given the significant gap between the time of the crime and the time at which a complaint is made by a victim of an alleged crime. For example, after a report of sexual assault that occurred a year previously, the officer might not arrest right away but refer the case to a detective, who can conduct interviews and gather evidence. Investigations can also uncover additional crimes, sometimes involving other youth or adults.

Once investigations are complete, the prosecutor reviews the report to determine whether substantial evidence of a violation of law exists. When a prosecutor determines a high likelihood of a commission of a crime, the youth is charged and set on the juvenile court calendar for an arraignment. Approximately 54 percent of the cases referred to the prosecutor result in formal charges (OJJDP 2014). In such cases, a summons to appear in court will be sent to the juvenile. During an arraignment, the juvenile enters an initial plea; is appointed or has the opportunity to hire an attorney; future court dates are set, including a trial date; and conditions, or bond, are reviewed and set. According to the same ODDJP report, 19 percent of delinquency cases in 2011 were dismissed, while an additional 24 percent were handled through a diversion program (2014). As Sarah Hockenberry (2016, 1) explains, "two-thirds of youth held in residential placement in 2015 were committed to the facility as part of a court-ordered disposition; the remaining youth were detained pending adjudication, disposition, or placement elsewhere, or were in the facility as part of a diversion agreement."

As discussed in Chapter 2, the Canadian Youth Criminal Justice Act (YCJA) establishes community-oriented practices as a national priority. The provincial and territorial governments have some degree of latitude in implementation. and much of the funding is from subnational sources (Bala and Roberts 2006). Two principles guide implementation of the act: 1) if possible, extrajudicial measures should be employed, and 2) such measures are presumed sufficient consequences for first-time non-violent offenders (Bala and Roberts 2006). A youth who has previously received extrajudicial measures may still be eligible for community-based services rather than detention. A record of offences and consequences is maintained to guide systematic decision making in the event of the youth's repeated difficulties with the law (Department of Justice Canada 2013). The YCJA also requires police officers to explore extrajudicial matters before charging a juvenile with a crime. Extrajudicial options include 1) no action; 2) informal warning; 3) a police caution – a more formal written or oral communication from the police to the juvenile, along with their families; 4) a Crown caution, under which the prosecutor delivers the communication to the juvenile and their family after police refer the case; 5) referral of the juvenile to community programs specializing in services designed to prevent criminal behaviour; and 6) extrajudicial sanctions. This latter category may be used only if the youth takes responsibility for the offence(s) and agrees to the sanction. The youth must understand the sanction and have an opportunity to consult with counsel (ibid.).

As well as prioritizing community-based responses, the YCJA narrowed the conditions under which youth could be detained on either a pretrial or post-adjudication basis. This narrowing came partly in response to the fact that, by the turn of the twentieth century, Canada had one of the highest rates of juvenile detention and incarceration of any of the Western nations (twice the rate of the United States). Furthermore, many stakeholders found it concerning that youth were four times as likely to be detained or incarcerated after criminal activity as were Canadian adults (Canadian Children's Rights Council 2005). If detained today, the protocols and conditions youth face closely mirror those in the United States, discussed above. As in the United States, court processes rarely involve only a single appearance (Humes 2015). Similar to the United States, around half (48 percent in 2014) of cases involving youth result in formal charges. In recent years, bifurcated sentiment about the severity or leniency of the juvenile justice system exists in Canada, with some stakeholders calling for harsher consequences and others finding the system still overly oriented toward harsh punishment.

Contemporary strategies under the YCJA rely on conferencing. Conferencing involves sustained interfaces involving the youth and connected stakeholders (parents, teachers, probation officers, social workers, specialists, etc.). Teams develop activities that hold the youth accountable while also providing targeted services in the hope of addressing the youth's unmet needs underlying antisocial behaviours (Bala, Carrington, and Roberts 2009). Similar efforts exist in parts of the United States, especially in jurisdictions practising restorative justice. Conferencing may include family group meetings, victim-offender mediation, restitution activities, counselling, or other services. The broad legal definition of "conferencing" promotes variability in approaches to serving youth among the provinces and territories (Corrado, Gronsdahl, MacAlister, and Cohen 2010; Hincks and Winterdyk 2016).

In addition to creating new demands of both parents and professionals, conferencing under YCJA brought broader discretion to juvenile justice practitioners, especially youth probation officers (Corrado, Kuehn, and Margaritescu 2010). Such discretion can correlate with more intensive workloads. For example, in Alberta, many probation officers' caseloads decreased with YCJA, but personnel faced increased complexity in the expectations regarding the quality of casework. The intensity of the clinical work with youth and the diversity of community-based resources and organizations increased work demands without concomitant increases in training (Hincks and Winterdyk 2016). YCJA also requires balancing of the roles of officer of the court and trusted adviser to the youth in order to hold juveniles appropriately accountable while attempting rehabilitation. Despite increased professional discretion, research on practices in British Columbia suggests that recommendations tend toward uniformity (Corrado et al. 2010). Such uniformity suggests a return to a focus on the efficiency side of the diversity-efficiency dilemma following the implementation of policy clearly intended to diversify responses to youth crime.

Parents can attend court proceedings in both Canada and the United States. Ongoing attendance may prove challenging for employed parents given factors such as the lack of notice or provision of a specific time for the case and given that most court proceedings involve mulitple appearances on different days. Especially if a youth becomes repeatedly involved in the justice system, parents may be unable to attend all appearances while remaining employed. Parents caring for younger siblings or without reliable transportation could find appearing in court similarly challenging. Finally, in some cases, parents play dual roles as both support person for the child and victim of the crime itself, naturally complicating their attendance at court proceedings. Attending to the factors affecting parent presence in court improves the handling of cases and supports restorative efforts for youth. Unfortunately, the temptation to jump to harsh conclusions about families exists. Perhaps as a result, a relative paucity of direct support for parents of youth involved in the juvenile justice systems, as compared with those available for other court proceedings or parenting activities, persists in North America (Walker et al. 2015).

Court participation involves sustained public self-regulation and the ability to comprehend the developments as they unfold over several proceedings. The question of whether an individual with autism or autistic individual can receive a fully fair trial is worth raising (Brewer and Young 2015). As mentioned, people on the autism spectrum may be asked to portray a non-autistic persona in court in order to be deemed in respectful compliance. Furthermore, juvenile justice practitioners influence the course of court proceedings, potentially favouring youth with less-autistic interaction styles. Examples of behaviours expected in the context of neurotypical ethnocentricism reinforced by North American culture include understanding frequent eye contact as a prerequisite of both respect and attention; preference for bodily stillness in the presence of persons in authority unless specifically directed to make formal movements, such as standing when a judge enters a courtroom; and relating events in narrative format, with an emphasis on the lead actors. Although juvenile courts aim to provide the least restrictive environment possible, jurisdictional culture and the personalities of the court employees present on a given day can impact the outcomes of cases, resulting in the uneven and unpredictable practice of neurodiversity.

Overrepresentation of youth with disabilities in the juvenile justice system appears to result in part from discriminatory decisions made by court personnel (Tulman 2003). Contemporary judges follow policies limiting detainment to circumstances involving flight risk or a specific danger supported by evidence provided by the prosecutor or probation officer. Consideration of these factors in the context of autistic diagnosis is complicated because related characteristics "may not become fully manifest until social demands exceed limited capacities or may be masked by learned strategies in later life" (Autism Speaks, n.d.[a], n.p.). Atypical coping strategies, including eloping unexpectedly and repetitive self-injury, are employed by some people on the autism spectrum. Gauging the appropriate level of caution challenges even the most enlightened courts.

Furthermore, youth with autism and autistic youth may struggle when working with novel adults. Defence attorneys represent many clients. Time and other resource limitations complicate interactions often already involving divergent communication strategies. Public defenders may not have adequate time to spend with their clients to achieve advocacy (Tulman 2003). Practices such as ad-hoc meetings with attorneys, at times in sensory-rich environments such as courthouse hallways, defer to the public defender's need for efficiency over the practice of neurodiversity. Less than satisfactory representation results when attorneys and youths fail to reach common understandings of events and proceedings.

As Edward Humes (2015, ix) writes, "juvenile court is still the unwanted stepchild of the justice system, still understaffed and underfunded, still struggling between the opposing poles of rehabilitation and punishment, still deeply misunderstood by public and policy makers alike." Even so, efforts to rebalance efficiency and diversity and to reduce neurotypical ethnocentrism exist. Materials designed to assist young people with disabilities and disabled youth through the judicial process, including those with autism and the autistic, have been deployed in both Canada and the United States. For example, the Ohio State Bar Foundation created a series of videos explaining the processes for, and rights and responsibilities of, young people with disabilities and their families. The foundation also wrote a resource guide "for the general public" (Ohio State Bar Foundation, n.d.). The intended audience includes not only youth but also other stakeholders, including court professionals. The document opens with a discussion of appropriate communication styles, including a bullet-point guide to communication with youth with neurological differences. Including teachers in the list of stakeholders in a guide created to help in negotiating court systems might seem odd at first glance. However, as is discussed later in this book, this connection reflects the reality of contemporary primary and secondary school educators, especially in the United States (Amstutz 2015). Public school teachers working in the schools today are far more likely to be involved in the court process and to have multiple students in court than in previous generations.

Going a Separate Way: Diversion Programs and Therapeutic Courts

Diversion programs intend the expansion of diversity in judicial practice and the deepening of the restorative ethos in juvenile justice systems. Diversion programs increased in the first decade of the twenty-first century (Sickmund, Sladky, and Kang, n.d.). Two types of diversions exist: pre-charge diversions and post-charge diversions.

As discussed, allowing police officers discretion in response to a crime or crisis constitutes pre-charge diversions. Especially for youth with disabilities and mental health disorders, pre-charge diversions can address a crisis without lengthening the juvenile's criminal record. In Canada, YCJA greatly expanded the options for police officers in responding to youth crime. Most provinces report greater use of warnings, extrajudicial measures, and extrajudicial sanctions than before the 2003 implementation (Campbell 2016; Corrado et al. 2016; Department of Justice Canada 2013). At least one in every five incidents is cleared using extrajudicial measures (Allen et al. 2014). Police officers weigh several factors when considering pre-charge diversion, including but not limited to type of offence, number of police contacts, and existence of a safety risk to keeping the youth in the community. Lack of community resources challenges the effective implementation of this option. Wait times for medical treatment for youth in crisis situations also create deterrents in both Canada and the United States. Officers weigh spending hours in a hospital or treatment centre against the minutes involved in detention-centre drop-offs. In already resource-constrained units, affording this time proves difficult at best. Officers become pressured to choose efficiency over diversity.

Post-charge diversions are presently more common. Such programs stay charges, postponing court appearances and instead providing for community support services. Necessary qualifications for these programs vary among court systems, but typically focus on first or second offences involving a misdemeanour or gross misdemeanour crimes (Bala, Carrington, and Roberts 2009). For example, a diversion program might require a youth charged with minor in possession to meet with a chemical-dependency treatment provider. Emphasis on placing as many youths as possible in the community has dramatically enhanced the resources dedicated to youth in some Canadian communities (Morris and Enstrom 2016). In Ontario, the Mental Health Court Worker program grew from thirteen to forty-five sites as a way to fulfill YCJA's mandated emphasis on community treatment (Campbell 2016). These workers facilitate mental health services between justice-involved youth and the community organizations providing services. Rights-based disability policies also serve to expand diversity in courts' practices. For example, the Accessibility for Ontarians with Disabilities Act, passed in 2005, requires courts to adapt practices for youth with disabilities and mental illnesses so that their court participation reflects and responds to the juvenile's capacities (CAMH 2013).

Post-charge diversion programs also include the creation of specialty courts. Therapeutic courts centre on the provision of services to address population-specific needs such as drug abuse, mental illness, veterans in distress, and families in crisis. Professionals involved in therapeutic courts tend to include a judge, probation officer, counsellor or psychologist, prosecuting and defence attorney, and treatment provider (Wiener and Brank 2015). Therapeutic courts establish an alternative to incarceration following voluntary opt-in to the program by entering a plea of guilty or agreeing to an assumption of guilt. Participants must follow the program structure and attend frequent court hearings to review their progress. The Canadian Mental Health Association provides the juvenile court with treatment and resources for the program participants. As of 2015, fifteen such therapeutic courts existed in Canada (Lamoureux 2015).

In May 2015, Vice Media released a story about the shortcomings of the court systems in Canada and the need to expand therapeutic courts.

The article included a narrative about the experience in the court system for Donald Kushniruk, who committed a minor offence and was housed in a holding cell for two years and seven months while his case was pending in a standard court (Lamoureux 2015). There were several indicators that Kushniruk was mentally ill, including unusual behaviours, his refusal for legal services, and his insistence on representing himself. Shortly after he was released to the community, he committed a new offence and was sent back to jail. After being incarcerated for two weeks, he committed suicide. Kushniruk's story illustrates the importance of therapeutic courts to address the needs of offenders under state authority (ibid.). Chris Hay, the executive director of the John Howard Society of Alberta, states that "jail and the justice system [aren't] set up at all to deal with addiction, with mental health, with poverty, with all of the social aspects that we know directly correlate with juvenile delinquency and adult criminality … Mental health courts are a recognition that mental health issues aren't best served in a residential setting … but best served with a multi-faceted approach" (ibid., n.p.).

Mental health courts appear effective when funded and managed well. For example, a comparison of the recidivism rates in New York's Brooklyn and Bronx areas concludes that mental health court participants recidivate less than those involved in standard court processes (Rossman et al. 2012). Perfecting the use of therapeutic courts remains challenging. Engaging neurodiversity and proactive approaches to inclusion, integration, public safety, and disability rights rest at the core of success with these courts. Several obstacles stifle expansion of diversion programs. For courts outside large metropolitan areas, resource deserts challenge the creation of the most basic diversion programs. Furthermore, in larger areas, demand for existing services overwhelm service capacity or mismatch with available programs. Diversion programs often require family or individual therapy or other services from health care professionals. Many court jurisdictions lack sufficient suitable practitioners to handle all referrals within practical time frames. However, as a researcher from Eastern Canada stated in an interview for this book, law enforcement and juvenile justice practitioners in rural communities can be better equipped to respond to youth with autism and autistic youth because of familiarity with all the individuals living in their community (interview conducted by Whitney Littlefield on March 24, 2017). Although urban areas tend to have more funding and resources, discretionary decisions generally involve less specific knowledge of individuals. Negotiating implications of these perpetual differences between communities rests at the centre of continuous improvement of speciality courts and diversion programs.

Tipping the Balance: Training on Trial

Practising neurodiversity and avoiding neurotypical ethnocentrism both require insight into neurological difference. Juvenile justice practitioners in Canada and the United States broadly report insufficient training regarding autism and neurodiversity more generally (Dicker and Marion 2012; Mallett 2012). The Centre for Addiction and Mental Health reports that police training is "limited and inconsistent" (CAMH 2013, n.p.). Furthermore, training varies substantially between jurisdictions across North America. For example, in Ontario, mental health and disability training are incorporated into the mandatory training for the Ontario Provincial Police and other municipal police services, while other jurisdictions provide autism training for first responders only after a critical incident involving an autistic or a person with autism (Burke 2014).

Juvenile justice professionals can pursue elective training to strategically enhance their professional profile. The elective training or continuing education provides training hours to enhance skills (American Probation and Parole Association, n.d.). In British Columbia, first responders such as police, emergency personnel, nurses, and firefighters receive training at the Justice Institute of British Columbia (Justice Institute of British Columbia, n.d.). The institute delivers both basic and advanced training for persons in these positions. As is the case with several training curriculums, autism training is not a standalone program, however. Rather, if it exists, it is likely combined with a general mental health curriculum (Hovbrender and Raschke 2010). In the United States, Washington State offers juvenile probation officers and detention officers about twenty-eight topics covered in a forty-hour-block training curriculum at the Criminal Justice Training Commission (Washington State Criminal Justice Training Commission, n.d.). Mental health is covered briefly, but no mandatory requirement specific to neurological differences exists. This lack of training impedes many practitioners' ability to effectively respond to and communicate with autistic youth and youth with autism. Even those with good intentions can be completely ineffective in the absence of understanding the difference or disability (Dicker and Marion 2012). Unintended consequences connected to gaps in training include misinterpreting behaviours typical of autism as criminal; youth with autism being accused of committing crimes that have resulted from difficulties in adapting to their environment; trauma when reasonable considerations of differences are not met; and an inability to recognize situations in which community-based responses or diversions are more appropriate (Dicker and Marion 2012).

Lack of disability-focused training has been a long-term challenge across the criminal justice system. For example, in 1993, the United States Office of Special Education and Rehabilitative Services (OSERS) released an article highlighting the training desert regarding disability and the resulting social and legal consequences. The OSERS report states that 12 to 70 percent of juveniles incarcerated had a diagnosable disability, including developmental, learning, mental, or emotional (Curry, Posluszny, and Kraska 1993, 5). More recently, OSERS (2017, n.p.) reports, "though precise figures are difficult to come by, it is estimated that the percentage of incarcerated youth with disabilities typically range from 30 percent to 60 percent, with some estimates as high as 85 percent." The wide ranging estimate of prevalence highlights gaps in disability awareness in juvenile justice contexts.

OSERS identifies four perennial challenges relating to police discretion: 1) law enforcement missing invisible disabilities; 2) vulnerability of the youth with disabilities when overly compliant, leading to possibly admitting unfounded guilt; 3) youth not responding at all, which may be interpreted as non-compliance, resulting in harsher treatment; and 4) youth being arrested for minor crimes that are not a threat to community safety (Curry, Posluszny, and Kraska 1993, 6). To help address these issues, in 1990 OSERS released a training curriculum entitled ECHO: Effectively Communicating with Handicapped Offenders. ECHO served as an educational tool using videotapes and manuals to train all juvenile justice practitioners about disabilities and communication (Curry, Posluszny, and Kraska 1993, 6). Unfortunately, even thirty years later, tools such as these remain less than universally available. More typical is a decentralized approach using tools developed by autism advocates and experts and implemented by request within first-responding agencies. For example, the Autism and Informed Response curriculum was designed by South Carolina Autism Society to enhance autism awareness among EMS and police (Hall, Goodwin, Wright, and Abramson 2007). In this peer-to-peer program, the trainers are parents of children on the autism spectrum who also work as first responders.

As the public develops awareness of the perennial misunderstandings between people with autism and law enforcement, more demands are placed on the justice system for change through training. As discussed, need for better training begins with the moment at which law enforcement starts giving directives to an autistic or individual with autism and finishes well after the end of formal involvement with the justice system. Many people on the autism spectrum process language especially literally. Commands from law enforcement may be misconstrued, and instructions given for subsequent processes may be misunderstood. For example, Reginald "Neli" Latson, a person with autism, spent four years in prison after being interrogated by law enforcement and then trying to leave without answering their questions (Pasha 2017). In Neli's case, he also struggled with communication while in prison and spent a significant amount of time in solitary confinement for non-compliant behaviour. Training for juvenile justice practitioners and law enforcement personnel should be mandatory curriculum in order to increase the potential for just practice and reduce the cost of mistakes rooted in ableist ethnocentrism.

Conclusion

Long periods of normal policy development follow punctuations in the evolution of public policy in democratic systems (Baumgartner and Jones 2010). Punctuations of disability policy in Canada and the United States in the second half of the twentieth century positioned both disability policy subsystems squarely into rights-based policy frameworks. Substantial work on the part of a plethora of stakeholders infused rights-based approaches throughout disability policy infrastructures. This work remains incomplete. In the context of policy subsystems connected to but not defined by disability policy, ableist ethnocentrism continues to constrain full expression of disability rights. Such ableism also reduces the potential for a post-rights punctuation in disability policy more reflective of genuine diversity.

The policies, programs, procedures, and personnel shaping the initiation of involvement of youth with autism and autistic youth with juvenile justice systems exemplify this stage of the evolution of disability policy. In both Canada and the United States, gaps exist between the formed intention of procedural rights from arrest to sentencing and the capacity of the practitioner to effectively deliver on these dreams. Both nations have room to learn and develop better ways to address community-safety issues as they relate to youth with autism and autistic youth. However, law enforcements agencies and juvenile justice systems remain committed to carrying out the rights-based stage of evolution by adapting to a re-conception of the rights of the people they serve. A high-ranking sheriff working in the Northwest region of the United States commented that, although time and resources are always a constraint, "we are not limited in will, and will goes a long way" (interview conducted by Whitney Littlefield on March 24, 2017).

Law enforcement and juvenile justice personnel possess the will, passion, and desire to serve the needs of the community to the best of their abilities. However, resource constraints pervade in both nations, limiting both the time to pursue advancement of knowledge and the ability to provide educational resources. Furthermore, actual or expressed lack of ability to provide such support results from contrasting priorities, different ideologies, or a drained budget. Regardless of the systematic reality, individual public servants are in most cases going to do the best they can with the knowledge and resources at their disposal (interview conducted by Whitney Littlefield on March 24, 2017).

Ableism powerfully shapes understandings of best practices. Juvenile justice systems took root in an ecology of paternalism focusing on the identification and removal of individuals with disabilities and disabled individuals, either for the protection of the disabled or for the protection of society. Effects of mismatch between this paternalism and rights-based policy continue to this day. The observation of the challenges surrounding the planting of new policies into old ecologies have existed for decades. For example, in 1980, Fred Riggs (1980, 107) wrote:

> Whether the reasons are linguistic or cultural, I do not know, but the fact is that we sometimes have words for one side of the coin but not for the other – a fact that pre-conditions the way we think about some problems ... for example, the word "outline," which we use when drawing a profile around something, delimits the same thing as "inline" of whatever surrounds the subject, but English dictionaries do not recognize the latter word. Yet, clearly administrative performance is as much conditioned by the external environment and context in which it is carried out as by the preferences and choices of the immediate actors concerned.

Much has changed in the decades since Riggs made this point about the ecology of public administration in internationally comparative contexts. Ongoing work with law enforcement and juvenile justice system personnel asks these professionals to reconsider the commission and adjudication of youth-related crime in the context of neurological difference.

In considering the judicial processes involving youth with autism and autistic youth in the juvenile justice systems of North America, ecology matters. Much is similar (and similarly problematic) about these procedures in that the balance struck between efficiency and diversity precludes attention to neurodiversity and neuro-intersectionality. The cultural status of criminal justice professionals also affects relationships between law enforcement and the community. Particularly, community perceptions of police discretion depend on whether law enforcement is seen as responding appropriately to crime. Given that, quite apart from the social justice interests attendant in the fuller realization of disability rights, motivation for continued work in the diffusion of disability awareness derives from a desire to develop, protect, or, in some cases, recreate the positive cultural status of the police and the courts. Building awareness and recovering status will take time.

Finally, expressing right-based disability policy across the criminal justice systems requires (re)orienting law enforcement to the role of public guardian (Roth 2018). Officers in both Canada and the United States are routinely dispatched to school and homes where adults seek assistance with distressed children and youth. For example, a deputy from the Northwest region of the United States stated that their department responds daily to calls from homes where a youth with disabilities is out of control (interview with sheriff's deputy conducted by Whitney Littlefield on March 29, 2017). Furthermore, in the United States, twenty-one states have mandatory arrest laws for domestic violence, meaning that if a call is made, at least one of the participants in the altercation must be arrested. Mandatory charging policies also exist at both the federal and provincial levels in Canada. As well-intended but efficiency-oriented policy, laws so designed eliminate officer discretion. With regard to autism and juvenile justice, these laws place parents in the difficult position of needing assistance while fearing that their child will be incarcerated. Similarly, parents worry that restraining their child, even when properly done to keep the child safe, may be seen as abuse and therefore avoid calling on assistance from law enforcement for fear of facing charges or becoming involved with child protective services. Police, parents, courts, juvenile justice personnel, and individuals with disabilities and disabled individuals often still lack both the tools and the knowledge to transcend either idealism or ethnocentrism in the management of such high-stress circumstances. Understanding the complexity of implementing rights-based approaches to disability policy requires full, informed contemplation balancing the real capacities of all stakeholders with the necessity of improvement of the practice of neurodiversity.

Chapter 3 summary

1. **Why consider autism in the context of juvenile justice?**
   - Youth with developmental disabilities are seven times more likely to come in contact with law enforcement, which increases the likelihood that they will become involved with the juvenile justice system.
   - Youth with disabilities are more likely to be arrested and placed in detention than are their peers without disabilities.

2. **How does the juvenile justice system particularly affect youth with autism and autistic youth?**
   - The court hearing and process can be confusing for anyone. Often, youth with disabilities have difficulty understanding the legal proceedings and charges.
   - Police officers and juvenile justice personnel may mistake behaviours manifested by a disability for defiance or disrespect and respond to that, owing to a lack in training or experience working with youth with disabilities.

3. **How can circumstances be improved for youth with autism, autistic youth, and the personnel who interact with them in juvenile justice settings?**
   - Increase the amount of training for law enforcement and juvenile justice personnel regarding disabilities, screening, and communication.
   - Adopt technology such as SMART911 or encourage the use of the wallet card to assist law enforcement and other public services in serving people with disabilities.
   - Increase the use of diversion programs for youth with disabilities to keep them out of the formal court process but still hold them accountable for their behaviour.

4. **What does rights-based disability policy look like in the context of rehabilitation of children with autism and autistic children who have become involved with the juvenile justice system?**
   - Through the lens of punctuated equilibrium theory, due process was substantively enforced with the adaptation of Section 504 in the United States and adopted by the Charter of Rights and Freedoms in Canada.
   - Investing in the expansion of therapeutic courts and ancillary community-based services favourably rebalances diversity and efficiency.
   - The cultural status of law enforcement personnel is that of a public guardian.

Figure 2 Chapter 3 summary

4

This Kid Is Different
Health Care Management and Developing Empathy

Health care is a quintessentially domestic policy subsystem. Admittedly, contemporary trends such as the growth of international pharmaceutical companies, diffusion and coordination of medical research, medical assistance across international borders, disease transmission among nations, and the ability of some to seek out medical care in other nations necessitate multinational perspectives and global efforts in managing health care. Even so, health care systems reflect choices made by (national) governing bodies about the care of a populace. Autism and juvenile justice serves as a keyhole issue, reflecting differences and similarities tied to health policy design decisions as well as to the evolution of the politics of neurodiversity.

As discussed in Chapter 2, holding people in custody incurs state responsibility for meeting all daily needs of those jailed, including health care and accommodations necessary for an inclusive environment. Populations of youth in custody usually include a higher proportion of individuals with complicated health care needs than does the general population (Hogan, Bullock, and Fritsch 2010; Elliot and Katzman 2011; Campie et al. 2015). Providing accommodations for youth with disabilities and disabled youth can be especially challenging in circumstances of neurodiversity. Even barely adequate attention to complex and dynamic neurological differences increases the cost of running juvenile detention facilities above the (largely imaginary) baseline costs of running a facility in the absence of neurodiversity.

Juveniles have differential access to private health care owing largely to the socio-economic status and geographical location of their parents or guardians, especially in the United States. In both nations, the public health care systems predominantly affect the intersection of juvenile justice and autism owing to state responsibilities incurred through incarceration and to the goal of enhancing transition services to avoid a return to custody after release. This chapter explores how juvenile justice systems manage youths' health care from the time of their initial arrest to their completion of probation. This chapter also discusses the ways in which relationships and care are developed within juvenile justice systems, including how those practitioners and providers develop empathy, or sometimes lack empathy, for the population served.

Both Canada and the United States engaged in an iterative process of health policy development of ever-increasing intensity over the course of the last century and into the current one. Although a complete history of health care policy development in Canada and the United States is beyond the scope of this book, a brief overview of publicly provided health care assists in the comparison of the implications of these policies for autism and juvenile justice. In the context of autism and juvenile justice systems, issues relating to federalism and artificial distinctions between physical and mental health care have distorted the care of youth in juvenile justice systems. Understanding the context of public policy design choices lays the foundation for the planning and promotion of better practices in the juvenile justice systems of both nations.

Health Care in Canada

Health care in Canada exists as a positive right provided by the national constitution and administered primarily by the provinces and territories. It includes access to well-established and cost-effective health care practices. According to the Government of Canada (2017, n.p.), "all Canadian citizens and permanent residents may apply for public health insurance ... when you have it, you do not pay for most health care services as health care is paid for through taxes ... all provinces and territories will provide free emergency medical services, even if you do not have a government health card." The public health care system includes coverage for catastrophic illnesses and for more routine expensive life events, such as child birth.

Although substantial criticism of the Canadian health care system rightfully exists, and should be expected in the context of a healthy democratic system, Canadians do not experience medical tragedies such as bankruptcies resulting from medical costs, as commonly experienced in the United States (Hackney, Friesner, and Johnson 2016). Also, life expectancy is three years longer in Canada than in the United States (Conference Board Canada 2019), suggesting that a greater overall success in long-term health outcomes is connected to a lifetime of reliable access to health care. Discourse about and between the two systems is, nevertheless, complicated by the vastly different expectations about the role of governments in health care. For example, one commonly expressed drawback of the Canadian system is wait times for services (Reid 2010). Since Canadians typically consider access to health care a right, whereas those living in the United States are more apt to consider health care a product duly rationed through market forces, reactions to wait times differ. Different perceptions of wait times augment opportunities for misunderstandings of each nation's experiences, which exist on this issue especially. Canadians run the risk of misunderstanding that in the United States substantial wait times for services exist too, assuming an individual is lucky enough to gain access to a specialist at all.

Public health care in Canada is called "Medicare" (not to be confused with programs for the elderly in the United States with the same name). Efforts to establish this system began with provincial programs initiated in 1947 in Saskatchewan. In the current system, covered care still follows provincial and territorial formularies. These formularies often assume typical needs, at least at some level. In an interview conducted for this book, a Canadian researcher described how health care coverage falls short of supporting people with disabilities and disabled people. Additional special care through therapists, psychologists, and medications are not always covered, and as a result these services are often paid out of pocket (interview conducted by Whitney Littlefield on February 17, 2017). Youth are especially vulnerable to this dynamic, since individuals cannot apply for disability coverage under the Canada Pension Plan Disability benefits until having reached eighteen years of age. Furthermore, under some circumstances, coverage does not include assessments or may require a longer than desirable waiting period before assessment. In 2015, for Canadian children suspected of having autism, the average wait time between initial referral from a pediatrician and completed assessment was eight months (Penner 2016). Triaged and often extended wait times tend to exist in all population-based medical care. When and if these costs outweigh the benefits of quicker access to care for those who can afford to pay extra creates moral and ethical questions for health policy regimes of particular nations.

Even after diagnosis, triaging and rationing may add additional time before a particular treatment or service becomes available. According to a Canadian behaviour consultant interviewed for this book, wait periods for services can run as long as two years depending on the level of vulnerability of the individual, family, and community (interview conducted by Whitney Littlefield on February 17, 2017). This is in keeping with a standard of care focused on the needs of the population as a whole, rather than on relying more exclusively on supply and demand to determine order of access to limited services. Part of this circumstance also stems from a lack of consensus in the scientific and medical communities as to the most effective and appropriate interventions for autism (Madden et al. 2017; Cowan, Abel, and Candel 2017). Finally, as in the United States (and around the world), medical services provided for autism are affected by the behaviour basis or the diagnosis, disagreements on goals for young children, and, in some cases, a desire to wait until the child develops more before providing a formal diagnosis (Lo et al. 2017). Since each Canadian province and territory controls which protocols, medications, and treatments the public health care system covers, different opinions on particular interventions can be reflected across the country.

In 2004, the Supreme Court of Canada heard the case of *Auton (Guardian ad litem of) v British Columbia* on the question of whether provinces have a legal responsibility to provide a preferred intervention for autism (in this case, applied behaviour analysis). In a unanimous decision, the court held that provinces have the right under both the Canada Health Act and the Charter of Rights and Freedoms to determine which treatments and services constitute core services for particular conditions, including autism. Federalism rests at the heart of the complicated balancing act between a pronounced national commitment to health care and the desire to respect provincial and territorial autonomy (Sommers and Naylor 2017).

Several other factors affect access to services in Canada, even with an established diagnosis and authorized services. As in the United States, service approval can include time limits for service provision. Health care professionals sometimes recommend lengthier limits than those authorized. Scarcity of providers also restricts access, especially outside major urban centres. Many areas in the country lack specialized services for autism, resulting in some families relocating in order to access them (Ontario Ministry of Children and Youth Services, n.d.). Finally, as with the United States, grey areas exist in the classification of some interventions and services as either medical or educational. Once incarcerated, of course, providing services for youth with autism and autistic youth could appear be simplified by having only one facility involved. At times, this proves true. As is discussed below, the potential for negative feedback loops between educational and medical services provided under the auspices of a single entity within the juvenile justice system also pervade. Furthermore, relying on justice systems to finally bring services together runs counter to a rights-based paradigm inherently referencing community-based locations as fundamental to inclusion and avoidance of discrimination based on disability.

Health Care in the United States

In the United States, access to even basic health care services remains far from uniform. Health care is available through a conglomerate of public and private providers, governed by a patchwork of policies and practices, with substantial variance in administrative practice (T.R. Reid 2010). A person under the age of sixty-five has coverage of basic health care only if they are enrolled in an insurance program or qualify for a public program through poverty or other compromised status, including, sometimes, disability.

Unlike a universal health care system, where every person in a given locality can access the same care, an individual in the American health care system must deliberately enroll in a program based on the level of coverage for which they are willing or able to pay. Physicians employed by health organizations or in private practice generally predetermine which types of insurance they accept from potential patients and are generally free to reject forms of insurance if they so choose. When employers provide insurance, company officials select one or more options for health insurance for their employees from a plethora of options. Individuals can also purchase health insurance for themselves or their families directly or through health care exchanges run by the states. For people under the age of eighteen, a parent or guardian must deliberately provide them with insurance through employment or qualification for public health insurance coverage, meaning that some children and youth in the United States are left uninsured (Feldman et al. 2015; Flores et al. 2016). Some care for children is subsidized by the federal program through the Children's Health Insurance Program (CHIP), but access varies by state (Medicaid and CHIP, n.d.). Although free clinics and emergency care exist, the range and extent of these services are limited at best (Sommers et al. 2015). Furthermore, these well-documented gaps in coverage have historically been especially pronounced for mental or neurological conditions, especially in children.

Stratified access to health care incorporates a diversity in the level of care correlating with willingness or ability to pay. People living in the United States time and again risk forgoing medical care because of cost (Schoen et al. 2013). Despite the fundamental right of the people of the United States to life, liberty, and the pursuit of happiness, the right to liberty is at least as fundamental as the right to life. Some individuals interpret this fundamental right as *not* being forced to incur health care costs when they otherwise would avoid the expense, despite persuasive evidence of the quality-of-life gains anticipated as a result of making such care available (Schoen et al. 2013; Sommers et al. 2015).

Public health care policy and programs in the United States nevertheless expanded over the course of the twentieth century and the next. As early as the Progressive Era, efforts to create public health care existed in the United States. President Theodore Roosevelt was one early supporter of such programs. Early policy proposals coincided with labour and unionizing campaigns, ultimately producing the connection between employer and access to health insurance in the United States.

These early campaigns, unlike many later public policy developments designed to expand access, enjoyed the support of the American Medical Association (AMA). This support was short-lived. The first major national health care public policies successfully passed and implemented in the United States came during the Great Depression while Franklin D. Roosevelt served as president. Although a desire to include health care in the Social Security Act of 1935 existed, concern about opposition from the AMA thwarted its inclusion (Palmer 1999). However, in 1965, the Johnson administration implemented Medicaid and Medicare, creating health care programs for people living in poverty and the elderly. Medicare was expanded to include some people with disabilities in 1972. Medicaid programs are fashioned by states in collaboration with the federal government, resulting in substantial differences among the states. Thus far, the halting trajectory over time has been to expand the number of people covered under Medicaid and Medicare. Variance in eligibility continues to exist among states, and heated debate remains as to the appropriate size of the program, with positions ranging from program elimination to expansion to full coverage of the populace.

Owing to the existing public programs for children with disabilities, specific needs of children with disabilities or disabled children lie outside of the central concerns present in the creation of the Patient Protection and Affordable Care Act, colloquially known as Obamacare (Feldman et al.

2015). The legislation expanded access to health care in the United States through 1) the establishment of an individual mandate to secure insurance (or pay a fine), and 2) the creation of health care exchanges designed to expand purchase options for those not offered health insurance through an employer (or those previously ineligible for public programs). The legislation also provided the opportunity for states to expand Medicaid eligibility with financial support from the federal government. As of April 2017, thirty-two states had expanded Medicaid under the act. Even so, the structure of the law does not create a uniform health care system. The law instead created a uniform responsibility for citizens and businesses to acquire health insurance through various mechanisms, with tax penalties for those residents failing to comply with this requirement. Design elements of the law also included restrictions on the insurance companies' abilities to deny coverage. Importantly, the law maintained the core perception of health care as a market good in the United States. As then president Barack Obama (2016, 526) describes in an article written for the *Journal of the American Medical Association*, "Americans can now count on access to health coverage throughout their lives, and the federal government has an array of tools to bring the rise of health care costs under control ... however, the work toward a high-quality, affordable, accessible health care system is not over."

The Affordable Care Act (ACA) enumerates ten categories of services that must be covered by insurance companies, also known as "essential health benefits" (EHBs). Two out of those ten services hold particular relevance for autism and juvenile justice. One is mental health services. The second is habilitative services, which are defined by the US Department of Health and Human Services as "health care services that help a person keep, learn, or improve skills and functions for daily living" (*Affordable Care Act*, 45 CFR 156.115). These skills include behavioural, social, or mental abilities considered necessary for children to learn how to take care of themselves. The ACA leaves the details of how they will approach the EHB benchmark plan up to each state (ibid.). Finally, the ACA covers autism screening for eighteen- to twenty-four-month-old children (Autism Speaks, n.d.[a]). Unfortunately, many of these provisions may disappear with President Donald Trump's efforts to repeal Obamacare (Appleby and Agnes 2017). If President Trump and Congressional Republicans successfully achieve this goal, likely outcomes include denial of coverage of services for pre-existing conditions and a clawback of existing access under public programs.

As mentioned, Medicaid plays a key role in the context of autism and juvenile justice. Medicaid has also archetypally exemplified fiscal federalism in public health policy in the United States for more than fifty years. As Benjamin Sommers of Harvard's Department of Health Policy and Management, and C. David Naylor, of the Department of Medicine and the Institute of Health Policy, Management and Evaluation at the University of Toronto, explain, "in exchange for federal funding that covers roughtly 50% to 75% of Medicaid program costs depending on the state (the so-called match-rate), states agree to administer the program within broad federal guidelines" (Sommers and Naylor 2017, 1619). From before its enactment, the ACA affected this ongoing dynamic, especially because the design of the ACA promotes voluntary expansion of Medicaid to people with the promise of full federal coverage of the costs associated with newly created eligibility (Sommers and Naylor 2017). According to Chester and Wright (2016), "more than 45 million children have coverage through Medicaid and the Children's Health Insurance Program (CHIP). For the nation's youngest children, Medicaid and CHIP play an outsized role, covering 45 percent of children under the age of six, compared to 35 percent of children between the ages of six and 18." While not all youth involved with juvenile justice systems qualify for Medicaid, as discussed in Chapter 3, statistical overrepresentation of youth from constrained socio-economic backgrounds exists across juvenile justice systems in the United States (Leiber, Bishop, and Chamlin 2011).

Finally, some states create optional waivers (or state plan amendments) designed to increase access to Medicaid for children with disabilities from families with incomes too high to otherwise qualify for Medicaid programs. Services provided can extend beyond those covered (or, at times even available) through either private purchase or other health care plans. For example, wraparound services funded through Medicaid programs sometimes innovate beyond traditionally recognized services or pilot programs long proposed by scholars but not yet routinely available. However, such programs vary across states and over time. As a result, administration of health care in juvenile justice systems differentially intertwines with Medicaid programs across the United States.

Some legislators in the United States continually press for block-grant financing of Medicaid, meaning that states would be given only lump-sum financing to run these programs, regardless of actual cost of care (Sommers and Naylor 2017). Implications of such a shift prove difficult to predict but point to the rationing of care by some mechanism or another. Obvious parallels in the fiscal federalism exist between the Canadian system and block grants for Medicaid (ibid.). However, as expected in the context of comparative policy analysis tied to regime theory, effect and utility of similar policy tools could be driven by philosophical context even if the United States was not so habitually averse to policy learning across national borders. As Sommers and Naylor (2017, E1) explain, "block granting of social programs is not inherently good or bad ... rather it is a policy associated with specific economic and political trade-offs ... increased local control and predictability for the federal budget come at the risk of increased cost-shifting to states or provinces ... that, indeed, is the Canadian experience." Pushes for block-grant funding in the United States coexist with efforts to reduce the number of people who qualify for Medicaid.

Wait times for specialized services exist in the United States, as they do in Canada. Because of the variability in provider availability, coverage, plans, and access to publicly provided programs and services, duration of wait times vary substantially in the United States (Daniels and Mandell 2014). Such delays affect young people with autism and autistic youth in that country (Gordon-Lipkin, Foster, and Peacock 2016). On average, young children with autism in the United States receive this diagnosis between five and six years of age (Crais et al. 2014). This reflects the fact that services not available as health care, either through insurance programs or to those who do not have health insurance, become required as part of some individual education plans created for students under the Individuals with Disabilities Education Act. For example, occupational therapy may become available to a young person as a student but be unavailable, unless privately paid for, to a young person as a patient. In considering health care from a North American perspective, a simple understanding of the wait times for services proves important, since Canadian audiences tend to misunderstand their existence in the United States, assuming instead that privately funded insurance programs respond more immediately to paying clients. One relative advantage of the diversity of insurance programs in the United States involves opportunities for experimention with different management protocols, in the hopes of finding best practices for shortening wait times (Gordon-Lipkin, Foster, and Peacock 2016). Finally, over twenty-five hundred residential detention facilities exist for juveniles in the United States. As Leslie Acoca, Jessica Stephens, and Amanda van Vleet (2014, 2) describe:

> While these settings generally offer correctional and/or therapeutic treatment, there is currently no Federal law or standard definition that defines residential treatment programs ... therefore, these facilities vary widely

according to the offense levels of the girls and boys housed there, program goals, services provided, security features, such as locked rooms or cells, physical environment, facility size, length of stay, and targeted population.

This diversity of facilities existing in the absence of overarching administrative policies almost inevitably creates augmented disparities in health care regimes.

Health Care in Juvenile Detention

As discussed earlier, detention involves taking full responsibility for addressing a person's basic needs. While perhaps not a central focus on the general public's view of detention centres, any humane (let alone restorative) vision of incarceration includes adequate attention to the health care needs of residents. Meeting such needs involves both onsite services and interaction with the larger health care systems outside of facilities. In both Canada and the United States, gaps exist in the health care delivery to juveniles in custody. Both the coverage and the gaps reflect the overarching national character of the health care systems.

Keeping the population of youth detained as healthy as possible makes the operation of facilities less costly and simpler, at least in principle. In both Canada and the United States, access to appropriate health care has long alluded youth in custody, particularly in locations detaining youth for relatively short periods (Desai et al. 2006; Liebenberg and Ungar 2014). For example, a 2006 study of youth in custody in the Cook County, Illinois, Juvenile Temporary Detention centre found that only 16 percent of youth who needed mental health treatment while in custody received it, a figure only 5 percent higher than the percent of youth *not* determined to need treatment who received such treatment while in detention (Teplin et al. 2005). Similarly, in 2005, the Société Canadienne de Pédiatrie reported between 23 and 50 percent of youth entering detention facilities had unmet physical or mental health care needs (Canadian Pediatric Society 2005).

In a more recent study, Acoca, Stephens, and Van Vleet (2014, 3) reported that "a majority of juveniles who enter custody have unmet health needs." Furthermore, Linda Liebenberg and Michael Ungar (2014, 117) reported that "approximately 74% of girls and 66% of boys in the juvenile justice system meet the criteria for a current disorder." While autism in and of itself does not constitute a mental health disorder, no reason exists to suspect rates of need or experiences with services would be better for autistic youth and youth with autism. After all, as Liebenberg and Ungar point out, "the presence of more than one disorder, comorbidity, is consistently found in over half of young offenders" (ibid.). As Rava et al. (2017) explain, comorbidity constitutes a risk factor increasing likelihood of involvement with the criminal justice system for autistic youth and youth with autism, particularly if the youth in question exhibit externalizing behaviours such as emotional outbursts or aggressive behaviour. Given this, youth with autism experiencing incarceration likely need more mental health services than do youth with autism who are not in contact with the juvenile justice system. Finally, since the majority (72 percent in the United States in 2013) of youth in custody are male and autism occurs more frequently in males than in females, the proportion of youth with autism and autistic youth in custody would be anticipated higher than the general population of youth (Acoca, Stephens, and Van Vleet 2014; Puzzanchera and Hockenberry 2017). Even so, "girls experience higher rates of mental health and substance use disorders and are less likely than boys to have their medical needs identified, treated, or followed inside the juvenile justice system or after their release to their communities" (Acoca, Stephens, and Van Vleet 2014, 4). Given this, caution in planning around expected gender differentials remains important.

Access to appropriate health care beyond mental health proves similarly challenging in juvenile justice systems in Canada and the United States. It is important to note in passing that the distinction of mental and physical health care connects back to the largely disproven separation of mind and body largely attributed to Rene Descartes. Nevertheless, in both Canada and the United States, distinct providers, professions, policies, and infrastructures for physical and mental health persist and play an ongoing, ethnocentric, role in the national health identities. Autism does not inherently involve differences in physical health. However, as was shown in a twenty-five-year study of individuals first diagnosed with autism in the 1980s, having autism appears associated with "a high number of chronic medical conditions, regardless of intellectual ability" (Jones et al. 2016, 551). Finding effective health care proves challenging for some children and youth with autism, above and beyond those anticipated for all children, especially in the United States (Drapela and Baker 2014). Furthermore, treatment for comorbid conditions involves potential for physical side effects, augmented during periods of transition in providers. As a result of these and other factors, consideration of physical and basic medical care plays a central role in understanding autism and the juvenile justice system.

In 1976, the US Supreme Court held in *Estelle v Gamble* that denying medical care to incarcerated individuals constituted cruel and unusual punishment. Despite this ruling, denial of medical care persisted well beyond the 1970s, including in detention facilities for youth. For example, in June 2003, Omar Painsley died at age seventeen of a ruptured appendix without having received any treatment, including attempts to revive him, despite having repeatedly pleaded for help from staff at the Miami-Dade Juvenile Detention Center (Shirk 2009). Service delivery structures vary and sometimes involve less than desirable levels oversight or attention to patients' rights (Acoca, Stephens, and Van Vleet 2014). Provision of health care in US detention facilities frequently involves competitive government contracts awarded to profit corporations. Those in detention are at times assessed co-pays for medical care, similar to those paid by the non-incarcerated, sometimes producing a hesitancy to pursue care on the part of the patient. The vast majority (approximately 98 percent in 2007) of facilities detaining youth fail to comply with the National Commission on Correctional Health Care's voluntary standards established for health services provided in detention facilities (ibid.). As Elizabeth Barnert, Raymond Perry, and Robert E. Morris (2016, 103) explain, "the small size of many facilities, staffing challenges, limited availability of nearby specialty medical services, and budgetary constraints are some of the reasons that juvenile facilities may have difficulty meeting the standards set by NCCHC."

Not surprisingly, the structure involving competitive bidding for government contracts allows local monopolies to flourish (United States Department of Justice 2016). It also augments variation in both quantity and quality of care across facilities. In the United States, the level of care that juveniles receive also depends on whether the facility is operating under local, state, federal, or private funding. Privately funded facilities are less likely to provide a full range of services than those run through the public sector (Barnert, Perry, and Morris 2016). Some facilities provide care through local health departments, which collaborate with other agencies, including those in the private sector. As Barnert, Perry, and Morris (2016, 103) explain, "over recent decades, we have observed that there has been a shift away from partnerships with academic medical centres, possibly as a result of competing priorities within medical centers and training programs." Furthermore, some facilities do not provide in-house care for their residents for various reasons, whereas others have nurse and medical staff available around the clock.

Multiple turning points affect access to care during youth detention. A critical step in access to health care while in custody takes place during the intake or booking process. Both federal and state laws dictate specific medical questions that must be asked so staff are aware of conditions needing immediate attention. Many juveniles have untreated oral health needs when they arrive in detention facilities (Barnert, Perry, and Morris 2016). Furthermore, an estimated 80 percent of youth in juvenile justice systems are not enrolled with a primary care provider in their communities (Gergelis, Kole, and Lowenhaupt 2016). As Gergelis, Kole, and Lowenhaupt (2016, 24) point out, "many of these conditions are first identified upon entering the juvenile justice system, addressed while youth are incarcerated, and require continued care long after their release." Unfortunately, largely owing to the different bureaucracies and at times conflicting qualifications for public health programs, many juveniles lose existing publicly provided coverage while in detention and, therefore, have no health coverage on release (Barnert, Perry, and Morris 2016; Acoca, Stephens, and Van Vleet 2014; Sattler 2017). Although in many facilities across the United States youth receive quality health care while detained, coverage gaps exist, and formerly detained youth can fall off coverage in the absence of dedicated adult advocacy and resources.

Juvenile detention facilities are not typically set up for the treatment of complex health challenges (Kretschmar 2017). Health care services compete with a spate of other services and activities central to the institutional agendas of juvenile correctional facilities (Barnert, Perry, and Morris 2016). As Gergelis and her colleagues (2016, 26) explain, "juvenile detention and correctional facilities run on strict daily schedules with time for school, meals, and other programming, which can create time conflicts for medical and psychiatric appointments ... patients must be escorted to the clinic by correctional officers for supervision and safety, which requires sufficient staffing." As well, as Gergelis and colleagues further point out, this interruption of institutional scheduling combines with a highly variable length of stay in custody, potentially undermining both correctional and rehabilitation programming. As a result, investment in coordinating services on behalf of a particular youth at the expense of the organization as a whole can appear not worth the trouble the effort costs.

As discussed above, unlike in the United States, health care in Canada is a fundamental right for all people. Therefore, all people who are incarcerated have the right to health care. This right is further guaranteed through the 1992 Corrections and Conditional Release Act, which protects the rights of incarcerated people as being the same as those of all citizens, barring those that are suspended in keeping with the offender's sentence. Therefore, inmates and detainees have the right to be treated in a fair manner with respect to their gender, ethnic, cultural, and linguistic differences, as well as to have their health care needs met.

The Canadian juvenile justice system offers several programs for youth with mental illnesses and disabilities. As in the United States, youth involved with the juvenile justice system tend to have more complex health care needs than the general population of youth in Canada (Elliot and Katzman 2011). The Criminal Code of Canada contains procedures to determine the culpability of youth with mental health disorders or disabilities who commit a crime. A youth is found to be a forensic client if to a review board that consists of judges, attorneys, mental health professionals, practitioners, and community members, they are "not criminally responsible on Account of Mental Disorder" (CAMH 2013, n.p.). However, the Centre for Addiction and Mental Health states that screening practices in jails and detention centres are inadequate and inconsistent and, therefore, ineffective in identifying the need for accommodations or services that can be provided to those in detention (CAMH 2013). Compromised screening necessarily reduces the effectiveness of health care, even in the most resource-rich environments. Obviously, in environments of scarcity, effects of incomplete screening on the quality of health care can be even more damaging.

Risk Assessments and Services in Detention

Improved screening of youth entering juvenile justice facilities has long been recommended by professional health care organizations (Gergelis, Kole, and Lowenhaupt 2016). Juvenile justice personnel have many potential tools at their disposal to provide for the health care of youth. Risk assessments are one of the primary tools used to determine the likelihood that a juvenile will commit another offence, combining the goals of basic health care and rehabilitation. Risk factors are defined as aspects of the juvenile's life that increase the likelihood of engaging in criminal behaviour, for instance, substance use and abuse, mental health issues, attitudes, and beliefs (Wasserman et al. 2003). On the other hand, protective factors decrease the likelihood of committing crimes – for instance, good attendance and performance in school, prosocial ties to the community, and having a job or strong employment skills (Wasserman et al. 2003). Risk assessments serve as vital tools to protect the health and safety of youth in detention. For example, youth in custody experience far higher rates of suicidal ideation than do youth in the community (Gergelis, Kole, and Lowenhaupt 2016). Risk assessment can assist practitioners in procuring supports before a tragedy occurs.

Which risk assessment tools are employed by a juvenile court jurisdiction is determined by the judges and juvenile court executive staff (e.g., the juvenile court administrator or warden). Selection is far from simple. Laurence Steinberg (2008) argues that courts should not rely on just one process but should use a combination of both actuarial risk assessments and subjective clinical assessments. In addition, subjective assessments are made by the juvenile justice practitioner working one on one with the youth. Such observations are not empirically validated, but rather are hopefully clinically informed judgments about the youth's risk, needs, and care strategies.

Robinson et al. (2012) reviewed the screening instruments used in prisons for identifying autism with the goal of identifying why so many individuals with autism and autistic individuals are undetected in the criminal justice system. The research team also created a new screening tool tested in twelve Scottish prisons. The new tool demonstrated adequate construct validity for autism (meaning the test measures what it aims to test); however, the sensitivity measures are low and require further study to increase the scale's efficacy.

Designing an appropriate and time-sensitive tool proves difficult but could solve significant problems for youth, especially if they have yet to be diagnosed. The potential for a reduced workload for staff and better care for the juvenile could function as an incentive for juvenile court jurisdictions or their supporting agencies to develop these tools. Effective screening tools are essential for juvenile justice practitioners to justify getting the needed resources and exploring treatment options related to the juvenile's diagnosis. A common critique of clinical assessments is that the results can be biased or filtered by the interviewer's own skills, interpretations, and perspectives of the interviewees. Clinicians' perceptions can be negative because of the youth's race or disability status, or positive because of shared ascribed or demographic characteristics between the clinician and the client. Either source taints the clinical outcomes of assessment.

Actuarial assessments create a uniform set of closed-ended questions administered to all juveniles. These second-generation assessment tools classify individuals according to particular traits and aim to predict the odds of future law-violating behaviour based on the configuration of those traits (Schwalbe 2007). The efficacy of second-generation assessment tools depends on their predictive validity, or the accuracy of the tool to predict which juveniles among those assessed will go on to commit offences (Schwalbe 2008). In theory, actuarial assessments filter out the bias inherent in clinical assessments because the uniformity prevents clinicians' subjective perceptions of the juvenile from being the only official record of a youth's risk factors and non-criminogenic needs. While they promote greater objectivity and uniform data collection among raters, actuarial assessments lack the detailed historical information clinicians need to make an accurate judgment about a juvenile's risks and needs.

Risk-needs assessments are third-generation assessments incorporating both static and dynamic measures of the juvenile in question. Static measures are those conditions that usually cannot be changed, such as race, gender, family history, and past criminal behaviour. Examples of dynamic factors in assessment tools are the juvenile's associations with criminal others, educational aptitude, and attitudes about their futures. These assessments are not as cut-and-dried as actuarial assessments, and their results aid practitioners in intervention planning as well as in classification of juveniles' recidivism risks (Schwalbe 2007). Fourth-generation assessments use a combination of static and dynamic factors to comprehensively track the youth from intake to aftercare, allowing practitioners to link baseline measures of risk and protective factors to mid-sentence and post-sentence outcomes. These assessments provide comprehensive information about the youth throughout their time under the authority of the juvenile court but also capture offender change (Andrews, Bonta, and Wormith 2006).

Both third- and fourth-generation assessment tools enhance practitioners' capacities to engage in evidence-based practice. The principles of effective correctional treatment are as follows: interventions should be administered to offenders proportionately to their criminal risk to reoffend (R); should address the offenders' criminogenic needs (N), and should be delivered to the offender in such a way that they can understand what is being given to them and demanded of them (responsivity) (R) (Andrews and Bonta 2010). The RNR model used in some North American corrections facilities since the 1990s identifies eight risk and protective factors that practitioners should target when working with the offenders. The first four – known colloquially as "the big four" – are a history of antisocial behaviour, an antisocial personality pattern, antisocial cognition, and antisocial associates. The other four are family or marital factors, school or work factors, leisure or recreation interests, and substance abuse. Taken together, these factors for offender change comprise the central eight risk factors for recidivism (Andrews and Bonta 2010). Much of the research on the RNR model is on adults, however. How fourth-generation assessments apply the RNR model to youth in the juvenile justice systems remains a work in progress.

Balancing the subjective and actuarial processes to serve youth in the juvenile justice systems can be both challenging and counterintuitive. There are several obstacles in the risk assessment process. These include 1) inadequacy of screening tools, 2) not enough resources to meet the needs identified through the screening, and 3) insufficient training of juvenile justice employees to utilize these tools (Mallett 2013). Modern juvenile justice systems ask practitioners to treat each youth individually and without bias. The formal instruments evaluating risk strive to answer the following questions: Will this juvenile commit another crime? If so, what factors reduce that chance if properly addressed by staff and the youth in question? Neurological differences can confound risk assessment tools. The risk assessment tool might predict that a youth with autism or autistic youth is at low risk for reoffending because they do not present the standard factors associated with recidivism, such as parental abuse and neglect, attendance in school, and drug or alcohol use (Oliver, Stockdale, and Wong 2012). However, autistic youth and youth with autism may be vulnerable to a different set of risk factors, such as disruption of routine and having atypical fascinations and difficulty assessing social cues or understanding indirect language, affecting the risk that youth will have more contact with law enforcement (King and Murphy 2014). Given this, most people with autism and autistic people asked about their experiences with justice systems do not believe that their autism was taken into account throughout the various phases of the process, including arrest, court, jail, and probation (ibid.).

Autism-specific health services for youth in custody and related training opportunities for detention staff remain limited. A practitioner experienced in both community-based programs and juvenile custody remarked that his jurisdiction "had no targeted services for the autistic kids ... even community-based services are sparse. Some kids may be able to access something for autism ... but that's only if they are on Medicaid. The justice system should not be the primary provider for autistic kids in need – the community is the place for these kids" (interview conducted by Laurie Drapela on February 13, 2017). If anything, the practitioners in this jurisdiction would use their professional discretion to best serve youth with autism and autistic youth. The practitioner remarked that the best way to engage these juveniles was to

> learn how to roll with things ... to strike a balance between [the youth] obeying the rules and letting them have their routine their way. One kid in detention who I know was on the spectrum was very difficult to get up and

ready for school. He would stay in bed rather than getting himself ready and lining up for breakfast and then school. He would put up a real fight if he had to get up before he was ready ... the other DOs [detention officers] let me know that it wasn't worth the fight to get him up and ready. Just let him stay. (Interview conducted by Laurie Drapela on February 13, 2017)

This practitioner noted that other youth in detention could get upset with the staff in response to differences in rules, underscoring one of the challenges of using discretionary measures to work with youth with disabilities and disabled youth rather than implementing codified policies of the court or detention office.

However, such flexibility and professional discretion can also reduce conflict inside the facility. Flexibility has been employed to help facilities reduce liability during intake. For example, residents who are pregnant are not subject to the same cuffing policy as non-pregnant residents. Female youth are more likely than the general population to have experienced trauma, including sexual abuse, and are more likely to be pregnant than are youth not involved with the juvenile justice system (Kretschmar et al. 2017). Juvenile justice system personnel can (and sometimes do) also use other resources, such as parents, counsellors, doctors, and probation officers, to gain more information about specific conditions or medical needs.

Mental Health Courts

Many youth with disabilities and disabled youth enter the criminal justice system with insufficient support, including long-term plans for providing support for health care needs. When leaving detention, gaps in support may reemerge. As Carleton University professor of psychology Robert Hoge (2008, 57) argues, "criminal activity on the part of young people often represents social conditions that we find difficult to confront." Wraparound services intend to address such gaps.

One way to deliver wraparound services to youth in the community is through mental health courts. In the mental health court model, juveniles are diverted away from traditional court processing to a specialized courtroom workgroup using therapeutic justice (Redlich et al. 2006). The philosophy of therapeutic jurisprudence stresses that legal actions also have tangible social and psychological benefit for the person processed by the criminal justice system (Wexler 2010). Mental health courts achieve this by keeping people in their communities so they can receive mental health treatment using a peer-support model, maximizing social and emotional support as the individual moves through the stages of the program. Mental health courts also emphasize collaboration rather than adversarial professional roles among the members of the courtroom workgroup (judge, prosecutor, defence attorney, court coordinator, mental health professionals), and offenders are both praised for their successes and held accountable for their failures by the mental health court judge (Redlich et al. 2006).

Mental health courts developed in the 1990s in response to the increasing number of adults with mental health challenges in the criminal justice system (Almquist and Dodd 2009). During the same period, many jurisdictions began a process of "net widening" with juveniles who had mental health challenges. That meant that youth with mental health problems were being formally processed by juvenile justice systems, when during an earlier period they would have either been diverted out of court to home or another community-based resource, or sent to a full-time care institution. By the 1990s, the juvenile justice system became responsible for caring for these youth, as other care options were not available or their families could not afford to assist them in the private health care market (ibid.). Mental health courts for juveniles remain less common than for adults in the United States. One reason for this is the differences in legal context in which the courts operate. For example, many adults with mental health issues self-medicate with substances legal for them, such as alcohol. Juveniles who engage in the same behaviour may come under the authority of the juvenile court in violation of a status offence.

Canadian juvenile justice systems have implemented mental health courts for youth as well (Davis et al. 2015). Beginning in 2008, the Canadian government adapted the adult mental health court model to meet the mental health needs of juveniles under state authority. This model was amended for youth because "they face unique challenges with regards to diagnosis and treatment, as well as [to] how to involve families and address school-related issues" (ibid., 161). In their process evaluation of one of the first youth mental health courts in Toronto, Davis and colleagues note that only half of the sample had their mental health treatment needs met through targeted interventions delivered by community service providers. The rest of the sample either received generalized treatment, such as talk therapy or counselling, or were in the process of receiving a comprehensive assessment with the intent to treat once this process was complete (ibid.). Interestingly, 4 percent of the youth in this study were diagnosed with autism, mirroring contemporary population estimates of prevalence.

A critical element of any therapeutic court is the development of eligibility criteria that are used to consistently identify appropriate clients for the intervention. Davis and associates found that such criteria were not consistently being used by program personnel, resulting in program attrition. They recommend development of inclusion criteria with a strong goodness of fit to the mental health mission of the court, as well as better training for judges, defence counsel, and Crown attorneys, in order to better identify potential clients for the court. Finally, the authors suggest mandatory mental health screening for all juvenile justice clients, to improve identification of youths' needs and treatment planning. An added benefit of mandatory screening is to enhance due process protections for youth, because those who are not fit to stand trial can be more accurately identified than is currently the case (Davis et al. 2015).

Mental health courts can serve to improve coordination of services, even for youth served outside the specialized court, as professionals across organizations gain familiarity with one another. Coordinated efforts between the court, county non-profits, and other local service agencies assisting youth with mental health issues meet various needs, such as housing, medical care, food security, special education services, and mentorship programs. Coordination matters. For example, an outcome evaluation of a community-based mental health program for youth with mental health challenges administered through the Clark County Juvenile Court in Clark County, Washington, found that youth who had received services coordinated by both the juvenile court and the mental health system had significantly lower recidivism rates than youth who received standard mental health services but no coordination with the juvenile court (Pullmann et al. 2006). Youth who received coordinated services also spent significantly fewer days in detention than youth who did not receive coordinated services (ibid.).

Wraparound services highlight an important reality of the human experience. While systems often categorize human needs in the democratic systems of both Canada and the United States, all lived experience connects. Regardless of the prevailing national attitude underlying the design of a given health care system, youth involved in juvenile justice systems have intertwined, complex needs affecting their ability to reset their life course. Especially in the context of neurological difference, interagency coordination and consideration of the needs of the whole child in the context in which they must make their way are critical to rehabilitation.

Empathy and Juvenile Justice

Practice of health care turns on empathy (Mercer et al. 2016). Empathy constitutes a potentially triggering concept, especially for autistics (Prizant 2016). One of the most challenging aspects of living in a neurotypcial world as an autistic individual or individual with autism involves the expectation that people will effortlessly express understanding, excel in perspective taking, and follow culturally standard processes recognized as empathetic exchange. A related challenge is the assumption that people with autism and autistic people cannot be empathetic (Silberman 2016). Such judgments reflect hegemonic forces of "normal" individuals levied against those who are neuroatypical.

Behaviours interpreted by others as lack of empathy on the part of a person with autism or an autistic person can provoke neglect or abuse. As Matthew Lerner and colleagues (2012, 177) at the University of Virginia note, people with autism and autistic people "display atypical development of social reasoning and intuitions." Differences in the interpretation of events may result in their failing to notice the pain or harm of others, not because of a lack of empathy but because of a differing experience of the situation. Similarly, differences in sensory perceptions sometimes associated with autism can strain the empathy of individuals without autism. For example, one of the authors of this book once spent a long night with a youth with autism who woke her several times every hour to report noises such as beeping coming from lights not audible to the neurologically typical residents of the house. Despite prolonged experience with autism both academically and interpersonally, the neurotypical author involved in this experience found her empathy strained as the night wore on, and younger children in the house were awakened by the distressed communications of the autistic youth. In the context of health care, Western medicine routinely incorporates less focus on experience than in other, more traditional health care practices (Vance 2016). Empathy and sensory incongruities between those on and off the autism spectrum contribute to timeliness of the delivery of health care, if not also to the quality of care received.

Systems too require empathy to function. Empathy involves imagining feelings connected to the position or circumstance occupied by another. Systems and the organizations they encompass rely on interpersonal communication and relationship building, even in technologically developed settings. Interpersonal communications devoid of empathy and a failure to build healthy relationships between the humans involved characterize unhealthy organizations and systems. Institutions controlling the day-to-day lives of large numbers of people sometimes become pathological organizations lacking empathy (Steinberg, Chung, and Little 2004). While the design intention of justice systems encompasses compassion for those accused of or found to have committed crimes, justice systems have been noted by scholars and activists as lacking empathy for all stakeholders (Beal 2014; ibid.). One reason collective empathy proves challenging in public institutional settings involves bureaucratic organization and directives that originate outside the agency and which prioritize fiscal efficiencies and dispassionate employee-performance benchmarks. Other contributors to lack of empathy on the part of juvenile justice practitioners as a group include lack of training and job-related trauma.

Priorities communicated to practitioners in juvenile justice agencies rarely include empathy as an outreach tool for establishing rapport with youth under correctional authority (Crawford 2014). The exercise of empathy can be perceived as wasting time and frequently becomes one of the first habits sacrificed under stress. Whether the resource involved is actual time or emotional labour, empathy vanishes alongside increased institutional strain.

The diagnosis of neurological differences such as autism becomes a non-neutral event in such circumstances. Acquiring a diagnosis not only creates potential for negative stereotyping but also tends to incur additional performance burdens for both individual employees and the organizations as a whole (Brewer and Young 2015). As mentioned in Chapter 1, many of the youth who enter the system have disabilities that are undiagnosed, which can interfere with the ability for the juvenile justice system to work appropriately for the youth. Even in circumstances where juvenile justice systems and practitioners working within their programs exercise empathy, the career reward structure for practitioners in the system – from juvenile court judges and administrators to juvenile probation counsellors – does not necessarily incentivize the development of empathy as a professional goal. As such, many practitioners in the juvenile justice system know they should engage individuals with disabilities and disabled individuals better than they currently do, but either do not know how to achieve this goal or cannot find a time-efficient way to practise empathy alongside all other professional expectations.

This circumstance has been noted for some time. Kvarfordt, Purcell, and Shannon reported in 2005 that while many of the detention officers and probation officers surveyed knew they needed training to better work with youth with disabilities, the majority of the sample had not received training for this purpose in anywhere from three to eight years, with the average training lag being five years (Kvarfordt, Purcell, and Shannon 2005). Approximately one-quarter of these practitioners had received some training on autism spectrum disorder, but an average of seven years had elapsed since that training. Despite these training lags, 96 percent of those sampled expressed a desire for education about youth with disabilities and the disabled (ibid.). As with any resource-constrained public system, providing training proves challenging for juvenile justice organizations despite employee motivation. Whereas these practitioners expressed preference for multiday conferences, such efforts lay beyond the reach of jurisdictions because of factors such as overnight travel and alternate staffing needs. Even with onsite (in-service) training, staffing needs create barriers to opportunities for continuing education, even for the most urgent of topics.

Nevertheless, local successes exist, sometimes in response to mandates of one kind or another. For example, in July 2015, the Pennsylvania state legislature amended section 3118(A) of Title 42 of the Pennsylvania Judiciary and Judicial to include training for district judges, to assist them in the diversion of defendants who have mental illnesses, intellectual disability, and autism (Autism Society of Pittsburgh, n.d.). According to local media, this expansion of training to include autism took two decades of effort to realize, with the Autism Society of Pittsburgh and State Representative Tom Caltagirone working together to forge amended legislation that eventually became state law. The district judges joined their justice system counterparts, such as probation officers, public defenders, and magistrates, in mandated training curriculums for positively engaging autistic justice-involved clients. The Duquesne University Department of Counseling, Psychology, and Special Education collaborated with the Autism Society of Pittsburgh to implement the training mandated by the state (Gordon 2016).

Administrative policy requiring training for juvenile justice personnel delivered with intellectual fidelity can improve practitioners' empathy, understanding, and criminal justice practice with autistic individuals and individuals with autism. Such active pursuit of understanding neurodiversity tends to increase multilevel empathy, improving both collaboration and capacity to work through conflicts (Roberge 2013). Such local experimentation also reflects the tradition of iterative policy development in public health care. And it demonstrates how nebulous the boundaries of health care can become in the context of autism, and of neurological differences more generally. Positive interactions no doubt connect to well-being. However, definitively asserting such programs as components of health, education, social welfare, or other policy subsystems depend both on the qualities of the national health systems and the preferences, biases, and whims of subnational public efforts.

Conclusion

Health care in the context of autism and juvenile justice reflects complex, multifaceted decisions within a policy subsystem firmly tied to national identity. Some of the challenges facing health care in this context rather uniquely affect national policy subsystems, such as the complications of privatization in the United States and the concerns about wait times in Canada. Other challenges (and opportunities) come about as a result of the collision of institutional design with the implications of a more fully realized neurodiversity in contemporary societies.

Importantly, youth in custody inescapably constitutes a health care crisis. First, the youth finding themselves in custody are generally far from well, by one understanding of the concept or another. Youth in custody more frequently experience the effects of trauma than do the general population of youth (Gergelis, Kole, and Lowenhaupt 2016). This is particularly true in the context of disability. Compared with the general population, people with disabilities and the disabled are more likely to be victims of crime and are *less* likely to report a crime (Harrell 2015). The US Bureau of Justice Statistics reports:

> The rate of violent victimization against persons with disabilities was at least double that of the rate for those without disabilities ... for example, youths ages 12 to 15 with disabilities had a violent victimization rate of 139.1 per 1,000 persons, compared with youths without disabilities in the same age group; this group had a violent victimization rate of 37.5 per 1,000 persons. (Developmental Services Group 2017, 1)

Given this, youth involved with the juvenile justice system are likely to be both victims and perpetrators of crime. This serves to complicate their health care needs.

Going into custody in and of itself induces trauma. Enhancing the practice of juvenile justice to better address autism (and other neurological differences) requires improved training and more general knowledge of trauma. This recommendation serves not only autistics and people with autism. For the population at large, clinical care in juvenile justice works better if it is trauma informed (Branson et al. 2017), especially as a driving factor for substance abuse and mental health challenges. As Acoca, Stephens, and Van Vleet (2014, 8) put it, "given that incarcerated youth spend varying lengths of time in detention, frequently enter with a multitude of undiagnosed or untreated conditions, and a periodic cycle in and out of correctional facilities, continued attention to their physical and mental health care needs while in residential placement is important to their rehabilitation and reintegration into the community."

Second, responsibility for the health care of juveniles in custody extends beyond the juvenile justice system. Paying broader attention to the population rests at the core of improved health outcomes. No other developed country incarcerates as high a proportion of its youth as does the United States (Barnert, Perry, and Morris 2016). In the short term, closer work with and on the part of pediatricians is key. As Gergelis, Kole, and Lowenhaupt (2016, 24) say, "adolescents involved in the juvenile justice system represent a unique pediatric population, often hidden from public view." And as Barnert, Perry, and Morris (2016, 105) explain, "to reduce repeat offending, pediatricians will need to take an active role in facilitating successful reentry." Unfortunately, medical professionals are not trained and do not typically demonstrate a predilection to become informed about the population of detained youth. But the suggestion that pediatricians become better informed of detained youth's health care needs is not new (Société Canadienne de Pédiatrie 2005). As Barnert and her colleagues explain, "we have observed that in many medical schools and residency programs, trainees receive little or no education about incarcerated populations" (ibid., 106). Most youth involved with the juvenile justice system live in the community, even in the United States (Sattler 2017). Furthermore, as the majority of juveniles in custody return to the community, health care providers and policy must engage both the physical and mental health of justice-involved youth.

The provision of health care incurs participation in neurodiversity. Health care tends to be focused on treatment and cure, both of which may prove unsettling at best to autistic youth (Zolyomi and Tennis 2017). Modern medicine remains haunted by legacies of attempts to cure human attributes now considered well within the norm by the majority of society. Prominent examples include homosexuality, transgenderism, left-handedness, and, even being female. In the context of autism and juvenile justice, consideration of neurodiversity with regard to health care becomes further complicated by the generally incontrovertible fact that some circumstance of the youth's life went off course. Neither the universal health care system of Canada nor the market-oriented system of the United States produced circumstances in which autistics and individuals with autism receive an abundance of timely and appropriate health care. Given that, erring on the side of expansion of medical services for youth proves advisable. Even so, any such expansion must be conducted with as full as possible an understanding of hegemonic ableism alongside radical empathy. Involvement of adults with autism and autistic adults in the design and planning of health services for troubled youth with autism and autistic youth stands a good chance of contributing to the creation of treatments and services designed to address suffering while still being respectful of harmlessly different ways of being.

Chapter 4 summary

1. **Why consider autism in the context of juvenile justice?**
   - Laws dictate that detention staff pose specific medical questions to address immediate health care needs as well as accommodations. Effectiveness of these laws depends on the quality of health care screening assessments.
   - Therapeutic courts are an alternative to traditional court programs and can respond and specialize services based on the individual. The expansion of therapeutic courts allows the juvenile system to respond to crimes committed by individuals with disabilities in a restorative manner.

2. **How does the juvenile justice system particularly affect youth with autism and autistic youth?**
   - People with autism and autistic people involved in the criminal justice system report that their autism diagnosis was not taken into account through the court process.
   - Some 70 percent of people with disabilities have been victims of verbal, physical, sexual, or financial abuse or victims of neglect.

3. **How can circumstances be improved for youth with autism, autistic youth, and the personnel who interact with them in juvenile justice settings?**
   - Despite having different health care systems, both Canada and the United States fall short of covering medical and therapeutic needs of youth with disabilities, creating a burden for families to obtain assessments and diagnosis, and to receive services.
   - A substantial proportion of youth entering detention facilities have unmet medical needs; therefore, access to health care through onsite and community medical services is paramount in providing basic needs as required by juvenile detention facilities.

4. **What does rights-based disability policy look like in the context of rehabilitation of children with autism and autistic children who have become involved with the juvenile justice system?**
   - Part of the restorative process is providing access to services and new skills. In the United States, access to medical benefits such as habilitative services through the Affordable Care Act's essential health benefits will be crucial for youth who have a state or privately funded insurance plan. In Canada, youth can access services through the government financed health care system.
   - Systems and organizations that can embrace empathy will build healthy relationships between the justice system and the people it serves.

Figure 3 Chapter 4 Summary

5

Zero Tolerance for Difference
The Role of the Education System in Defining Delinquency

Like health, education involves quintessentially domestic public policy. Roots of public education practices in North America are particularly local and remain expected components of the domain of the sub-federal governments. High-quality and comprehensive education is routinely considered one of the best, most reliable defences against juvenile justice system involvement (Christle, Jolivette, and Nelson 2005). This chapter discusses broad issues in education policy in Canada and the United States, especially as they pertain to juvenile justice and the role of the educational system in defining and managing delinquency. Success of both the juvenile justice systems and education systems depends on youth learning rather than capacities of youth, stakeholders' intentions, or total investment of time, talent, and resources. After all, as stated in a training provided for Washington State practitioners in 2017, "we can never know if someone is unable to learn something ... we can only say if we are unable to teach it" (Washington Initiative for Supported Employment 2015). Education is a gamble. However, it is a gamble with consistently excellent returns from the perspective of populations as a whole.

The examination of the education of youth at risk and the administration of education in juvenile justice systems require calling particular attention to the school-to-prison pipeline. Police involvement in schools in the United States grew especially markedly after the April 1999 mass shooting at Columbine High School in Columbine, Colorado (Sutter 2009). However, increased monitoring magnifies implications of biases. According to *Discipline Disparities for Black Students, Boys, and Students with Disabilities*, a 2018 report from the United States Government Accountability Office (2018, 2), the justice and education systems are "responsible for enforcing federal civil rights laws that prohibit discrimination in the administration of discipline in public schools." Based on interviews with administration and school evaluations, the report concludes that schools continue to struggle considerably to meet this responsibility, especially in serving children of colour. In recent years, schools made more calls than in the past to law enforcement for incidents that occurred on school property and at school events, especially in the United States. Many of these calls helped strengthen the school-to-prison pipeline.

Law enforcement personnel serve on campuses across North America. The wide-scale implementation of zero-tolerance policies also inspired an increase in school security measures, including common assignment of police officers called "school resource officers" (SROs) to school grounds across North America (Weiler and Cray 2011). During the 2013–14 school year, 28.8 percent of public schools in the United States reported having a campus SRO (United States Government Accountability Office 2018). SROs wear distinctive uniforms and drive patrol-style cars (some with cages in the back), and some officers carry weapons on school grounds (Sneed 2015). The practice of police officers supervising the behaviour of youth while they attend school all but ensures an increase in criminal referrals to prosecute juveniles (Lawrence 2006; Theriot 2009).

SRO programs are not new, however. For example, Alberta began stationing officers at some schools forty years ago, with the goals of their serving as a preventive measure against juvenile crime, increasing trust in the relationship between the community and law enforcement, and providing support and security for schools (Edmonton Police Service, n.d.). Stationing police officers in schools in the United States took off with the Drug Abuse Resistance Education (D.A.R.E.) program. Created in Los Angeles in 1983, D.A.R.E. had dual intentions of educating young people on the dangers of drug use and creating a positive relationship between youth and law enforcement. Although early evaluation research on D.A.R.E. failed to support its prevention impact (Berman and Fox 2009), the reconfigured program from the early 2000s has shown some reductions in substance use among youth (Kulis et al. 2007). Independent of the evaluation research, the program influenced the perception of police officers and their relationship to the community (Berman and Fox 2009).

Recent observations of unintended negative consequences of placing SROs on campus increased markedly. As a result, some communities have decided that the benefits of having officers on campus are not worth the costs to the educational environment. For example, trustees of the Toronto District School Board voted in November 2017 to end its SRO programs following reports from students, especially minority students, that the program causes them discomfort at school (Nasser 2017).

Involvement with the juvenile justice system incurs an increased risk of imprisonment as an adult. Although a private residence is the most frequent location for criminal incidents, one in every ten incidents where a youth is accused of committing a crime happens during school hours (Allen and Superle 2016). Importantly, get-tough strategies in schools have not enhanced student safety. For example, in 2011, one in every five students reported being bullied at school, and one in eight students reported being involved in a physical fight (Sickmund, Sladky, and Kang, n.d.). Gun violence remains a serious problem, especially in the United States, where both much publicized massacres and less high-profile shootings occur with disturbing frequency (Gupta 2015). Balancing the goals of protecting children, improving overall relations between law enforcement personnel and the communities they serve, and providing for high-quality education proves particularly complex in the context of persistent ableism and the practice of neurodiversity.

Inclusionary Education

Contemporary children's rights include access to education. This right extends to all children, including those with disabilities and those served by the juvenile justice systems of North America. Both Canada and the United States signed the UN Convention on the Rights of the Child of 1989 (United Nations 1999). Article 28 of the convention establishes that education should be universally and freely provided and that secondary and higher education be available and accessible to all (ibid.). While the authority of international organizations such as the United Nations is regularly questioned, signing an international treaty holds meaning for many issue stakeholders.

A legal obligation to provide public education to all young people exists as a matter of law in both Canada and the United States (Tulman 2003; Ontario Ministry of Education, 2010). In both nations, historical exclusions from formal education on the basis of disability inspired the development, implementation, and reauthorization of statutes specifically protecting educational rights of individuals with disabilities and disabled individuals. In the United States, a right to a free and appropriate education given the presence of a disability is established primarily through section 504 of the Rehabilitation Act and through the Individuals with Disabilities Education Act (IDEA) (Leone and Meisel 1997). Both acts centre on maximization of inclusion in regular education programs. Furthermore, both acts, especially the IDEA, depend on the specified identification of a disability. Finally, special education includes a fiscal federalism component, where the federal government covers part of the cost associated with the implementation of federal policy, though never to the degree promised at the moment of IDEA's creation.

The design of Canada's special education policies is similarly inclusionary. Like other aspects of education policy in Canada, education for students with disabilities and disabled students is the responsibility of provincial and territorial governments per the Constitution Act of 1867. While some federal funding for public education exists, the management of education includes no federal administration except for the Council of Ministers of Education, which serves in an advisory board capacity. As in the United States, public education, including special education, is free and considered a public good. Provinces and territories have mandates following the disability rights established in the Charter of Rights and Freedoms.

Even so, across North America, in order to receive appropriate special education services, parents of youth with disabilities and disabled youth must usually specifically advocate for their children. Schools are too often driven by ensuring the process of providing special education accommodations follows the letter of the law rather than determining if the outcome of the accommodation truly meets the needs of the individual (Tulman 2003; Baker and Leonard 2017). Without parents or guardians initiating, navigating, and monitoring the process, students with disabilities risk educational neglect by preoccupied school systems. This makes it especially difficult in intersectional circumstances, such as when the primary languages of school officials and parents or guardians do not coincide. Both Canada and the United States have large immigrant populations, adding another potential barrier to accessing services. Immigrant families often experience transcendent cultural differences and may not be aware of the special education process and special education programs (interview conducted by Whitney Littlefield on March 24, 2017).

Despite ongoing challenges, successes in special education flourished in recent decades. Many successes emerge from local experimentation.

For example, in an NPR interview entitled "Getting Students with Autism through High School, to College and Beyond," autistic student Colin Ozeki describes his experiences in New York City (Khan 2016). Ozeki attributes some of the success in student educational attainment to the fact that his autism was positively acknowledged by school personnel, creating a more understanding environment for the staff and peers. Ozeki further describes a school in New York City that adopted a program that integrates students with autism into regular classrooms. The program, called "ASD Nest," uses a co-teaching approach to support all students academically and socially (ibid.). Successful programs such as ASD Nest generally depend on targeted resources and coordination among behavioural specialists, school administration, and teachers to be considered worth the time, effort, and cost. Special education policies signal social public perceptions of disability. Despite progress in special education, some stakeholders express little sympathy for youth who have a disability *and* demonstrate behaviour issues that violate criminal laws, viewing such youth as undeserving or, at least, less of a priority than other youth in the context of perennially resource-strapped public education. Rights-based special education policy lays the foundation for success in all systems, providing education well-tailored to disability across North America.

Special Education in Canada
In Canada, provincial and territorial governments dominate education policy for non–First Nations students. As a result, the history of education policy varies across the nation. Even today, no entity exists to provide that a student who moves from one province to another will retain similar access to services (Kovacs Burns and Gordon 2010, 208). The absence of a federal education agency limits research on education in Canada as a whole (Kovacs Burns and Gordon 2010). A key piece of literature, *Obstacles*, published by a parliamentary committee in Canada in 1981, identifies ways to prevent discrimination on the basis of disability in public education (Kovacs Burns and Gordon 2010; Jongbloed 2003). *Obstacles* identifies three main goals in expanding rights of access for people with disabilities. First, people with disabilities and the disabled deserve to be treated with respect. Second, everyone deserves a sense of control over their lives. Third, disability should not bar participation in social life (Jongbloed 2003).

Provinces and territories crafted special education policies using a rights-based approach during the second half of the twentieth century. For example, in Ontario, the Education Amendment Act of 1980, commonly referred to as Bill 82, established inclusionary special education (Elkin 1982). Before Bill 82, students with disabilities and disabled students received education in segregated settings (Eaves and Ho 1997). Individual schools pioneered inclusive education before official legislation mandated it. A private district school board in Ontario, Hamilton–Wentworth Catholic, adopted the mission statement of "Each Belongs" in 1969 (Gallagher and Bennett 2015). The mission statement articulated that "every student has gifts that should not be neglected ... meeting the needs of all students is best achieved by an individualized and inclusive approach" (Hamilton–Wentworth Catholic District School Board 2015, n.p.).

Despite trends toward inclusion, segregation on the basis of disability persists. Some students (or their parents) choose segregated programs. Others, especially students with autism, segregate involuntarily. According to a Canadian researcher, "public schools will find every excuse to get them [students with disabilities] out [of general education classes]" (interview conducted by Whitney Littlefield on March 24, 2017). The researcher offered an example of a high school student with autism who attended a special needs program at a public high school. This student is non-verbal, and her teachers found it difficult to provide her with the appropriate education and care. Teachers' union contracts sometimes specifically state which services teachers are required to provide students with disabilities. At some point, this student with autism obtained braces, which required brushing and cleaning after meals. The teachers filed a grievance with the union stating they were not contractually required to help this student clean their braces. The student with autism was then forced to attend a separate high school for students with disabilities and disabled students, one where the teachers could attend to her medical and educational needs (interview conducted by Whitney Littlefield on March 24, 2017).

The work of developing policies that clearly identify disabilities, inclusionary education, and a framework for how educational systems can support students with disabilities and disabled students continues in Canada (Jongbloed 2003). Challenges, such as insufficiently trained teachers, persist, sometimes as a result of limited attention to inclusionary education in university programs (McCrimmon 2015). Furthermore, the composition of faculty credentials varies from school to school and district to district. In many parts of Canada, teachers outnumber jobs. Teachers enter special education positions by default rather than by choice, taking positions offered regardless of whether their professional goals include working with special education (interview conducted by Whitney Littlefield on March 24, 2017; Leone, Meisel, and Drakeford 2003).

Parents may tire of incompetent inclusion. Experience can raise questions about what inclusion entails in a given school. For example, seclusion rooms continue to be used as "time out" rooms from the inclusionary classrooms (Clibbon 2015). Broad diversity in design and use of seclusion rooms exists (ibid.). However, in a report published by the Family Support Institute of BC, 100 percent of parents surveyed said that seclusion was used as a behaviour consequence for their child (Family Support Institute of BC 2013). Unfortunately, communication failures between the school administration and parents are common, as many parents find out about the use of seclusion from other sources after the fact (ibid.). Furthermore, many teachers in Canada support banning the use of restraint and seclusion, since no proof exists for it having a positive impact on the student (Clibbon 2015). In circumstances where the practices of so-called inclusionary practices end in unmonitored and unproductive seclusion, parents may turn to other options.

Controversy surrounds segregated schools. Resource neglect abounds for segregated schools as compared with districts at large. Historically, such neglect has included provision of fewer professional development opportunities for teachers serving in segregated schools (Leone, Meisel, and Drakeford 2003). Furthermore, segregated schools can foster long-term disadvantage for students with disabilities and the disabled, given limited opportunities for social growth necessary for futures dominated by neurodiversity. Some families, however, find that the benefits of segregated schools outweigh limitations owing to the presence of specialized staff and families with similar experiences (McCrimmon 2015). In contemporary discussion of special education policies across Canada, best exercise of parent and student choice remains an open question.

Special Education Policy in the United States

As mentioned previously, education stands as a quintessentially domestic policy largely implemented in the United States at local levels of government. In 2016, there were over eighteen thousand local educational agencies in the United States, each involved in policy development and administration (Office for Civil Rights 2016). Even so, centralizing forces affect education across the nation. State laws and state education departments serve to homogenize curriculums and practices among these local districts through state policies and the distribution of education resources (Manna 2011).

Influential teachers' unions operate at both the state and national levels. Federal laws articulate broad mandates and restrictions, such as the provision of free and appropriate education for students with disabilities. Furthermore, since 1980, the federal Department of Education has influenced education policy through the disbursement of fiscal and technical resources, in exchange for subnational governments implementing desired content, programs, and approaches (Shipps 2008). The mission of the department is "to promote student achievement and preparation for global competitiveness by fostering educational excellence and ensuring equal access" (United States Department of Education, n.d.). As of November 2016, the department included over forty-four hundred employees distributed among agency divisions promoting civil rights and privacy laws, researching education access and policy in the United States, and coordinating federal assistance to state and local education entities.

The Elementary and Secondary Education Act of 1965 inaugurated the current-era federal legislation setting national education standards in the United States. Originally serving as a cornerstone of President Lyndon B. Johnson's War on Poverty, the act authorized funds for broadly cast strategies expected to improve schools, such as direct program support, promotion of parental involvement, and professional development. The 2001 reauthorization of the act, renamed No Child Left Behind Act (NCLB), pierced the public's consciousness, primarily owing to very public school ratings, dependence on standardized tests, and heavy-handed responses to perceived school failure. However, the reauthorization also forced school administrators to directly address achievement gaps based on student characteristics such as race, ethnic background, and first language, for the first time in US history. Furthermore, Part D of the NCLB improvement enhanced the commitment to services for youth at risk or who are delinquent or experiencing neglect (National Juvenile Justice Network 2016). The 2012 reauthorization, the Every Student Succeeds Act, sought differentiation from the deeply unpopular NCLB (ibid.). Revisions were aimed at several of the implementation challenges experienced with No Child Left Behind and enhanced flexibility for states.

Special education policy followed a similar course of increasingly complex federalism in the United States. Of particular consequence for autism and the juvenile justice system was the creation of the Education for All Handicapped Children, which would later reauthorize as the Individuals with Disabilities Education Act (IDEA). IDEA asserted unequivocal national authority to direct the education of children with disabilities and disabled children in the United States. Born as a largely unfunded mandate, the act established the right to a free and appropriate public education (FAPE) in the least restrictive environment (LRE). This legislation defined eligibility for access to the special education resources as well as the process of determining how special education would be delivered (through an individualized education plan, or IEP). To put an IEP in place, the youth must meet the eligibility requirements and the school must follow the statutory requirements in providing accommodations (Tulman 2003, 4; Mallett 2010, 9; Baker and Leonard 2017).

Individual education plans can influence the likelihood of the referral of a youth with disabilities and disabled youth to law enforcement for delinquent behaviour or school violations. Evaluating whether the discipline employed appropriately addresses disability is required under IDEA. In essence, if behaviours result from disability, the school cannot discipline the youth under the school's disciplinary code for exhibiting these behaviours without taking the disability into account (Leone, Meisel, and Drakeford 2003). For example, a juvenile with autism may respond to disruption in classroom routine through a physical outburst such as throwing classroom items against the wall or at other students. If this behaviour is a manifestation of autism, the school cannot immediately remove the youth or find alternative placement without following IDEA protocols (Tulman 2003). Usually, the school is thereby required to provide the youth with additional resources and attention to promote positive behavioural change. Given this, schools may choose to refer youth to the juvenile justice system to address the problem behaviour.

In stressful circumstances, teachers may feel too exhausted or time-constrained to engage in intensive behaviour modification strategies. Realities such as overpopulated classrooms, undercompensated and often undertrained teachers, increasing paperwork burdens, and successive budget cuts create environments where school staff do not have the time or resources to attend to provide needed services (McCrimmon 2015). Furthermore, when youth lack a formal diagnosis or are assigned to untrained paraprofessionals, their behaviours associated with disabilities are commonly stereotyped as insubordinate. Knee-jerk responses focus on characterizing behaviours as criminal violations rather than as manifestations of a neurological difference (Leone, Meisel, and Drakeford 2003). Even more extreme results include implementing the use of restraint and overuse of seclusion to control classroom behaviour. In 2012, 267,000 violent restraints were documented in public schools

(Suarez 2016). According to Lanette Suarez (2016, 869), "1,500 students are tied up or locked down every day by school officials." Seventy-five percent of those restrained or secluded students have disabilities. Students with disabilities are twenty times more likely to experience restraint and seclusion in public schools than their non-disabled peers (ibid. 2016; Gagnon, Mattingly, and Connelly 2017). Moreover, corporal punishment is still legal in nineteen states, blurring the lines between techniques used for punishment and methods of restraint and seclusion. As a result of disconnects between intention, capacities, and resources, situations involving difficult behaviours can devolve and end up in the juvenile justice system.

One way to reduce restraint and referrals to justice systems would be to replace law enforcement presence at schools and replace them with mental health professionals (Suarez 2016). Currently, school administrators bring in law enforcement or juvenile justice personnel when they and their staff become desperate for help with students causing disruptions. In order for such students to access juvenile justice services and resources, their alleged crimes must be referred to the juvenile court and charged by the prosecutor. In the example of a student throwing items, charges could include numerous criminal violations, including malicious mischief or assault. While targeted programs can at times help, as is discussed below, juvenile justice referrals can also reinforce school-to-prison pipelines. In response to pipeline-related concerns and mass-casualty gun incidents, some states have developed alternatives to detention for behaviour violations. For example, Florida adopted the Baker Act, directing police to divert people with mental illness to an involuntary psychiatric exam (Gurney 2018). Unfortunately, the Baker Act appears overused as a punishment, contrary to the original intent of assisting those lacking mental health care. For example, an article in the *Miami Herald* published February 2, 2018, describes an incident where the Baker Act was invoked, sending a seven-year-old boy to receive a psych exam, apparently as a punishment for disability-related behaviours rather than out of genuine concern for the student and the community (ibid.). Such practices ignore the basic fact that "there is no amount of force that can make someone less disabled ... all you end up doing is intensifying trauma" (Suarez 2016, 878).

The pursuit of control leads staff and administrations prone to use forceful tactics ever more unsympathetic to differences. Schools that do not develop appropriate responses to delinquent behaviour leave students with disabilities at risk of whimsical disciplinary procedures (Wald and Losen

2003). As mentioned, restraint and seclusion, arguably the most immediate and severe methods to address unwanted behaviours, are routinely used in public schools (Suarez 2016). A case investigation conducted by the US Government Accountability Office (2018, 33) found that the use of seclusion and restraint was "severe, persistent and pervasive." According to its report, students with disabilities were physically restrained either mechanically or physically 48,811 times and secluded 19,857 times (ibid.). This case also found that one student with disabilities was held face down 92 times in an eleven-month time span, including one restraint incident lasting ninety-three minutes (ibid.). Such extreme cases highlight the need for effective alternatives to safeguard students from civil rights violations while also addressing the immediate safety, security, and educational concerns of all students and staff.

Currently no specific federal law provides guidance, limitations, or best practices for the use of restraint and seclusion (Marx and Baker 2017). In 2009, the Preventing Harmful Restraint and Seclusion in Schools Act was proposed to Congress but was unsuccessful in the Senate (Gagnon, Mattingly, and Connelly 2017). The bill, although not adopted, nevertheless left a few positive legacies. It created public awareness about the abuses of restraint and seclusion, and twenty-seven states have since adopted or modified their laws on seclusion and restraint (ibid.). Furthermore, the Department of Education released a resource document in 2012 providing guidelines and principles for states to incorporate into policies (Marx and Baker 2017). School districts, administration, and boards should also ensure that district policies align with the US Department of Justice recommendations that would allow restraint and seclusion only if there is imminent danger and completely ban mechanical restraints (Suarez 2016). Developing positive behaviour interventions and support is paramount in preventing situations from escalating to a point where restraint or seclusion are warranted (Clibbon 2015). However, as Gagnon and authors astutely describe, policies are not always the most meaningful way to address the misuse and abuse of these practices. Training and education foster proper skills and illuminate tools for staff and practitioners working with all students (Suarez 2016). Across North America – but particularly in the United States – manifesting best practices in the context of autism and juvenile justice depends on the hard-won and well-supported professional expertise of teachers, which will lead students away from the juvenile justice systems whenever possible.

Youth with Disabilities and School-to-Prison Pipelines

Education transmits culture. School systems in North America perform two critical functions: 1) teaching young people how to participate effectively in democratic societies, and 2) improving employment prospects of adults (Lleras-Muney 2002; Tulman 2003). These motivations predate the twenty-first century (Doepke and Zilibotti 2005; Lleras-Muney 2002). Since juvenile justice systems centre on restoration, they cannot exist as intended in the absence of formalized education. Given this, active interactions between agencies charged with public education and those charged with juvenile justice are desirable. Nevertheless, troubling elements of such interactions continue to this day in the form of school-to-prison pipelines.

The school-to-prison pipeline describes the systematic dislocation of youth from schools to incarceration facilities (Bahena et al. 2012). Harsher school discipline came into vogue in the last decades of the twentieth century following a period of relaxation during the middle of the twentieth century. School discipline standards became more rigid, and rates of disciplinary suspensions and expulsions increased (Cramer, Gonzalez, and Pellegrini-Lafont 2014; Mallett 2015). For example, a study of Texas schools found that a third of all students received suspensions between seventh grade and their senior year (Suitts 2014). While causality in such circumstances is obviously difficult to pinpoint, youth are more likely to become involved with law enforcement or the courts after suspension or expulsion (Suitts 2014; United States Government Accountability Office 2018). The school-to-prison pipeline emerges from a cluster of unintended consequences of new policies and procedures with discriminatory outcomes against youth of colour, youth in poverty, disabled youth, and youth with disabilities in the absence of appropriate resources to implement the policies and regulatory oversight to ensure stakeholder accountability (Mallett 2015).

Direct referrals to juvenile court from schools are rarer in Canada than in the United States. Police remain less frequently stationed at Canadian schools as compared with in the United States, reducing the potential for immediate law enforcement intervention in student-discipline protocols. Also, policies and programs focused on alternative programs exist in many districts. In Toronto, schools followed up on 95 percent of expulsions in the district with school-based intervention for these juveniles (Zheng and DeJesus 2017). As well as contacting the students' families, schools offered guidance and opportunities to meet with a social worker, to engage in the restorative practice, and to access special education support services (ibid.). The Toronto District School Board adopted the Caring and Safe Schools Policy, which conceptualizes expulsion as evidence of a student's intensive need for rehabilitation. Similarly, the Peel District School Board in Mississauga, Ontario, requires all expelled students to attend a Fresh Start program, in which students can continue their academic studies while receiving psychological support, anger-management therapy, and personal skill development (Peel District School Board, n.d.). Even with these supports, however, the school-dropout rate remains disconcertingly high for students in alternative school programs (Zheng and DeJesus 2017). School dropout increases the risk of juvenile justice involvement through pathways such as more unoccupied time to spend with friends making delinquent choices. Additional innovation is the key to building on existing success of these programs, especially for students with disabilities and disabled students.

Intersectionality matters in the school-to-prison pipeline in Canada. Aboriginal youth, Native youth, and Caribbean youth are disproportionately affected by the school-to-prison pipeline in Canada (Rankin, Rushowy, and Brown 2013). Pooled data for the 2011/12 school year through the 2015/16 school year showed that black students had the highest rate of school suspensions (48 percent of suspended students), followed by mixed-race students (15 percent of suspended students). White students accounted for only 10 percent of suspended youth (Zheng and DeJesus 2017). Also, during the 2015–16 school year, youth with disabilities comprised 60 percent of juveniles suspended from school (ibid.). Overrepresentation of youth with disabilities and disabled youth and youth of colour in Canadian school expulsions presents an urgent cause for concern.

The school-to-prison pipeline exerts substantial force in the United States. Students who either voluntarily leave school or are forced to leave too often quickly transition to juvenile justice systems. Especially for girls, the largest predictor of recidivism is being suspended or expelled from school (Wald and Losen 2003). According to a study conducted by the National Center for Education Statistics, during the 2013–14 school year, approximately 5.2 percent of students enrolled in Grades 10 to 12 left high school before degree completion (McFarland, Stark, and Cui 2018). Youth with disabilities and disabled youth, especially those with emotional regulation differences, are particularly vulnerable to dropping out of school because of unmet educational needs, leaving them at greater risk for entry into the juvenile justice system (Sinclair, Christenson, and Thurlow 2005). Youth of colour are even more vulnerable to being swept up in the school-to-prison pipeline, given higher average dropout rates (Annamma 2014).

Leaving school does not necessarily happen entirely by choice. The number of youths suspended from school almost doubled during the last quarter of the twentieth century, even though the absolute number of children in the nation increased only about 8 percent during the same time (Wald and Losen 2003). Suspension threatens a sense of connection to school, which for many of the youth in question was weakened already. Despite a common belief that special education somehow precludes disciplining students with disabilities and disabled students, in the United States, suspension is common for students with known disabilities. Whereas students with disabilities and disabled students are often treated differently in discipline processes for non-dangerous behaviour, these differences do not necessarily mean less severe consequences for behaviours (United States Government Accountability Office 2018; Suarez 2016). Almost 12 percent of all students suspended have a known disability (United States Government Accountability Office 2018). Of course, whether a student drops out after a suspension or is expelled, once out of school, the youth runs greater risk of involvement with the juvenile justice system (Mallett 2013; Mallett 2015). As described in *A Study of Juvenile Justice Schools in the South and the Nation*, "the juvenile system has become a dumping ground where troubled children and youth are sent beyond any accountable system of education" (Suitts 2014, 25).

Less formal exclusion also reinforces the school-to-prison pipeline. Too often, community members reflexively resist interactions between their children and children considered dangerous. These characterizations frequently reflect and reinforce systemic prejudices against historically oppressed groups. Some scholars describe this as being "raced in schools," the process of school systems recreating societal strata inside institutions, with poor children of colour occupying the least desirable status (Annamma 2014). Black youths in urban poverty form the bottom of this strata because parents and community members unfairly perceive them as a threat to the social order of the neighbourhood and the school (Rios 2011; Winn and Behizadeh 2011; Annamma 2014). Such racist perceptions give those with biases against poor youth of colour permission to see them as dangerous persons destined to become involved in criminal activity and therefore best taken up in the school-to-prison pipeline for the sake of community safety. In reality, these injustices rob all juveniles of the benefits of the others' life experiences and social support. Deliberate and systematic reduction of adult tolerance of youthful behaviours during the late twentieth and early twenty-first centuries played an influential role in formalizing the effects of these exclusionary attitudes.

Zero-Tolerance Policies and the School-to-Prison Pipeline

Zero-tolerance policies aim to routinize punishment of students involved in adverse events with no or limited consideration of the details of the specific event. Mandatory suspension or expulsion from school represents a cornerstone practice under these policies. Such punishments are designed with the intention of preventing youth from committing future crimes on school grounds and to send a message to other students that serious crimes in school will not be tolerated (Mallett 2015). Importantly, the policies have been advertised as a mechanism for addressing historical injustices, such as the exploitation and harassment of girls, too long ignored by schools. In reality, zero-tolerance policies extend and enhance implications of social inequalities and historical injustices. Fifty percent of suspensions are for behaviours considered minor, such as disobedience and insubordination (Suitts 2014). Zero-tolerance policies result in a disproportionate amount of youth with disabilities, particularly learning disabilities, being referred to the juvenile justice system (Mallett 2013).

One Canadian example of a zero-tolerance policy is Ontario's Safe Schools Act of 2000 (Bhattacharjee 2003). This legislation enhanced the power of school teachers, principals, and administrators to suspend and expel students for misbehaviour such as selling drugs or violent acts. Students accused of minor infractions such as inappropriate touching or cursing also risked suspension under the policy. Suspensions from Toronto public schools increased 40 percent during the first year of implementation (Boyle 2003). Schools even suspended students for behaviours off school grounds. In one case, a young black male student received a suspension for answering the door at his home with a knife. During the investigation, family members described the knife as a butter knife the child had inadvertently carried with him to answer the door during the dinner hour (ibid.).

Empowering school personnel to more easily implement disciplinary actions, including those previously reserved for administrative entities outside the school, signalled increased rigidity in adult expectations for student conduct and a strong desire to separate students believed unworthy from the rest (Raby 2005). A study of perceptions of school discipline among high school students shortly after the act's implementation found black and South Asian students perceiving that they were treated worse at school than were other racial groups in that they were more likely to be suspended and that the school was more likely to call the police than it was in circumstances involving youth of different backgrounds (Ruck and Wortley 2002). Attending a racially segregated school, being male, and being an immigrant also increased the odds of students' perceptions of the likelihood of being suspended, police involvement at school, and being treated poorly by the police at school under this act (ibid.; Daniel and Bondy 2008).

Furthermore, advocates for students with disabilities and disabled students expressed concerns that the act discriminated against youth with neurological differences. For example, students with Tourette's syndrome articulated vulnerability to being suspended or expelled for cursing loudly and having emotional outbursts connected to this neurological difference. Qualitative research conducted with school personnel in Ontario elementary and high schools affirmed these concerns. While some teachers and administrators felt that the increased rigour of the school's disciplinary standards helped correct negative behaviour among typical students, students with chronic behavioural problems and school disciplinary histories were another matter (Daniel and Bondy 2008). An elementary school teacher remarked, "you have to be a disaster before you get help. Things have got to change. We are not going to make any dent with the [Caring and] Safe Schools Policy. No matter how we change it, no matter how we save, no matter what we do, until we get away from reacting and start looking at prevention" (ibid., 12). Ontario's law permitted school administrators and teachers to identify mitigating factors in a student's case that would prevent mandatory suspension or expulsion from school (Bhattacharjee 2003). Even so, the Ontario Human Rights Commission quickly found that despite this safeguard in the legislation, students with disabilities and disabled students disproportionately faced being forced from school on behavioural grounds (ibid.).

In the United States, zero-tolerance policies were encoded in the Gun-Free Schools Act of 1994 (Cramer, Gonzalez, and Pellegrini-Lafont 2014). This policy also provided for widespread stationing of school resource officers, underscoring the relationship between school discipline and formal justice authority. As in Canada, zero-tolerance policies increased the number of youths expelled or referred to the juvenile justice system.

Local preventive alternatives have been developed in the United States as well. For example, in 2000, the Salem-Keizer public schools, part of the Oregon School District 24J, developed a Threat Assessment System currently gaining popularity in surrounding states. According to the Salem-Keizer

Public Schools website, the threat assessments are designed to systematically address violence or harmful behaviour that poses a threat to students and school staff by designing an individual intervention and action plan. The model constitutes a preventive attempt to proactively manage concerning behaviours that are disturbing a sense of safety at school for others (Van Dreal 2011, 5). John van Dreal (2011, 34) describes the assessment as of the "unique interaction and dynamics between the perpetrator, the target and the situation they share." These tools are also used for youth who have committed a violent offence in the community to determine whether it is safe for them to return to school.

The response process under the Student Threat Assessment model is initiated by the school or a school staff observing significant concerns with a student's level of aggression. The behaviour in question must be realistically perceived as a threat to others or as aggression toward others. The design of the model separates assessments into two types of threats: Level 1 and Level 2. The assessment process begins with teachers and parents completing forms that identify specific concerns and behaviours. A meeting is then scheduled with the school and parents to determine actions and roles the involved adults will take to help the student be successful (Van Dreal 2011). Level 1 threats are addressed in-house by teachers, school administrative staff, and parents and usually do not involve other community partners.

If the behaviours exceed capacity for in-house management, the school will schedule a Level 2 assessment. Examples of Level 2 threats include a student bringing a weapon to school, escalated bullying or harassment toward a student or staff where the person does not feel safe, and outbursts of anger with damage to school property. The Level 2 meetings include various stakeholders, such as parents, school administration, a mental health counsellor, a juvenile justice practitioner (usually a probation officer), the Ministry of Children and Families-Child Protection, a school resource officer, and any other relevant law enforcement personnel. The multiagency team can use resources from several sources in the community in order to create an intense intervention plan (Van Dreal 2011). Intervention plans include specialized classes, skill building, random safety checks of personal items, and time accountability cards, to name a few (Salem-Keizer System 2017).

A student threat assessment coordinator estimated that 15 percent of the requested threat assessments are for students with autism (interview conducted by Whitney Littlefield on April 7, 2017). Examples of behaviours resulting in students with autism and autistic students being identified as a threat include disconcerting fixation on one person or one event that appears to provoke an aggressive response, and maladaptive coping skills from overstimulation or disruption from routine. The coordinator reported commonly encountering students who are undiagnosed with a disability. In such circumstances, threat assessments can be helpful, as the process focuses on the behaviour changes and choices as opposed to focusing on clinical diagnosis (interview conducted by Whitney Littlefield on April 7, 2017). Unfortunately, as a school resource officer interviewed for this book reported, schools sometimes delay requesting a threat assessment for youth with autism in an attempt to avoid causing disruption or trouble with that student. From the officer's perspective, however, this can negate the underlying purpose of the assessments because the school's request is submitted too late, after there is an actual emergency (interview conducted by Whitney Littlefield on April 25, 2017). Properly conducted threat assessments occur before an emergency, with the aim of helping students safely go on in school.

Learning Differences and Juvenile Justice Systems

Percentages of incarcerated youth who have a disability or are disabled prove shocking at best. Youth with disabilities relevant to appropriate education strategies are disproportionally represented in the juvenile justice system. Studies show that up to 70 percent of youth involved in the juvenile justice system have a learning disability (National Juvenile Justice Network 2016; Skowyra and Cocozza 2007; Wald and Losen 2003). A number of theories exist that attempt to explain why youth with disabilities and disabled youth are more vulnerable to entering the juvenile justice system; however, explanation for the phenomenon remains debated (Quinn et al. 2005; Suitts 2014).

School failure theory suggests that unsuccessful academic experience will almost necessarily introduce students with disabilities and disabled students to the juvenile justice system. School failure theory, however, falls short of explaining whether it is the disability itself that contributes to the failure in school. Christopher Mallett (2011) suggests that factors such social isolation, negative peer group, and low self-esteem strongly contribute to the likelihood of failure.

Susceptibility theory asserts that as a result of neurological differences, youth with disabilities and disabled youth behave differently from other youth in consequential ways. Example behaviours include lack of future thinking, impulsivity, and vulnerability to peer pressure. These differences in behaviour are perceived by their peers and adults as being delinquent and, therefore, the youth become more susceptible to having their behaviours characterized as deviant or criminal (Mallett 2013; Quinn et al. 2005).

Differential treatment theory suggests that youth with disabilities and disabled youth are overrepresented because adults with authority over the youth approach differences punitively (Quinn et al. 2005). For example, teachers both inside and outside juvenile justice systems are more likely to label youth with education-related disabilities as "delinquent" for any behaviour atypical in a normal classroom, even if that behaviour is a known expression of disability (Tulman 2003). Furthermore, schools tend to have more concentrated interaction and supervision for students with disabilities and, as a result, are more likely to observe delinquent behaviours from that youth (Mallett 2011).

As discussed in Chapter 4, labelling matters. Students with disabilities and disabled students are in part disproportionally represented in juvenile systems because teachers and school staff label them as delinquent (Rutherford et al. 2002). When teaching staff label these youth as delinquent, the risk of students with disabilities internalizing these labels and acting out accordingly increases. As a result, these youth may understand the differences between themselves and their peers as deviant or delinquent in and of themselves. Students may also seek out the label of delinquency. Youth with neurological differences may experience difficulty with social-cognitive development, rendering them more susceptible to the influence of delinquent peers and delinquency (Quinn et al. 2005). After all, having a delinquent peer group can appear more appealing than having no peer group at all.

Case in Point: Educational Programs inside Juvenile Justice Facilities in the United States

Education programs should be a keystone of juvenile justice institutions. Above and beyond nations' obligations to educate youth as discussed above, depending on the approach taken, "juvenile court schools can be the first stop on moving young people into the prison pipeline, or they can be an opportunity to intervene" (Challet 2017). Education reduces recidivism (Leone, Meisel, and Drakeford 2003). For youth with disabilities and disabled youth, education should include addressing behavioural challenges, involving parents or guardians in the process, and providing adequate transition services for re-entry into their home community (Challet 2017). Even so, the reality has long been that youth entitled to receive special education services will most likely go without adequate education while incarcerated (Leone and Meisel 1997).

There are approximately twenty-five hundred juvenile justice residential facilities in the United States, and each site must provide education for youth in custody (United States Departments of Education and Justice 2014). Schools in juvenile detention centres and residential facilities are generally called "court schools" or "juvie schools." In the United States, these schools provide education for over sixty thousand youth per year (National Juvenile Justice Network 2016). The educational structure and management differ between facilities within a jurisdiction and across jurisdictions. Delivery of special education remains heavily influenced by the policies and procedures of the facility in which a school is located (Leone, Meisel, and Drakeford 2003).

Schools face challenges in administering education to incarcerated juveniles. Many detention centres and juvenile prisons personnel focus on accountability and rehabilitation over providing educational services. Compulsory education or attendance laws vary between states but have long commonly included these minimum conditions: minimum graduation requirements, a set term for the school year, and a framework for coursework (Leone and Meisel 1997). Although schools are regulated by educational statutes set forth by the state and federal governments, schools run within the juvenile justice system are intermittently neglected in state oversight protocols (Challet 2017; Twomey 2008). For example, many states require students to attend school for a certain number of hours per day (Fritz and Brown 2012). However, the institutional schedule of the detention centre or residential facility impact whether those hours can be routinely met. Many schools working in the juvenile justice context provide considerably less instructional time compared with local public schools (National Juvenile Justice Network 2016). The credentials and other qualifications of the teachers providing the education in court schools also vary (Fritz and Brown 2012). Lack of attention to and investment in schooling of incarcerated students contributes to the failure of many youth after their release from confinement (Suitts 2014).

Arguably, incarceration could provide the best chance for some youth to get an education, considering the difficulties associated with skipping class while in detention. A key step in providing education involves proficient use of screening tools to assess disabilities and determine eligibility for special education. This step incurs numerous responsibilities for staff. Youth may not know or understand the full extent of their disability and may have difficulty relaying that information to intake officers and other personnel. Some justice system personnel lack familiarity with typical traits and behaviours indicative of disability (Grisso and Underwood 2004; Robinson and Rapport 1999, 19). Furthermore, when possible, parents and guardians are required to be included in the process of developing an IEP, even if that IEP is developed while the youth is in custody (Macomber et al. 2010; Robinson and Rapport 1999).

The importance of communicating and sharing information about each youth cannot be overstated. The burden of responsibility to seek out information related to disability and education for youth involved in the system lies with the juvenile justice practitioners (Mallett 2010). In particular, juvenile intake officers in probation and detention are tasked with coordinating with the court-ordered school and the public high school to ensure that educational needs are met. Christopher Mallett identifies five strategies for juvenile justice practitioners to use to help youth with learning disabilities: take note of identified disabilities; if no identified disability exists, employ a screening tool as appropriate to assess for a disability or refer to the school district to complete an assessment; consider comorbid issues; create reports including individualized and specific needs of the youth with disabilities and disabled youth; and facilitate parental participation education (ibid.).

In *Alexander S. v Boyd*, the Fourth Circuit Court of Appeals permitted short-term confinement facilities, such as detention centres, to use the IEP from their public school (Robinson and Rapport 1999). However, challenges surrounding exchanges of records at confinement or release have existed for decades (Robinson and Rapport 1999; Twomey 2008). The pervasive lack of communication between schools in the juvenile justice system and community public schools increases the likelihood an existing IEP will not follow the youth into custody (Tulman 2003). Especially for short-term care facilities, requesting records could save the teachers and educational administration time and resources by transferring the IEP from the public school.

Whether or not a designated space for schooling exists within a correctional facility can depend on the size, funding availability, and typical length of sentence of the youth in residence. Many smaller facilities do not have the space, funding, or resources to accommodate designated school areas. Under those conditions, resident youth complete school assignments in spaces shared with other detention-centre activities. Longer-term-stay facilities tend to have more comprehensive school systems. Regardless of the type of facility or where the classroom is physically located, each youth with a disability and disabled youth is entitled to a free and appropriate education. However, the flexibility to manage educational accommodations that are assumed to be straightforward in special education policies has historically conflicted with both the infrastructures and routine administration of the secure care facilities (Robinson and Rapport 1999).

Even in the best of circumstances and most modern of institutional infrastructures, providing special education services remains challenging. Court schools prove no exception to this general rule. Of the students with learning disabilities attending court schools, more than 25 percent did not have their special education needs met (Suitts 2014). According to the 2016 annual report of the US Department of Education's Office for Civil Rights, during the 2016 fiscal year, "OCR processed nearly 17,000 complaints – exceeding last year's record high by more than 60 percent – and opened nearly 4,000 investigations (29 percent more than last year)" (ibid., 4). Of course, such increases do not necessarily mean that the cause for complaints surrounding special education delivery increased, as such rises in observed instances can also be owing to improved awareness of the rights of children with disabilities and disabled children and of what constitutes appropriate delivery of education services. Also, not all of the complaints involved students with disabilities. Even so, the introduction to the report includes a paragraph highlighting some of the heinous instances represented by statistics:

> I will be forever haunted by some of the facts we uncovered during our investigations, including resolutions involving a student with a disability whose teacher told her to kill herself; a nine-year-old whose school subjected him to prone restraint or recovery from restraint for more time than he received instruction, and whose mother heard him crying in a restraint room while she was outside the school in the parking lot on her way to pick him up; an Arab American student whose peers hurled slurs including "terrorist" at her in school hallways; a recent immigrant student being taunted "Welcome to America" as he was physically assaulted, sustaining severe injuries; and a college student whose university, despite her reporting she had been sexually assaulted by a campus security officer, failed to investigate appropriately the potential risk to other students. These facts underscore our ongoing need to safeguard the civil rights guaranteed to all students. (Office for Civil Rights 2016, 4)

Although examples such as those noted above are the exception rather than the rule, civil rights safeguards are not naturally occurring and tend to atrophy quickly when not actively maintained.

Even the best-intentioned and well-prepared teachers employed in juvenile correction schools face challenges with implementing curriculums (Twomey 2008). Many schools in correctional facilities incompletely follow state curriculum guidelines, causing issues with credit transfer and academic progress (National Juvenile Justice Network 2016). One teacher may be tasked with teaching a class comprising youth at varying academic levels. According to *A Study of Juvenile Justice Schools in the South and the Nation*, about half the students juvenile schools serve are below their grade level (Suitts 2014). The age, maturity, and abilities of each youth can vary drastically, forcing the teacher to create separate individual requirements or standards above and beyond mandated IEPs. To best serve the youth, schools should provide several programs suited to the individuals' needs and goals of the youth (National Center for Education, Disability and Juvenile Justice, n.d.). Where possible, schools may use virtual academies or online programs to provide a state-approved structured curriculum and allow each student to work at their own pace. Programs might include GED (General Education Diploma) preparation, vocational education related to specific interests, literacy skills, and academic courses aligned with earning a diploma.

An estimated 40 percent of students enrolled in the schools in the juvenile justice system in the United States do not make any academic progress while incarcerated (Challet 2017). The US Department of Education found that, in 2009, youth attending school while confined for over 90 days "failed to make any significant improvement in learning and academic achievement" (Suitts 2014, 4). In 2014, the Department of Justice and the Department of Education together developed a strategy for improving schools in the juvenile justice system. *Guiding Principles for Providing High-Quality Education in Juvenile Justice Secure Care Settings* lays out five guiding principles to provide quality, particularly applicable to residential facilities providing long-term confinement: creating an environment conducive to and supportive of learning; provision of adequate funding to provide the educational services comparable to public schools; hiring qualified teachers and staff to provide the education in confinement settings; developing a cohesive and appropriate curriculum for court schools comparable to the education received in public schools; and providing services for re-entry into the public school systems after incarceration. These guidelines aim to increase the number of youths released from a secure care facility who graduate from high school. Getting a high school diploma or GED remains one of the most important protective factors for preventing future crime (Suitts 2014).

The transition back to public schools after release from custody can prove less than smooth. Too many students do not receive credit for the work they completed while incarcerated (Challet 2017). When students do earn credits, community schools might still overlook transferring those credits back to the home school district (Twomey 2008; National Juvenile Justice Network 2016). Furthermore, obtaining transcripts and interpreting requirements prove difficult for even admissions coordinators and counsellors when trying to work with youth transitioning from custody. Some schools also actively attempt to prevent court involved youth from returning to their schools (Wald and Losen 2003). Sixty-six percent of youth who are released from a secure care facility do not return to school (National Juvenile Justice Network 2016). Graduation rates for previously incarcerated youth have historically been very low. For example, one study found that only 12 percent of youth previously detained receive their high school diploma or GED (Bullis, Yovanoff, and Havel 2004).

Litigation offers one way to address the inadequacies of the formal education provided through juvenile justice systems. By 1997, more than twenty class-action lawsuits had been filed to address the educational services youth receive in juvenile detention (Leone and Meisel 1997). Other cases were specific to individual youth. For example, in *Johnson v Upchurch* (1983), the US District Court for the District of Arizona found that the Catalina Mountain School violated several procedural protections (Taylor, Decker, and Katz 2013). Violations included the school's failure to provide adequate education, including failure to comply with IDEA (Puritz and Scali 1998). The court handed down an injunction, plus guidelines for what Catalina Mountain School was required to do, such as complete mandatory assessments and provide work programs, with continual program monitoring.

The following year, the US District Court for the Southern District of New York heard *Andre H. v Sobol* (1984), which brought to light violations of disability rights at the Spofford Juvenile Detention Center in the Bronx, New York. Specifically, Spofford failed to conduct any screening to identify disabilities for their residents and made no request for public school records. It also did not have any administrative process or agenda to put in place special education services. The court required that Spofford Juvenile Detention Center develop a multidisciplinary team to ensure compliance with IDEA (Puritz and Scali 1998).

Youth continued to prevail in court cases involving education in juvenile detention facilities. In 1987, the US District Court for the District of Connecticut reviewed the conduct of the Long Lane School, a juvenile correctional facility located in Middletown, Connecticut (Puritz and Scali 1998). In *Smith v Wheaton*, the juvenile centre was found to be out of compliance with statutory timelines for completing evaluations for special education students in its custody. As well, detention personnel did not allow parents to participate in the educational decisions of their children while they were incarcerated, in direct violation of law. Absence of transition plans and implemented IEP programs also existed (ibid.).

Cases specific to autism that are outside of the provision of education in juvenile justice systems continue to occur and unfold. In 2017, parents requested that the school district reimburse them for expenses acquired for their child with autism, who was forced to attend a private school after long-term inadequacies of the IEP program provided by the public school system. The case was eventually brought to the Supreme Court after the lower courts ruled in favour of the school district. The court affirmed education rights for the student with autism and overturned the lower court ruling. In *Endrew F. v Douglas County School District (2017)*, the court unanimously ruled that students with disabilities have the "chance to make meaningful appropriately ambitious progress" (Kamenetz and Turner 2017, n.p.). The essence of this ruling places the responsibility on the school districts and expands the interpretation of appropriate education. In the majority opinion, Chief Justice John Roberts stated, "it cannot be right that the IDEA generally contemplates grade-level advancement for children with disabilities who are fully integrated in the regular classroom, but is satisfied with barely more than *de minimis* progress for children who are not" (ibid.). Students in juvenile justice settings poignantly represent this latter category of children.

Conclusion

Education matters, especially for children and youth already restricted from their homes and communities through the exercise of juvenile justice. Juvenile facilities must aim to function more like residential educational facilities (Suitts 2014). Reorganizing the system to appear and operate more like a school campus could foster a higher level learning for some youth with autism and autistic youth. However, several factors render this approach both more difficult and potentially less successful if not expertly managed. Many youth who enter the facility are facing critical challenges such as chemical dependency and other addictions. Furthermore, youth who enter detention from off the streets or other life-threatening circumstances often come in with various physical and mental issues that have gone untreated. In such circumstances, stabilization and safety become the main priority for correctional staff. For youth with disabilities and disabled youth in juvenile justice systems in particular, school settings too often mean nothing but failure and exclusion to the youth, meaning that staff seeking to educate them must also overcome trauma and manage triggers associated with formal education. Building more success into the education of incarcerated youth will take time and expertise above and beyond the capacity of current systems.

One important step in providing better education and transitions out of custody involves developing stronger relationships with the public schools and other community-based education providers. This serves to increase the cooperation between the entities in the hope of shared information, resources, and a smoother transition for youth who transition out of secure care facilities. Re-entry into the community and public school system remains a primary goal of rehabilitation and a key to reducing recidivism. The report *Improving Education Outcomes for Youth in the Juvenile Justice System,* published by the National Juvenile Justice Network (2016), presents several recommendations for a successful re-entry. Suggestions include focusing on cooperation among facilities, public schools, and other agency support services; reducing the time gap between release and enrolment back to public school; ensuring successful and rapid record transfers; and increasing the number of reengagement programs available.

Education is one of many daily concerns faced by administrative staff of a secure care facility. The management style and jurisdictional power of the administrative staff assigned to the facility can heavily dictate the success of the educational programs inside juvenile justice systems. Schools need to have the support of the facility's administrative staff to provide the special education needs of the youth in custody. Without support, schools are hard-pressed to address each individual need of students and tempted to shortchange vulnerable students. Even the best-intentioned school and administrative staff can feel overwhelmed by the politics and policies of the juvenile justice system. Budget concerns and fiscal limitations hinder efforts on the part of schools in the juvenile justice system in providing an education comparable to the public schools for youth with disabilities and disabled students. Financial independence from the facility has long been cited as potentially helpful (Leone and Meisel 1997; Leone, Meisel, and Drakeford

2003). However, to serve justice, such autonomy must come from a place of expertise and neurodiversity.

The school-to-prison pipelines must be turned off. This work most crucially affects youth in intersectional circumstances. Success in addressing overrepresentation depends not only on sustained commitment to "promote higher levels of academic and behavioral competence" (Quinn et al. 2005, 6) but also on a genuine commitment to all youth and across all manifestations of human diversity. One example of such an effort is an awareness campaign called "Rethink Discipline," introduced in 2004 as part of President Obama's My Brothers' Keeper initiative, aimed to reduce the rates of student removal as a disciplinary tool. Rethink Discipline establishes collaborations with schools to help them recognize disparities, reduce discriminatory outcomes of the disciplinary process, and stop SROs from administering school discipline. The campaign promotes alternatives strategies and evolving the relationships between law enforcement, schools, and students (United States Government Accountability Office 2018). Improving education in the context of autism and juvenile justice system starts with sustained and concerted effort to reconsider the realities and developmental purposes of youthful behaviours with the aim of reducing the rates at which young people interact with justice systems in the first place.

Finally, full attention to the connections between autism and juvenile justice system includes sustained re-examination of the role of schools in the lives of children and youth. Over the past several decades, expectations of teachers rose dramatically as other fundamental elements of youth community engagement faltered. Importantly, the peak time for juveniles to commit crimes is between the hours of 3 and 4 p.m. (Sickmund, Sladky, and Kang, n.d.). The hour after school release is the most vulnerable time for youth to be offenders *and* victims. For many, this could be an unattended time where they are travelling alone. During this time, young people may also become more influenced by their peers to break the law or make ill-advised efforts to address concerns that they or one of their peers is an intended victim. In either case, reliance on schools as (sometimes) exclusive sources of moral education and development is unlikely to prove a fully successful strategy. Responses ranging from extending the school day to reintroducing traditional freedoms of movement to contemporarily heavily and consistently monitored children have been suggested. Whichever strategies are determined most promising, avoidance of romanticizing the past, sustained attention to intersectionality, and best-practices-oriented analysis of local experimental with programs form the foundation of future successes.

Chapter 5 summary

1. **Why consider autism in the context of juvenile justice?**
   - There is a severe lack of coordination and communication between public schools and the schools that operate within juvenile justice facilities, creating several barriers for youth to receive the educational services they need while incarcerated and after release.
   - The assignment of school resource officers to public schools creates a heavy reliance on law enforcement, rather than school personnel, to handle any behavioural and discipline issues, in turn increasing the number of referrals to the juvenile justice system for incidents that occur while at school.

2. **How does the juvenile justice system particularly affect youth with autism and autistic youth?**
   - Policies like zero-tolerance remove discretion from schools to address behaviours and incidents that violate those policies without law enforcement.
   - In the United States, youth with disabilities are not receiving adequate education while in custody, and court schools are not able to fully comply with IDEA.

3. **How can circumstances be improved for youth with autism, autistic youth, and the personnel who interact with them in juvenile justice settings?**
   - Reduce the number of referrals to law enforcement for youth with disabilities, and find alternative ways to address and consequences for the behaviours in order to reduce the disproportionate number of youth with disabilities involved with the juvenile justice system.
   - Remove the circumstances that promote the school-to-prison pipeline.

4. **What does rights-based disability policy look like in the context of rehabilitation of children with autism and autistic children who have become involved with the juvenile justice system?**
   - Use interventions and methods, including those from the Salem-Keizer Threat Assessment System, to adopt a new way of addressing problem behaviours before referring the youth to law enforcement.
   - Increase education and training for school personnel and law enforcement about disabilities, to strengthen their skills in addressing undesirable behaviours at school.

Figure 4. Chapter 5 summary

6 The Social World of Juvenile Custody

Human beings are social animals. Incarceration, most poignantly juvenile custody, involves the initiation, nurturing, management, and, often, dissolution of human relationships. Lived experiences of incarceration for people with disabilities and disabled people remain incompletely understood (Ben-Moshe 2011; Humes 2015). Individuals with autism and autistic individuals are a historically oppressed minority group, particularly with regard to social interactions. Therefore, both youth with autism and autistic youth deserve targeted attention to whether and how they can participate safely and effectively in the social worlds of juvenile custody.

Social differences saturate many autism experiences. As Brewer and Young (2015, 50) explain in their discussion of the social world of autism:

> Friendships may exist but these are typically maintained because the other person tolerates the quirky and often inappropriate behaviour of the person with ASD [autism spectrum disorder] ... they will accept the person with ASD despite the relationship often being one-sided and the person with ASD appearing self-absorbed ... persons with autism may sometimes appear to have learned to read the emotions of others and modify their behaviour to address issues such as those outlined above, but the behaviour often appears scripted rather than intuitive ... this learning of skills can perhaps be likened to learning a foreign language in adulthood: metaphorically speaking, the social skills will always have an accent.

Without question, the above description reflects a bias toward the neurotypical perspective on social bonding with autistics or persons with autism. Full practice of true neurodiversity involves consideration of autistic definitions of relationships, including friendships. However, the context of autism and juvenile justice systems remains most shaped by standardized (and neurotypical) and often institutional social worlds. For the time being, the safety and success of justice-involved youth with autism and autistic youth require a focus on helping both youth and systems use standard social skills, even if accented.

Environmental conditions of confinement can be tormenting for any youth. For autistic youth and youth with autism with sensory sensitivities, atypical approaches to communication styles, or non-standard ways of relating to others, the torment can be especially acute. Administrative decisions and confinement conditions can either attenuate or augment the sources of distress. Relations with facility personnel make a definitive difference. Juvenile justice system employees may struggle to effectively and differentially relate to juveniles with disabilities owing to limited resources, procedural codes, and mandatory job duties (Haqanee, Peterson-Badali, and Skilling 2015). Even so, social worlds led, shaped, and nurtured by adults in charge remain as fundamental to the success of youth in custody as for all young people.

Relationships depend on shared communication. The lack of training or an ableist bias can intensify communication barriers for both personnel giving directives and juveniles trying to understand instructions. This limits the potential for success of even well-established interventions. For example, youth with autism and autistic youth may prove especially vulnerable to communication challenges while participating in custody-based therapeutic programming built around standard communication styles and capacities. Clinical dosage, performance measures, and therapeutic progress for youth receiving services through the juvenile court may be calibrated, or normed, to so-called typical youth (Bellini et al. 2007), rendering progress in such activities more difficult to determine given autism. Not only can this strain communication in therapeutic relationships but effects of the communication on the youth's progress may prove difficult to detect.

As discussed in Chapter 3, correctional programs exist both in communities and in confinement. Correctional programs aim for "the adjustment of behavior from a pattern that is criminal or antisocial to one that is more law-abiding or pro-social" (Motiuk 2012, 15). Perceptions of an individual youth's motivation to reform factor into decisions about the appropriateness of particular programs. After all, youth showing high levels of motivation for behaviour change pose less risk of reoffending and appear more likely to succeed in community-based correction programs (Clark 2005; Feldstein and Ginsburg 2007). On the other hand, youth judged as having low levels of motivation for behaviour change or as resisting programming efforts are more likely to be held in custody. For youth with disabilities and disabled youth, relationship-driven assessments of motivation can mislead. If juvenile justice personnel misunderstand disability, they may misperceive that the youth is fighting the program and therefore requires a higher level of security and care in custody. Since incarceration can have devastating effects on youth with autism and autistic youth, including sometimes reversing hard-won progress in socially desirable behavioural changes made prior to involvement with the juvenile justice system, the decision to keep a youth in custody based on misperceptions of motivation hinders the goals of juvenile justice systems.

Importantly, difficulties in social interactions can and do originate in all parties involved in social interactions, not just in the individual with autism or the autistic individual. Equally important (and sometimes missing from the discourse on disability inclusion) is the recognition that flexibility and change require effort on the part of those persons, programs, and policies built around the neurotypical experience. Such efforts can prove exhausting. While certainly not an excuse for the continuation of historical discrimination and exclusion, resilience grows when exhaustion is minimized, and attention to the needs, disadvantages, and rights of the neurologically typical are also considered. In other words, although everyone involved should be expected to reduce ableism, reducing ableism does not involve infinite patience and exclusively unilateral change on the part of those considered typical. Furthermore, it is crucial not to assume that all juvenile justice personnel are neurologically typical. The social worlds of juvenile justice systems can best serve youth with autism and autistic youth if expectations of the youth, justice system personnel, and other adult stakeholders all remain human, humane, and attentive to the politics of neurodiversity.

Well-Being in Juvenile Custody: Detention and Residential Placement

Well-being involves multiple dimensions. In their meta-analysis of research into the well-being of families that include youth with autism, Tint and Weiss (2016, 264) examined five domains of well-being, including "family interaction, parenting, health and safety, family resources, and support for family member with disabilities." While alternative constructions of taxonomies of well-being exist, this breakdown covers the broad scope of human needs and transfers readily to instances where institutions (ideally temporarily and partially) stand in for family in the lives of young people in custody. Even so, especially in an comparison of two distinct nations, relying too much on any taxonomy runs the risk of oversimplifying complex issues and failing to appropriately address the diversity of issues attendant in considering groups from different racial, ethnic, gender, and tribal affiliations, and from different nations. Understanding this diversity of diversities present in both Canada and the United States involves consideration of the experience in custody from a largely intersectional standpoint (Poteat et al. 2016; Strand 2017). The relative importance of dimensions of well-being can be understood only as both dynamic and varied.

Incarceration ensnares identity. For example, a lesbian Latinx youth from a poor neighbourhood may experience the social process of negotiating detention very differently than would a straight white male from a middle-class background. Furthermore, incarcerated youth may self-segregate by gender, age, race, or ethnic background, and by region of origin, resulting in differing experiences, both incidental and planned. Especially in the United States, for-profit entities pervade detention systems, resulting in for-pay perquisites ranging from the ability to make phone calls to access to food, bathing, or recreational products. As a result, disparities tied to differences in family-of-origin resources serve to concentrate negative effects of custody on traditionally marginalized economic groups such as youth of colour, members of First Nations, and women (Younhee and Price 2012). For example, female youth incarcerated in the juvenile justice system experience additional difficulties meeting gender-specific needs. A study of detained adolescent females found that many girls in the system need education about pregnancy, sexually transmitted diseases, and safe choices in order to effectively manage coercive social pressures to engage in risky sexual behaviour and become pregnant (Johnston et al. 2016). The social world of youth in detention involves multiple bureaucratic systems and complex, emerging identities situated in the dynamic sociological worlds of the twenty-first century.

As discussed in Chapter 2, policy changes in the Canadian juvenile justice markedly decreased the use of custody during the first decade of the new millennium. The 2003 Youth Criminal Justice Act (YCJA) reduced the number of youths in custody by requiring diversion to the community for all first-time offenders and non-serious offenders, as well as by allowing some youth to split their sentences between custody and the community.

YCJA recommended custody only for the most serious of youthful offenders (Bala and Roberts 2006; Bala, Carrington, and Roberts 2009). Juvenile corrections statistics indicate actual movement away from incarceration. The youth incarceration rate in Canada dropped from 12.5 per 10,000 youth in 2002–03 to 6 per 10,000 in 2014–15 (Statistics Canada 2016; Reitano 2004). YCJA also reduced the standard length of detention. In the 2015–16 school year, 45 percent of incarcerated youth served one month or less in custody, and 91 percent spent six months or less in detention (Malakieh 2017).

As is the case with any federal system of governance, the implementation of national policy varies across subnational borders. Since 2011, most Canadian provinces and territories experienced large reductions in the proportions of justice-involved youth serving any time in custody (Miladinovic 2016). Newfoundland and Labrador experienced a 58 percent drop in juvenile incarceration during this time, one of the largest in Canada. Not all stakeholders believed the effects of these changes were exclusively positive. For example, a study of Newfoundland and Labrador Youth Centre (NLYC) showed increasingly holistic treatment approaches aimed at meeting as many of youth needs as possible (Morris and Enstrom 2016). Some NLYC practitioners praised reduced custody lengths. However, the shorter lengths of stay in correctional confinement frustrated some practitioners, who felt that youths with complex issues related to mental health are best addressed with longer stays in correctional environments (ibid.).

Similarly, in Ontario, the proportion of youth receiving custody sentence reduced under YCJA. Between 2003 and 2014, custody admissions in Ontario declined by 72 percent (Ontario Ministry of Children, Community and Social Services 2016[b].). After the passage of 2003 legislation, Ontario created the Ministry of Children, Community and Social Services, combining child welfare, youth justice, community support, and child mental health services (Campbell 2016). The Youth Justice Division, created to support youth under juvenile justice authority, includes youth services officers who receive specific training in counselling and the mental health needs of youth. Ontario also created the Intensive Rehabilitative Custody and Supervision Program, providing mental health services for youth while in custody and treatment plans for transition to the community as part of the custody-based continuum of care (ibid.).

Similarly, the Juvenile Justice and Delinquency Prevention Act of 2002 establishes four key standards for juvenile justice systems in the United States: deinstitutionalizing status offenders and non-offenders, sight and sound separation, jail and lockup removal, and reducing disproportionate minority confinement (Sickmund and Puzzanchera 2014). Essentially, the act aims to reduce time spent in detention, ensure there is no contact between youth and adults in detention, and ensure that effects of intersectionalities are minimized across the nation. Even so, use of detention varies by the offence committed, gender, race, and age (Sickmund and Puzzanchera 2014). The social world of youth in detention remains inconsistent.

Length-of-stay statistics prove elusive, since data on release cohorts are not tabulated in the United States (OJJDP, n.d.). However, the average length of stay in a long-term juvenile facility in that country is about six months. One census found that only 11 percent of juveniles remained in detention a year later (OJJDP 2019). Different facilities usually exist for short- and long-term stays. Short-term detention centres are used on a temporary basis while juveniles are awaiting court proceedings or if they were sanctioned by the court for a violation of court order, also known as a "probation violation." Youth are held in detention while their case is pending if they are considered to be likely to fail to appear at the next court hearing, to be a concern for community safety, or to be a risk to themselves or at risk if returning to the community (OJJDP 2014). Given these factors, social worlds of short-term facilities matter and make a difference.

Placing a youth in custody is costly. According to Lauren Kirchner (2014, n.p.), "average costs of the most expensive confinement option throughout the 46 states surveyed is $408 a day, or $148,767 per year – per person." Estimates of the long-term costs of juvenile confinement among forty-six states ranged between 8 to 21 billion dollars per year (ibid.). In addition to these costs, as discussed in previous chapters, incarcerating juveniles increases the risk of recidivism, increases the risk of poor school performance, and weakens employment prospects later in life (Maggard 2015). Furthermore, estimates of rates of incarceration tend to exclude youth held in psychiatric hospitals, mental institutions, and other homes that provide ongoing medical care (Ben-Moshe 2011; OJJDP 2019). Youth from historically excluded backgrounds are more likely than their non-Hispanic white counterparts to receive treatment while in juvenile detention (Barnert, Perry, and Morris 2016). Since the prevalence of serious mental illness among youth who are found to have violated the law ranges from 60 to 80 percent, such sites also contribute to the social world of youth involved with juvenile justice systems (Perry and Morris 2014). Interactions between the mental health systems and juvenile justice systems are complex, especially in the United States and in the absence of a national health care system. A broad spectrum of sites house the social world of youth with autism and autistic youth while incarcerated, sharing key commonalities, including restrictions on movement, limited access to outside friends and peers, and structured schedules.

Intersectional Vulnerabilities

Juveniles with autism and autistic juveniles are vulnerable populations for both reoffending and victimization while in custody. As discussed, these risks intensify when youth also embody intersectional characteristics historically associated with oppression or exclusion.

In social interactions and in the building of the social self of youth, intersectionality can play a particularly important role (Ben-Moshe 2011). Intersectionalities involving gender include relevance in the social world of youth with autism and autistic youth. As is reflected in known rates of diagnosis and self-identification, autism is more prevalent in boys and men than it is girls and women (Lai et al. 2015). Although it is not considered an accurate description in contemporary thinking, some have even described autism as an extreme version of maleness, owing to the stereotypical approaches to social interactions among individuals with autism and autistics (Baron-Cohen 2002). In the early twenty-first century, the known population of individuals with autism was 75 percent male and 60 percent white (Cha 2015). As a result, autism has also been historically mischaracterized in some corners as predominantly affecting white males (ibid.; Lai et al. 2015). While such disparities likely reflect diagnosis bias as opposed to exclusively underlying epidemiology, autism still appears more prevalent in males than in females (Christensen et al. 2016).

Such gender differences also exist in juvenile justice systems. In the formative moments of youth specific justice systems in North America, a misogynistic failure of imagination framed juvenile justice as an issue almost exclusively affecting boys. Although far less of a gender gap exists today, boys remain overrepresented in contemporary criminal proceedings. For example, a study of court cases conducted by students at California State University Channel Islands relating to juvenile justice and disability between 2004 and 2018 conducted by Wendy Goolsby, Michael Worman, Kazim Jafri, and Madison Harden (forthcoming) found that over 95 percent of the case narratives in which gender of the juvenile defendant was discussed involved boys or young men. In the context of the juvenile justice systems, these dual gender imbalances underlie twin challenges of male overrepresentation in targeted programs and programs designed with boys in mind. While gender is neither truly binary nor determinative, females with autism may struggle to benefit as anticipated from services predominately geared toward males.

Furthermore, autism in girls may be missed by juvenile justice system personnel who are planning social supports for incarcerated youth. Lower recorded percentages of mental health conditions among females in custody relative to males may in part reflect screening biases. As discussed in Chapter 3, the use of screening tools varies from jurisdiction to jurisdiction and from facility to facility. Access to treatment and programs varies from one facility to another even under the unlikely circumstance of equal access to financial resources. Some facilities do not have in-house medical staff available to assist with screening. Medical staff involvement during admissions processes can make the difference of whether a youth with autism or autistic youth will receive appropriate services and accommodations while in custody. A girl's behaviours may be dismissed as emotionality, deception, or simply a penchant for drama, rather than as a sign of neurological difference or mental health challenges. Probation officers and psychologists have been found to use gender, racial, and ethnic stereotypes to rationalize how they serve young women under their care (Gaarder, Rodriguez, and Zatz 2004). Many psychologists and probation officers perceived these young women as whiny, manipulative, and trashy and consistently failed to consider behaviours in the context of their lives in the community or neurological difference (ibid.). Probation officers articulated a need for additional training to work more effectively with girls and described the lack of resources for gender-specific programming as a barrier to rehabilitation practice in juvenile detention.

Some jurisdictions have implemented gender-responsive programming in their courts to improve outcomes for girls in the system (Chesney-Lind, Morash, and Stevens 2008). In such approaches, both risk assessments and treatment approaches are modified to consider the co-occurring nature of girls' risk factors for recidivism. Most of the risk and needs assessments used by juvenile justice practitioners are statistically normed on boys despite being routinely used with girls in juvenile justice systems (Vitopoulos, Peterson-Badali, and Skilling 2012). For girls, risk factors for delinquency, such as a history of physical and sexual trauma, as well as a history of homelessness, tend to associate with increased risks for self-harm, rather than with the potential victimization of others (ibid.). Girls tend to have different needs than boys, often related to social support, trauma counselling, substance-abuse recovery, domestic violence, and pregnancy (Walker et al. 2015). Finally, a strengths-based approach to rehabilitation services appears to be especially helpful for girls – particularly those in adolescence, when self-esteem drops precipitously (ibid.).

LGBTQIAA+ youth also interact differently with the social worlds of custodial settings. Crucially, these youth have been found twice as likely as other youth to experience an adverse childhood experience such as child abuse, homelessness, and foster-care placement (Irvine 2010). LGBTQ-IAA+ youth receive pretrial detention more often than do heterosexual youth, rendering them more likely to interact with the social world of juvenile custody earlier in their experiences with a juvenile justice system (Poteat, Scheer, and Chong 2016). Moreover, sexual-minority youth experience more peer victimization than do heterosexual youth, later associated with higher rates of punishable offences and institutional infractions while incarcerated (ibid.). Juvenile justice practitioners may be particularly challenged to create social services for youth with trauma histories whose autism presents in ways inconsistent with commonly understood notions of this neurological difference.

Transcending such challenges with the goal of creating just and successful social worlds in juvenile justice systems involves appreciating both neurodiversity and intersectionality. As discussed in Chapter 1, neurodiversity rests on the inherent worth of every human being and necessarily incorporates the celebration of all human differences (Armstrong 2011; Baker 2011). In keeping with the ethos of the disability rights movement, the neurodiversity paradigm argues that neurological atypicalities produce valuable social, emotional, and cognitive contributions to humanity (Baker and Leonard 2017). Neurodiversity theory argues that neurological differences carry advantages, thereby strengthening the human ecosystem (Armstrong 2011). As such, this theory conceptualizes neurodiverse individuals as self-reliant humans advocating for their rights and the rights of others to ensure full inclusion in modern-day legal, social, and political life (Charlton 1998). Given this, social services and rehabilitative programming for youth with autism and autistic youth can be appropriately designed only with advice and counsel from autistic adults, ideally well versed themselves in juvenile justice systems.

Intersectionality theory describes how certain combinations of human characteristics experience greater levels of prejudice (negative attitudes) and discrimination (denial of rights and liberties) because of the cumulative effects of historically marginalized statuses (Roberts and Jesudason 2013). Black women scholars and activists pioneered the intersectional approach, arguing that they were doubly invisible to the various rights-based social movements owing to the cumulative effect of two historically subordinate statuses (hooks 1981). Queer women of colour represent an additional intersectionality typically overlooked in mainstream rights movements centring on positive and negative rights for sexual minorities (Alimahomed 2010). For example, scholars theorizing on the combination of disability, race, and gender assert that historical notions of disability connoted caregiving tasks relegated to women working in a service capacity (mothers) or a servant capacity (women of colour working as domestics) (Ben-Moshe and Magaña 2014). Such constraints in analysis have hampered efforts on the part of too many thinkers and stakeholders to understand these individuals as fully human. Analysis constraints limit potential of current programs and policies shaping the social worlds extant in juvenile justice facilities.

Disability has been less consistently incorporated into intersectionality conceptual frameworks than have race, class, gender, and sexual identity (Strand 2017). Strand (2017) notes that the Black Lives Matter movement presents an opportunity to blend intersectional theory and neurodiversity theory in a way that expands theoretical breadth as well as builds coalitions among advocacy organizations serving specific intersectionalities. On a theoretical level, advocacy organizations for persons with disabilities, disabled people, and persons of colour find common ground in their quest to end police brutality. In the case of the neurodiversity paradigm, this movement embraces persons of all races, religions, sexual orientations, and nationalities under an umbrella of rights, respect, and dignity for all neurological configurations of the human mind. In solidarity, all may be strengthened. Disability rights organizations are jouing forces with Black Lives Matter to demand police training for non-violent de-escalation techniques and education on how to recognize the signs of autism in order to prevent officers from confusing such traits with intentional non-compliance (Strand 2017). As traditionally marginalized groups form coalitions for positive change, critiques of limited relevance to social programs owing to a narrow scope of inquiry weaken (Warner 2008).

Juvenile justice policy and practices still reproduce national societal inequalities inside juvenile detention facilities. As discussed, Aboriginal youth are overrepresented in Canadian juvenile detention relative to the proportional of Aboriginal youth in the population (Statistics Canada 2016; Kong 2009; Malakieh 2017). In the United States, youth of colour have long been disproportionately detained (Kempf-Leonard 2007). In both countries, youth in detention are afflicted by poverty and family strain, and experience difficulties in school more frequently than non-detained youth (Corrado, Kuehn, and Margaritescu 2014; Leiber, Bishop, and Chamlin 2011). These trends have proven difficult to erradicate despite effort to curtail these effects. In 2015–16, admissions into the youth correctional system among Aboriginal youth in Canada increased 6 percent from the year before (Malakieh 2017). In the United States, research on disproportionate minority contact continues to show racial disparities in juvenile confinement facilities, albeit at reduced rates than in the past (Davis and Sorensen 2013; Leiber, Bishop, and Chamlin 2011; Puzzanchera and Hockenberry 2017). Webster and Doob (2007) argue that, on the whole, Canadian culture is less punitive in its justice orientation than is that of the United States, relying on community-based solutions for all but the very serious of criminal acts for both adults and youth. A less punitive orientation supports greater potential for social worlds, including those found in juvenile justice systesms. Differences in overarching social attitudes toward crime and punishment influence the likelihihood of acceptance and the success of neurodiversity- and intersectionality-informed strategies aiming to improve social worlds in juvenile justice systems.

Social Failure and Deterrence

The justification for the use of detention facilities for youth involved with juvenile justice systems depends on the jurisdiction, political climate, and stakeholders in nation-states (Webster and Doob 2007). Traditionally, five models dominate: incapacitation, retribution, restitution, rehabilitation, and deterrence are relied on to keep correctional facilities in operation (Mays and Winfree 2006). Incapacitation means to physically ensure that an offender does not commit another crime by putting them in prison or jail. Incapacitation is usually the primary argument for legitimizing correctional facilities, as it is believed that incarceration is the best way to guarantee that a person will not commit another crime, though arguably they can still commit crimes while in custody.

Retribution connects to the ancient *lex talionis*, or an eye-for-an-eye principle, which focuses on punishment for the offender's actions similar to the victim's experience. Restitution constitutes ordering that the juvenile cover monetary losses the victim or community suffered as a result of the juvenile's actions. Rehabilitation is the concept of seeking help and resources for the offender in the hope of solving the issues that led to the offender committing a crime in the first place. Some perceive this as being soft on crime. However, research shows that rehabilitation is the most effective approach to preventing future crime (Lipsey and Cullen 2007).

Deterrence theory holds that swift, severe, and sure consequences prevent future criminal behaviour (Matsueda, Kreager, and Huizinga 2006).

This approach has two dimensions: specific deterrence involves a legal punishment delivered directly to individual, in the expectation that this prevents further law-violating behaviour because of the harmful effects of the lived experience. General deterrence occurs when the legal punishment for a crime is widely communicated either in writing or through vicarious experience, setting an example for other youth and discouraging them from committing crimes. Deterrence appears of to be limited effectiveness (Paternoster 2010; Schneider 2012). For example, juvenile crime is not lower in states that frequently transfer juveniles to criminal court and try them as adults (Steinberg 2008; Griffin et al. 2011). Deterrence doctrine can be complicated to implement in an adversarial legal system that emphasizes a due process model of deciding criminal cases. Furthermore, previous involvement with justice systems shifts the ratio of risk-to-reward assumed in deterrence. Deterrence reinforces adverse elements of social engagement, often working quite counter to the goals of social services programming and further compromising the potential to nurture prosocial social worlds for justice-involved youth.

Deterrence theory also presumes that people link criminal behaviour to legal consequences and adjust planned behaviour accordingly. As well as this basic cognitive linkage, the theory assumes that as the severity of punishment increases, so does the potential for deterring criminal activity. Research on the efficacy of the theory's claims has been less than completely supportive of these hypothesized causal chains of events, especially for youth who have already engaged in illegal activities (Loughran et al. 2012). The research also generally does not fully consider neurological differences. What is perceived logical varies alongside neurological differences (Sprague and Kobrynowicz 2006). Since autism often links with challenges in executive functioning and planning, evidence of the deterrence theory would have to be particularly persuasive to appear likely to overwhelm the influence of other social factors on the potential for youth with autism and autistic youth to engage in illegal activity.

Standpoint theory postulates that ways of making sense of the world are best achieved by considering each individual's embeddedness in time and space, as well as socio-economic context. This framework may prove a more useful perspective in understanding how persons with autism and autistic persons define and experience legal consequences in combination with all others factors in their social worlds (Sprague and Kobrynowicz 2006). Exploring how the perceptual worlds of people with autism and autistic people are distinct from neurotypical individuals when applying deterrence theory's rationality assumption may broaden practitioner and scholarly knowledge about this theoretical perspective. The case of Andrew, described in Chapter 2 (a youth with autism charged with sexually molesting his sister) illustrates how an individual on the autism spectrum may even reject the entire causal chain articulated in deterrence when the charged offence does not overlap with the individual's perceptions about the nature of the transgression (Thompson and Morris 2016). Andrew's attempts to make sense of his social world relative to his desire to continue with disfavoured activities contributed to, as opposed to prevented, tragedy. Greater reliance on standpoint theory could provide opportunity for understanding contexts and risks when it comes to autism and juvenile justice system involvement.

Unfortunately, in recent decades, the political popularity of deterrence theory grew, despite improvements in the general comprehension of youth development and the social construction of disability. In Canada, Prime Minister Steven Harper's conservative government amended the Youth Criminal Justice Act (YCJA) in 2012 when it created the Safe Streets and Communities Act (Correctional Service Canada, 2012a). The revisions reflected a get-tough approach to juvenile crime centred on deterrence; legal punishment rested at the centrepiece of this decision (Mann 2014). These revisions moved YCJA away from a policy of diverting youth away from formal juvenile justice processing. The criteria by which youth could be held in pretrial detention were broadened. Deterrence, as well as denunciation, became legitimate sentencing goals, in addition to those of rehabilitation and community re-entry (Mann 2014). The YCJA's emphasis on strict interpretations of offender accountability signalled a reliance on the power of legal punishments to achieve desistance from criminal behaviour among youth in the Canadian juvenile justice system.

Some research findings support tough-on-crime policies. In reviewing YCJA five years out, Bala, Carrington, and Roberts (2009) characterize it as an effective piece of legislation. Even so, legal punishments reduce criminal activity only for certain kinds of offenders (ibid.; Loughran et al. 2012). Furthermore, some research has found an intensifying effect of delinquent behaviour after youth exposure to legal punishments delivered under the deterrence doctrine (Bouffard and Piquero 2010; Petrosino, Turpin-Petrosino, and Finckenauer 2000). In her study of teenaged Canadian youth with extensive histories of violent delinquency, Mann (2014) found no evidence that the severity of sanctions delivered by the correctional authorities had any impact on the youths' desire to stop engaging in criminal behaviour. Younger offenders were enjoying their forays into delinquency and violence too much to consider stopping this behaviour, and other youth were angry and had bought into the power that violence could bring them so they refused to consider stopping (ibid.). When asked what kinds of things would lead them to stop committing crimes, most of the youth responded that social supports, education, job training, and assistance managing mental health challenges or negative affective states (e.g., anger) would be most helpful (ibid.). Finding balance between punishment and assistance has long challenged juvenile justice systems. This balance rests at the very core of the social world of juvenile justice systems, not only affecting all programs and services but pervading the tone of interpersonal interactions extant throughout the system. Remembering that the social world of justice systems always both reflects and affects the quality of life throughout a given society should also factor into considerations of this balance.

Juvenile justice systems inevitably require all juvenile justice practitioners to continually balance between punishing for the offence and preventing future crime by addressing the individual needs of the youth. In the context of modern democracies, proportionality requires that the culpability of the offender must be taken into consideration to create a fair and just process (Scott and Steinberg 2008). Proportionality asserts that the substantive nature of a juvenile's sentence must correspond to the offence they have committed. Known as the "just deserts" model of punishment, this philosophy holds that punishment follows actions deserving such consequences (Frase 2005). Moreover, the punishments range in severity depending on the nature of the offender's crime, rather than exclusively on the needs of the offender, because part of the goal of legal action remains to extract retribution on the offender by the state (ibid.). This retributive function often creates cognitive dissonance for practitioners inside the juvenile justice system as they grapple with the state's requirement for punishment against the stipulation that juvenile offenders experience a separate legal system prioritizing the plight of the child. Responding to the suffering of young humans with care is a deeply human response. One coping mechanism when forced to act against this natural instinct involves othering or dehumanizing the young person in question. Owing to historical oppression and bias, young people with autism and autistic youth prove especially vulnerable to such othering. Creating effective and just social worlds in juvenile justice systems depends on tending to the associated angst of providers. The too-frequent absence of this necessary support of professionals underlies and exacerbates many failures and abuses in the social worlds of juvenile justice systems.

Proportionality also shapes social worlds in juvenile justice systems as a result of added (perceived) complexities with regard to how the system treats the young people in given facilities and communities. The exercise of proportionality can appear less fair, especially to casually informed observers and tangentially involved stakeholders, because two young people committing the identical crime might receive unequal sentences. Proportionality can also feel less fair to victims, since consequences tied to a particular criminal event depend on who committed the crime rather than exclusively on some measure of the suffering caused by the actions of the perpetrator. However, all just social worlds, including society at large, involve some measure of proportionality. Just as an individual's ability to enter into a legal contract or vote is limited by age, so too is their ability to participate in the adult justice system as an offender. Similarly, a youth who has had previous opportunities to learn from the consequences of criminal activity through earlier involvement with juvenile justice systems likely requires different interventions than does a youth with no previous involvement. Supporting success in the social world of juvenile justice systems requires as much focus on individuation of young people as safely possible within large, institutional organizations engaged in one of the most complex and uncertain of human social efforts.

Blameworthiness critically shapes appropriate response to a crime. Blameworthiness is distinct from that of cause and even that of responsibility (Shaver 2012). A person can be responsible for a criminal event that occurs but may not have had a negative intention for the offence to come to pass and therefore may not be blameworthy for the offence (ibid.). For example, if one juvenile provides information to another about an individual and that individual is later victimized by the youth who received the information, the information sharer can be said to bear some responsibility for the crime but is not to blame for it. A key component of assigning blame involves assessing the existence of an intention to have a negative event occur. Blameworthiness closely mirrors the legal concept of mens rea, or criminal intent, discussed in Chapter 2. These complicated distinctions perform crucial functions in society, as both legal systems and members of the public risk miscarriages of justice given misunderstandings of blame. Blame produces shame, thereby compromising for most people a positive self-image. Misplaced shame adversely affects most social systems. Well-crafted social services programs attend actively and progressively to blame and shame.

Working with blame and shame proves especially challenging given neurological differences. For youth with disabilities and disabled youth, incapacitation can differentially increase the likelihood for trauma and future crimes (Mallett 2013). Penal systems have been designed around the thought processes ascribed to typical capacities. To the degree that empathetic attempts to understand the lived experience of juvenile custody factors into design decisions woven into the juvenile justice system, these attempts have generally been made by those identifying as neurologically typical. Adult autistics are rarely, if ever, consulted. Especially when it comes to contemplations of the resulting social worlds within juvenile justice systems, the exclusion of input from autistics and individuals with autism increases the risk of victimizing neurologically distinct individuals. Examples of effects of such potential oversights include inadvertently emphasizing difference (such as when autistic youth have an unusual reaction to the sensory environment) and increasing the risk of non-compliance because the youth cannot as efficiently comprehend the dynamics of the institution as anticipated by program and institutional design.

As discussed in previous chapters, policies aiming to stop discrimination by design on the basis of disability exist in both Canada and the United States. In Canada, the Charter of Rights and Freedoms establishes protections against discrimination on the basis of disability, including while held in a correctional facility (1982 Charter of Rights and Freedoms, section 15). Similarly, in the United States, reasonable accommodations are required under the Americans with Disabilities Act. Even so, how those accommodations are made varies depending on the facility, resources, and abilities of the correctional staff. Limitations to the Americans with Disabilities Act have been long recognized (Baker 2011; Pitney 2015). Despite the Americans with Disabilities Act Amendments Act of 2008 seeking to maximize accessibility in the context of disability, establishing such rights for vulnerable populations such as the incarcerated remains challenging at best (Ben-Moshe 2011; Smith 2005). Paucity of input from across the spectrum of human neurodiversity in both nations augments such challenges.

Crisis Considerations: Juvenile Justice Systems as Social Services

Incarceration risks negative effects on children and youth regardless of environment or facility (Sugie and Turney 2017). Even so, potential for positive outcomes for juveniles in detention exists when youths receive services addressing a condition or need not previously met. Detention centres wear many hats, roles that include providing medical and mental health services, school services, and a safe place to detox, and meeting basic needs such as food, shelter, and showers. It is vital to remember that for some youth, detention remains the only time they have access to these essentials. As examples, detention and correction officers regularly treat juveniles for lice and schedule dental appointments for abscess teeth, provide twenty-four-hour monitoring for youth detoxing from drugs, and restart youth in school. Although some of these needs could be met without detaining youth, persistent gaps in community services ensuring access to some of these basic services exist (Maschi et al. 2008). Considerations of the social world of juvenile justice systems exist necessarily in reference to the social world faced by youth while in community. Of course, healthier, stronger communities stand out as a broad goal for all societies. Juvenile justice systems play a key role in this fundamental social goal.

As discussed in previous chapters, youth entering detention in Canada or the United States go through an intake or booking process. This generally involves a sequence of mandated forms and tasks, completed to ensure safety and security in the facility and to address the youths' needs and accommodations (if applicable). Federal and sub-federal governments in both Canada and the United States set minimum guidelines and standards for facilities to follow. In Canada, Corrections Canada "contributes to public safety by actively encouraging and assisting offenders to become law abiding citizens, while exercising reasonable, safe, secure and humane control" (Correctional Service Canada 2012b, n.p.). Corrections Canada evaluates this mission according to five values: respect, fairness, professionalism, inclusiveness, and accountability. Specifically, Canada seeks to foster inclusivity by "welcoming, proactively accommodating and learning from cultural, spiritual, and generational differences, individual challenges, and novel points of view" (ibid.). Implementing this goal involves specialized programs, policies, training, and specialized staff charged with ensuring that individuals under the care of Corrections Canada do not suffer discrimination.

In the United States, the National Institute of Corrections (NIC) provides guidelines, process, procedures, and support services for all areas of incarceration. The NIC is part of the Federal Bureau of Prisons within the US Department of Justice. Since 1930, the Federal Bureau of Prisons (n.d., n.p.) has been tasked with "management and regulation of all Federal penal and correctional institutions." The agency's mission statement reads: "We are an agency like no other. We protect public safety by ensuring that federal offenders serve their sentences of imprisonment in facilities that are safe, humane, cost-efficient, and appropriately secure, and provide re-entry programming to ensure their successful return to the community" (n.p.). The Office of Juvenile Justice and Delinquency Prevention (OJJDP), part of the Department of Justice, also manages programs and facilities for detained young people. OJJDP's mission is to

> provide national leadership, coordination, and resources to prevent and respond to juvenile delinquency and victimization. OJJDP supports states and communities in their efforts to develop and implement effective and coordinated prevention and intervention programs and to improve the juvenile justice system so that it protects public safety, holds justice-involved youth appropriately accountable, and provides treatment and rehabilitative services tailored to the needs of juveniles and their families. (OJJDP, n.d.)

Facilities and state agencies use federal agency support services, mostly online trainings and guides, to ensure compliance and standards. For example, the NIC has released the *Desktop Guide*, written by Anne M. Nelsen, to support agencies with their intake and admissions process. The guide defines several mechanisms to juvenile detention, one of them being "the services that address immediate and acute needs in the educational, mental, physical, emotional and social development of juveniles" (Nelsen 2014, 1). The NIC establishes admissions documents criteria, including obtaining information about special medical problems or needs.

As discussed in previous chapters, Canada and the United States use juvenile assessments to determine appropriate programming for all youth involved with juvenile justice systems, both in custody and in the community. Mental health challenges and, often, neurological differences fall into the risk category employed in risk-need-responsivity (RNR) models popular in contemporary conceptions of social services provided in juvenile justice systems (Andrews, Bonta, and Wormith 2006; Thompson and Stewart 2006; Schwalbe 2007). As outlined in Chapter 4, linking the youth with specific programs and services based on their level of risk to reoffend, their criminogenic needs, and their abilities to intellectually and emotionally engage treatment lays the foundation for their beneficial interactions with social worlds in custody and beyond (Thompson and Stewart 2006). Rehabilitative services should reduce associations and identifications with others engaging in criminal activity, while directing youth toward more positive social choices (Bonta and Andrews 2016).

RNR models centre on eight dimensions of risk and protective factors for youth delinquency: a history of antisocial behaviour, an antisocial personality, antisocial cognition, antisocial associates, family factors, school or work factors, leisure or recreation interests, and substance abuse (Andrews and Bonta 2010). Recent scholarship broadens the conceptualization of mental health under the RNR model by considering mental health as a criminogenic need (rather than exclusively as a risk) that when met can reduce recidivism risk by taking difference-specific responsivity into account. This approach deeply considers cognitive capacities of the individual receiving services, as well as the psychological nature of those services. In a study of Canadian youth in juvenile detention, McCormick, Peterson-Badali, and Skilling (2017) argue that reductions in recidivism risk could be achieved through mental health treatment when treatment matches criminogenic needs related to mental health issues in reference to the social world surrounding the youth both in detention and in their home communities. Youth who simultaneously received mental health services and programming to reduce criminogenic risk factors (such as impulsivity or anger-management challenges) experienced lower recidivism rates than did youth who needed both services but received either one or neither of these services, as well as youth who needed both services but received neither (ibid.).

Unfortunately, even in recent years, many youths with disabilities and disabled youths received limited or generic social services while living in correctional facilities. In a qualitative analysis of Vermont state prisoners who self-identified as having a disability, Phil Smith (2005) found that most inmates believed themselves to have received little to no services to assist them in their adjustment to prison life. These prisoners established a relationship with disability advocates (Vermont Developmental Disabilities Council, Alliance for Prison Justice) and rehabilitation professionals as a way of documenting their unmet needs. Common complaints include benign neglect, such as prison therapists being annoyed during therapy sessions, as well as abuse, such as being placed in solitary confinement in response to mental health episodes (Smith 2005). In a case history of two youth with autism in juvenile detention, researchers noted that strict adherence to facility routines benefited one youth, but only to a point. After lunch, this young man's sensory and social sensitivities heightened and he engaged in conflict with other youth. Subsequently, he stayed in his cell in the afternoons, an exception to facility policy (Paterson 2007). The second youth profiled exhibited limited abstract language proficiency and suffered from depression. He struggled to express empathy when participating in therapy and withdrew to his cell (ibid.). Withdrawing from social services and social worlds while in detention constitutes a failure in service and reduces the anticipated benefit of incarceration.

Even if participation is maintained, providers struggle to make existing programs work in neurodiverse contexts. For example, in an interview with Laurie Drapela, a juvenile probation counsellor working with detained youth who have mental health diagnoses noted this about an inmate with autism during a moral reasoning exercise:

> The whole purpose of the exercise is to ... get them thinking about how they can share with another person ... Give to another person. It's like this: there are two kids walking in the desert – one kid's water bag breaks ... How do both kids survive the desert? Most kids ... figure it out ... share the water in your bag so both survive. Not this kid [with autism]. He came up with everything but sharing. Find a cactus and get the water out. Let the other kid drink urine to get water ... This kid [with autism] would not share his water bag and it began to disturb the other kids in group. (February 13, 2017)

Despite the programming services offered by the county to youth with mental health conditions, both a juvenile probation counsellor and a community care coordinator stressed that services for youth with autism insufficiently address needs of youth on the spectrum seeking services through the juvenile court and the community (interviews conducted by Laurie Drapela, February 13, 2017 and February 16, 2017).

Autism advocates' assistance, training, and support of justice practitioners enhance practitioner knowledge and promote human dignity of neuroatypical people in correctional confinement. As mentioned, involvement of both autistics and autism specialists makes for better program design and delivery. Precedent for such steps exists. For example, in 2013, the United Kingdom's National Offender Management Service (NOMS) commissioned the National Autistic Society to review the quality of correctional services delivered to prisoners with autism in both the juvenile and adult custody systems (Lewis et al. 2015). NAS noted that general staff knowledge of autism was respectable, but misunderstandings of autistic inmates' behaviours occurred nevertheless. NOMS's goal was to transform "pockets of good practice" (ibid., 69) into a total correctional system adaptation for inmates with autism.

The National Autistic Society designed an accreditation program to educate criminal justice practitioners (police, corrections, probation) about the needs of adult inmates who are people with autism or autistics. Autism Accreditation is a decades-old certification program signifying autism acceptance, education, and appropriate outreach in institutional and community settings. At Feltham Prison, a juvenile facility in the United Kingdom, researchers estimated the prevalence of autism at 4.5 percent, which is in keeping with contemporary population estimates (Thinking Person's Guide to Autism 2017). Prison administrators allowed outreach educators into Feltham; they then familiarized prison staff with autism, worked with staff to modify autistic prisoners' routines so they could use common areas at quieter times, decluttered parts of the buildings to ease anxiety, and emphasized to line staff and prison administrators that integrating persons with autism and autistic people into correctional life involved the entire prison – not just certain pods or isolated areas. Delivering autism training as standard operating procedure for all practitioners working in the system – but especially those working in custody, with its bright lights and loud sounds – integrates neurotypical and neuroatypical in social space, promoting respect for one another (Des Roches Rosa 2017).

This accreditation example speaks to the benefits of open systems recognizing the inevitably intertwined nature of all social worlds. Organizations functioning as deliberately open systems achieve homeostasis by the constant exchange of resources with the local environment, permitting inflow and outflow of energy through porous boundaries (Burke 2014). Youth detention centres such as Feltham Prison function as open systems when administrators invite experts into the facility to enhance practitioners' abilities to work with autistic inmates. Such importation of energy and insight allows youth with autism and autistic youth to better adjust to the custody environment, reduces likelihood of conflict between staff and detained youth, and increases the overall safety of the correctional environment (ibid.). This results in a healthier organization supporting the provision of (too often novel) social services and more positive social worlds for youth in juvenile justice systems.

Conclusion

The social worlds of juvenile justice systems resonate with complexity. Persons with autism and autistic people are diverse and, often, intersectional, with other characteristics associated with contemporary or historical oppression. Theoretical perspectives articulating rational applications of rewards and punishments consistently fail to efficaciously decrease adolescents' participations in delinquent acts, regardless of where they fall on the neurological continuum.

The social world of juvenile confinement incurs additional complexities for both detained youth and correctional staff. Autism can add or deepen dimensions to these complexities, providing opportunities for staff and correctional administrators to further diversify efforts to meet the needs of youth in their care. Staff training opportunities can be limited in both quantity and quality. In addition, mental health screening tools can vary widely in their abilities to accurately identify incarcerated individuals with autism, thus making it more difficult for correctional staff to identify exactly which youth should receive interventions. As well as these staff-youth challenges, juveniles with neurological differences may exhibit communication challenges with peers in custody and therefore often stand to benefit from deliberate peer-to-peer assistance and sensory-friendly correctional environments.

Social worlds in juvenile justice system can be strengthened and enriched through ongoing experimentation and active consultation with autistic adults. Current systems provide ample opportunity for experiments, whether natural or, to the extent legal and just, planned for the purpose of gaining better insight into best practices. No single assessment tool is consistently used in both Canada and the United States to identify youth with autism and autistic youth, for example. Rather, youth detention facilities use various assessment tools to identify criminogenic risks and needs for all youth, including youth with autism and autistic youth. Juvenile corrections practitioners and clinicians target services to reduce these risk factors and increase youths' chances of successful detention completion, often with considerable room for local decision making. Improving efficacy of correctional programming for youth with autism and autistic youth starts with autism training for all persons working in the facility, with the goal being a total institutional acceptance response toward persons with autism and autistic people. From there, joint, active attention to what works promises to enhance success in the social work of autism and juvenile justice.

Chapter 6 summary

1. **Why consider autism in the context of juvenile justice?**
   - Ironically, probation services and other enrichment activities require social interaction and skills and may destabilize youth less able to easily engage with these services. Practitioners should keep this in mind when evaluating youths' participation in referred services.
   - Deterrence theory largely influenced the development of the juvenile justice system, processes, and procedures. Deterrence implies rationality, which assumes that every person makes a decision based on a cost-benefit analysis of likely effects of actions. This potentially negatively impacts youth with autism and autistic youth, who may make decisions differently.
2. **How does the juvenile justice system particularly affect youth with autism and autistic youth?**
   - Lack of trained staff can intensify communication barriers for both the officer giving directives and the juvenile trying to understand them.
   - Screening tools can be helpful in recommending accommodations and services so long as the person conducting the screening is not biased and asks questions appropriately to the individual (considering age and comprehension ability).
3. **How can circumstances be improved for youth with autism, autistic youth, and the personnel who interact with them in juvenile justice settings?**
   - Incarceration can have devastating effects on youth with autism and autistic youth and can often *reverse* progress in behaviour change. Finding alternative ways to address the behaviour that include skill building may better promote long-term change.
   - Programs that do exist for youth with autism should be designed responsively to the groups it serves, to acknowledge the intersectionalities that exist with youth in these groups.
4. **What does rights-based disability policy look like in the context of rehabilitation of children with autism and autistic youth who have become involved with the juvenile justice system?**
   - Synthesizing intersectional theory and neurodiversity enhances our conceptual understandings of coalition building to bring positive change for all persons.
   - Penal systems have been designed around the thought processes ascribed to individuals of typical capacities. They can increase the risk of victimization of neurologically distinct individuals by inadvertently emphasizing difference (such as when youth with autism and autistic youth have an unusual reaction to the sensory environment), or by increasing the risk of non-compliance because the youth cannot make sense of the policy directive of the institution.

Figure 5 Chapter 6 summary

7
Transitioning beyond Juvenile Justice Systems

Juvenile justice systems strive for youths' permanent discharge from the system, after which they cease involvement in criminal behaviour and thereafter contribute positively to society. While many other well-intentioned and just reasons for services provided through juvenile justice systems exist, the primary purpose for the systems' existence remains keeping youth who have broken the law out of jails and prisons as adults. In both Canada and the United States, success in achieving secondary goals of substantial improvement of the quality of the lives of justice-involved youth and their families has been mixed at best (Dowden and Andrews 1999; Vieira, Skilling, and Peterson-Badali 2009). Even so, on the whole, modern systems do successfully decrease the odds of involvement with crime as adults for justice-involved youth (Borum 2003; Bullis, Yovanoff, and Havel 2004).

Juvenile justice systems aim to (re)integrate youth from custody and probationary services back into local communities to the fullest extent possible. What a specific juvenile needs for this engagement depends greatly on developmental stage, home environment, and community of origin (Altschuler and Brash 2004). For example, a homeless fifteen-year-old transgender boy may need vastly different services and supports than a cisgender ten-year-old girl from a household with employed parents. While differences in life experiences, social capital, peer groups, and resources also occur in adult populations, the intersectional effects of the developmental stage and these differential socio-economic and environmental factors can be a considerable challenge for practitioners working with youth. Organizations providing for the reintegrative needs of youth span a broad spectrum of government agencies, private non-profit organizations, and private corporations, as well. Thus, the process of juvenile re-entry into community life is affected by the individual youth's motivation, personality, resources, connections, and abilities relative to the organizational directives, types of assistance, and quality of monitoring of the adolescent's behaviour by both public and private entities.

Theories rooted in intersectionality provide conceptual frameworks for understanding how to better serve youth with autism and autistic youth in juvenile justice systems. In addition, regime theory sheds light on national-level factors influencing youth and community experiences. Organizational theories examining organizational power sharing and describing interactions between formal and informal institutions provide a conceptual basis for understanding collective responses to the risks and needs of youth returning to their communities. Finally, restorative justice theories and wraparound service frameworks provide insight into working with transitioning youth and enhance understanding of the re-entry experiences of youth with autism and autistic youth. Caution surrounding change is especially important for youth with autism and autistic youth who may experience it in a traumatic way, even if the change is typically interpreted as positive, such as moving out of a detention facility or completing probation. Change can potentially disrupt any life progress achieved while in juvenile justice programs. Attention to transition trauma is key to understanding most autistic experiences, including autism in the context of juvenile justice systems.

Theory and Transitions: Accessing Health Care and Community Resources

In comparing aspects of interactions between autism and juvenile justice systems in Canada and the United States, regime theory illuminates how state actors and non-governmental stakeholders collectively identify problems, design, and implement policy solutions to those problems (Wijen and Ansari 2007). Regimes are "defined as social institutions consisting of agreed-on principles, norms, rules, decision-making procedures, and programs around which actors' expectations converge in specific issue areas" (ibid., 1083). Regime theory views causality as reciprocal, rather than recursive. The theory assumes that institutions both shape and are shaped by economic, political, and social forces. Human agency works with these forces to serve as a catalyst to produce innovative adaptations to societal problems (Shipps 2008). In short, regime theory explores how "policy challenges from the larger world – including the global economy, social movements, and more" are mediated by local institutions and action (Stone 1998). Macro- to micro-level interactions lay at the centre of regime theory.

Although it is difficult to imagine a policy subsystem unrelated to the juvenile justice transitions, as discussed in Chapter 4, health policy subsystems provide essential support services for youth needing mental health assistance as they move from custody to the community. Regime theory predicts persistently differential health care access issues in developed nations. For example, in their development of a public health regime in the United Kingdom, Asthana and Halliday (2006) underscore the necessity of considering intersectional variables such as race, social class, and gender as they affect the state of national health care inequalities. In national systems, social context – particularly social factors affecting health outcomes over the life course – plays a definitive role in reducing the uniformity of services received. Despite this, research identifying evidence-based practice for improving health outcomes sometimes overlook the social context in a regime involving single-payer, national systems.

Regime theory anticipates differences in all policy subsystems sustaining healthy living conditions for a given population. For example, access to healthy food helps establish and maintain health for all humans, but societies vary widely on how much access to healthy food poor people receive (World Health Organization 2017). Food production systems differ among nation-states. The United States is an example of a highly corporate, aggregate farming system where the food supply is heavily supplemented with additives, preservatives, and the occasional nutrient (Steele et al. 2016). Countries in Europe exhibit stricter controls and oversight over food production methods, some of which date back centuries (Kurzer and Cooper 2007). Under a regime theory approach, these types of macro-level contextual factors linked to micro-level food-access factors provide a more complete framework for examining and improving health outcomes in developed and developing nations than do individual factors alone. Potential for success in transitioning youth to communities is sculpted by the avenues and limitations created by national policy regimes.

Health policy regimes bring together many organizational units to address public and individual health concerns (Asthana and Halliday 2006; Bambra 2007; Meagher-Stewart et al. 2012). Scholars expanding on classic variants of welfare regime theory to health outcomes among citizens in nation-states argue that the provision of health services takes place in a socio-political context that intersects with individuals' natural and learned capacities (Bala 2007). Policy responses to health needs should incorporate upstream policies as well as downstream interventions (Asthana and Halliday 2006). Such an approach blends traditional epidemiological research strategies with those of other social sciences. Barriers exist to such integration, which lies outside established medical models of health policy research (Raphael, Curry-Stevens, and Bryant 2008). Nevertheless, successful precedents exist. Community activist responses to the AIDS crises during the late twentieth century yielded advocacy groups, partnered with medical organizations, to save the lives of gay men (and others). CATIE in Canada and Gay Men's Health Crisis in the United States delivered safe-sex education curriculums, coordinated medical testing with health organizations, provided social support, and modelled humane treatment of sexual minorities for medical professionals in traditional organizations. Since transitioning youth out of juvenile justice facilities necessarily involves a similar need for coordination and power sharing between policy regimes, academic disciplines, and organizations, attending to lessons learned from such previous efforts holds considerable promise.

As with all issues relating to the politics of neurodiversity, the dynamics of transitions are situated in social and ecological contexts that provide (or do not provide) support, treatment, education, and financial assistance to these youths and their families. For example, in the United States, when youth transition out of juvenile justice custody facilities, they often no longer receive services from the state itself but from community-based organizations under contract with the state (if at all). Regime theory's emphasis on multiple levels of organizational support within government and between government and non-government organizations promotes efficacious case planning and service delivery for youth with autism and autistic youth transitioning out of custody (Meagher-Stewart et al. 2012).

Health regimes shape the potential for the blending of mental health service delivery with the juvenile justice system. Health sector personnel typically understand autism as a medical condition deserving of clinical interventions, describing persons with autism or autistic persons as having a developmental delay. Such a moniker often disparages persons with differences and neglects the politics of neurodiversity. As discussed, the term "handicap" reflects and fosters a negative perspective of disability, assuming lowered social status. This interpretation does not sit well with many activists and advocates, particularly some in the activist corner of the neurodiversity movement (Baker 2011). Autistics generally resist this neuro-hegemonic characterization of autism as a developmental delay because such a term presumes that neurotypical development is the standard by which all other youths should be assessed (Orsini and Smith 2010). Such concerns illuminate the important consequences of delivering services for autism within a medical context. As youth with autism and autistic youth move out of juvenile custody facilities and into communities, no choice of services except those provided through this limiting lens may be available. A widespread understanding of autism as a neurological difference that is part and parcel of a developing body occurring in a naturally neurodiverse human population could enhance the youths' adjustment to their local environments. Health regimes incorporating neighbourhood and school-level attributes and neuro-progressive attitudes can assist community practitioners in viewing these youth through a developmental rather than medical perspective.

Theories of Development and Transition: Macro-Level and Micro-Level Perspectives

Contemporary practice of neurodiversity celebrates differential developmental paths across the human population. Despite valid concerns that developmental models mistake so-called typical development as normative, using developmental models as a loosely held map for understanding youth progress may assist in evaluating transition programs. Theoretical perspectives with a developmental focus help in articulating needs of youth because they take into account ages and stages (Altschuler and Brash 2004), as well as the intersections of race, class, gender, socio-economic status, and disability (McLeod and Owens 2004). Developmental theories conceptualize age as not just a chronological concept but a time-bounded series of developmental milestones occurring in close temporal proximity to one another. Grouping temporally proximate physiological, sociological, and psychological changes together is referred to as a stage, typically occurring within a series of successive years of life.

Each stage contains distinct sets of developments, the focal points of which vary by scholar. Jean Piaget (1951) articulated four stages of physio-emotional development emphasizing the interplay between neurological development and the social environment. Piaget hypothesized that all youth move through the same stages at roughly the same rates. Moving through the stages involves transitioning from the sensorimotor stage at birth to the formal operational stage, in which the mature brain uses deductive reasoning, advanced logic, and abstract ideas (ibid.). Similarly,

Erik Erikson (1993) described human development as maturation across eight developmental stages possessing competing objectives, such as trust versus mistrust (Stage 1), autonomy versus shame and doubt (Stage 2), and ending at the final stage of ego integrity versus despair (Stage 8). Piaget and Erikson's theories fundamentally changed conceptions of intellectual and social development, prompting researchers to reconsider how humans form self-esteem, self-efficacy, and the capacity to bond with others. While the precise nature of stages remains hotly debated, modern profiles of human development tend to revolve around a defined set of stages.

Developmental theories also articulate the necessity of both formal and informal institutions in meeting the needs of youth, blending macro-level entities (such as role of the country, state, or city) with those at a micro-level (e.g., family, neighbours, peer networks, and schools). Criminologists integrated developmental theory into criminological theory to explore why juvenile participation in crime increases during the tween years, peaks in the late teens or early twenties, and declines by the thirties (Shulman, Steinberg, and Piquero 2013). The overall empirical regularity of this age curve, as well as the development of longitudinal studies of youth, allowed researchers to track youth over several decades (Jennings et al. 2015; Piquero, Farrington, and Blumstein 2003). Youths' offending histories were found to be usually short-lived and confined to the late teen years, despite some chronic offenders initiating criminal behaviour at an early age and consistently criminally active through late adulthood (Farrington 2003).

Sampson and Laub (2016) articulate life's journeys among youth as a series of age-graded transitions that affect the likelihood of finding them on either delinquent or non-delinquent trajectories through a framework described as life-course theory. In this theory, both formal and informal institutions play a crucial role in eliminating or providing for youth to engage in delinquency. For example, in the early years of life, the major influencing institutions for young children tend to be the family and the school. Youth in the middle and later stages of development also engage the formal institutions of school, early labour force participation, and the informal institutions of family and peers. Formal institutions for persons in early adulthood typically include the labour force, training and higher education, marriage, and parenting.

Life-course theory seeks to explain not only the rise in adolescent delinquency common between the ages ten and the early twenties but also the marked decrease that occurs among many youth as they enter early adulthood (middle twenties), also known as "desistance" (Sampson and Laub

2006). Following a cohort of youth for at least sixty years showed that marriage, employment, parenting, and military service are age-graded transitions placing those formerly in trouble with the law on non-delinquent trajectories (Laub and Sampson 2003). Yet as Sampson and Laub (2003) point out, the potential exists for simplistic group-dependent interpretation that life-course theory predicts one's destiny as opposed to other sociological trends. Perhaps most infamously, the notion of the juvenile super-predator crafted during the 1990s describes a future society in which a substantive portion of youth committed multiple acts of horrific violence without remorse (Dilulio 1995). Policies and programs designed around this unproven and often racist construct harmed both communities and societies. In using stages theory to contemplate parameters for promising transition services for youth with autism and autistic youth, the theory best serves to provide guideposts rather than tests of youth potential. Stages theory provides insights into how to best plan guidelines for transition services.

Youth who commit crimes often do so because of failures to successfully engage in the stage-appropriate activities needed for success inside formal institutions, and because of a lack of support from informal institutions such as friends or family (Jennings et al. 2015). Steinberg, Chung, and Little (2004) build on this developmental focus, arguing that, in most Western industrialized societies, the period between ages sixteen and twenty-four sees the most critical psychosocial advance in a youth's life because this phase contains the transition to adulthood. Family disruption, adverse childhood experiences, and school failure constitute three powerful factors that can disrupt smooth transitions between life stages, starting in early childhood and producing a potentially delinquent trajectory (Baglivio et al. 2014). Building relationships with already delinquent peers increases the likelihood of the delinquent trajectory (Warr 2002). Youth with disabilities and disabled youth may also experience higher rates of aggression and bullying from peers than do non-disabled youth, compounding their other risks factors for delinquency (Mallett 2014). Well-planned transition programs include a focus on peers and peer relations, particularly for youth in a developmental stage parallel to that of a typically developing teenager or young adult.

Furthermore, children and early adolescents from low-income families with a family history of law-violating behaviour who incur criminal charges at an early age, and who are African American males, are at particular risk of being on delinquent trajectories as they age (Zhang et al. 2011). This persistence connects not only to the experiences and decisions of the youth but also to systemic racism reflected in the responses to initial violations of the law and other human behaviours (Kempf-Leonard 2007). For example, youth of colour and those experiencing poverty remain much more likely than other youths to be charged with crimes regardless of the behaviour in question (Leiber and Mack 2003; Wordes, Bynum, and Corley 1994). These children and youth also often receive more severe consequences once charged (Davis and Sorenson 2013). Life-course theory focuses on the formal and informal sources of social control for youth from the juvenile justice professionals to teachers to society at large and thereby serves as an important reminder that, to date, systemic characteristic-based discrimination has misdirected far too many lives. As juveniles transition from confinement to the community, success of contemporary services depends on facing up to and making amends for these intersectional realities.

Transitioning Tensions: From Juvenile Confinement to the Community

Transitioning to adulthood represents a murky and blurred process in modern Canada and the United States. Both nations' dominant cultures largely abandoned formal rites of passage ceremonies. Classic research from developmental psychology suggests modern young people do not use a specific maturation event or chronological age to assess maturity. Instead, young people gauge themselves as adequately mature based on the collective weight of their self-perceptions in the societal context (Steinberg, Chung, and Little 2004). In circumstances relevant to juvenile justice systems, youth perceive themselves maturing out of delinquent behaviour and change their role expectations for themselves by adopting adult role expectations and responsibilities. This sense of psychosocial capital develops in late adolescence and helps youth transition successfully to early adulthood (ibid.).

Practitioners working with justice-involved youth are expected to assist youth develop mature psychosocial capital in order to reduce risk of recidivism. Transitioning out of juvenile justice systems proves challenging for many youth (James et al. 2013). In both Canada and the United States, facilitating this transition is especially complicated given autism or other differences in capacities. As discussed, leaving juvenile systems can involve losing the services received there, without receiving adequate transitional services in their place. As a result, services end before articulated service goals are attained. Service loss augments risk and susceptibility factors for ongoing justice system involvement. Intersectional circumstances heighten the risk of transition service gaps, especially for youth growing up in neighbourhoods with concentrated disadvantage. Disadvantages experienced in these neighbourhoods can include very low employment rates, high poverty rates, low-performing public schools, dilapidated housing, high crime rates, and low levels of social cohesion among residents (Sampson, Raudenbush, and Earls 1997; Wasserman et al. 2003).

Importantly, community circumstances can and do change for the better. Services for youth constitute the most commonly resources leveraged by communities re-establishing themselves (Henry 2009). Obviously, the quality, density, and effectiveness of these services vary. Service quality tends to depend heavily on the charisma, dedication, preferences, and luck of community leaders. Temporary and competitive funding sources also make a difference and are tied to luck and the capacities of community influencers. Even jurisdictions with robust resources experience challenges to successfully reintegrating youth from custody into communities. Substantial social capital can be necessary to convince community members to invest in a particular child, especially if the particular youth has been connected to difficult or painful community experiences. Already stressed and burdened individuals, families, organizations, and communities can come to prefer to focus on more apparently promising recipients of their time and efforts than the youth returning from custody. This dynamic becomes especially complicated when family members have also been victimized by the youth and when services for coping with this experience are ineffective, unproven, or unavailable. In such cases, youth may find little welcome in either their home or schools, seriously compromising potential for transition success.

As mentioned, youth with disabilities and disabled youth can have an even more difficult time reintegrating than youth without disabilities. Transitions necessitate changes in routine that may prove challenging for all children, especially youth with autism and autistic youth. For example, in a longitudinal study of youth in the Pacific Northwest released to a mid-sized city in the state of Oregon, approximately 40 percent of the 531 juveniles returned to juvenile detention within one year after release. Youth with disabilities returned to Oregon's detention facilities at nearly two and a half times the rate of non-disabled youth during the first six months of the study (Bullis et al. 2002). However, receiving special education services while in custody decreased the odds of engaging in school or work on release (ibid.).

Youth transitioning from residential facilities to communities may require an array of sustained services to be successful in the long term. Needs include academic enrichment and skill development, vocational education support, connections to support services in the community, family support, and client-specific transition plans (Unruh and Bullis 2005). Partnerships between the court and local community stakeholders underscore critical transition services for youth. However, service gaps between the court and community providers, as well as within the web of willing community partners and providers, can stand in the way of successful transitions.

Transitioning Youth from Confinement to Community in Canada

During the early twenty-first century, governments in both Canada and the United States increased attention toward transitions between life stages. In 2003, Ontario created the Ministry of Children and Youth Services to support youth and families by providing services to help youth to grow into productive adults in society. As part of its mission, the ministry hopes for "children and youth [to] have the best opportunity to succeed and reach their full potential" (Ontario Ministry of Children and Youth Services 2016[a]). The ministry operates approximately twelve juvenile corrections facilities and also manages the Ontario Autism Program, which assists families in navigating services and providing tools for parents.

The Ministry of Children and Youth Services aims to prevent youth from becoming or remaining delinquent. Generally, the Canadian approach focuses on early contact with youth under juvenile justice authority still in the community. This early contact partners with quality transition services to reduce future involvement in delinquency (Day et al. 2012; Weinrath, Donatelli, and Murchison 2016). Another way in which Canadian practitioners work toward this goal involves initiating reintegration when the youth enters the criminal justice system, rather than waiting until after they have been sentenced or the court process is completed (Ontario Ministry of Children and Youth Services 2016[b]). Reintegration plans are designed to individual youth and work proactively with entities, including school, employment, the family home, and the community. Furthermore, the guide suggests that the plans be "holistic, structured, individualized and focused on the youth's strengths" (ibid., 8). Plans aim to empower youth to work with their reintegration team, which could include family, a probation officer, education partners, community providers, and municipalities, creating goals that will prevent the youth from re-entering the system (Ontario Ministry of Children and Youth Services 2015). The Ontario Ministry of Children and Youth Services also created the Autism Intervention Program to provide support services, including preparing the child for behaviour intervention programs such as intensive behavioural intervention and applied behavioural analysis (ABA) to assist youth with autism and autistic youth in increasing their skills in communication, emotional regulation, and interpersonal skills (Ontario Ministry of Children and Youth Services 2016[c]).

Across Canada, various government-funded organizations employ professionals, such as crisis coordinators, advocates, and behavioural consultants, to individuals and families with autism. If a youth with autism or autistic youth engages in destructive or harmful behaviours, a behavioural consultant may be engaged. This is vitally important because, as one behavioural consultant in Canada explains, youth with autism or autistic youth often tend to be involved with the juvenile justice system as a result of a social mistake, as opposed to deliberately criminal behaviour (interview conducted by Whitney Littlefield, February 17, 2017).

Behavioural consultants meet with individuals and families to provide both formal assessments and skill building. Consultants spend time observing the person with autism or autistic person to better understand any biopsychosocial issues. The consultant uses a functional assessment to explore the nature of any problematic behaviours and any potential harm to the youth or people surrounding them. A behavioural consultant, through observation and assessments, seeks to understand why the youth is engaging in damaging behaviour and then creates a plan that includes interventions and skill building to try to eliminate that behaviour. Consultants then develop strategies to reduce those behaviours (University of British Columbia, n.d.). Crisis coordinators and behavioural consultants also assist youth with autism on probation. A probation officer can solicit services from behaviour consultants to help the youth transition back into the community without court supervision. Unfortunately, primarily because of a lack of funding for behavioural programs, wait lists impact the ability of the families to access transitional services. Youth on the wait list may be selected based on the severity of circumstances, as opposed to time spent on the wait list. Protocols permit some youth on probation to bump to the top of the list for services.

For youth transitioning out of custody environments, governments ideally coordinate services to fortify juveniles' relocations back home. Strategies including cross-sectional training between multiple policy systems (such as foster care and juvenile justice), bail conditions minimizing disruptions of therapeutic practice, education for non-justice clinical workers about the juvenile justice process, and educating each professional in the process of getting youth from one system to another about each system may prove particularly useful (Scully and Finlay 2015). In particular, focusing on youth involved in both the child welfare and juvenile justice systems, including providing the therapeutic techniques as needed for challenges related to autism, could substantially enhance the successes of these youth both within these two systems and in the community (Ruiz-Casares, Trocmé, and Fallon 2012). Informed coordination around hope and good intentions promises to maximize potential for the success of youth in transition.

Transitioning Youth from Confinement to Community in the United States

In the United States, because of the decentralized nature of juvenile probation services, transition programs for youth in juvenile custody vary widely from jurisdiction to jurisdiction. As discussed in Chapter 2, juvenile courts in the United States are administered by state or local governments, with the federal government providing research and program-implementation funds for rehabilitation programming and practice. Quality of transition services for youth leaving custody to reside in the community exhibits diversity both within and between juvenile court jurisdictions. Despite this variability, many probation officers and transition case planners generally share the perception that successful re-entry for youth in custody depends on well-planned transition services.

In the past twenty years, state and local governments made some measure of progress in providing more complete services for youth coordinated within and between the juvenile justice system, social service agencies, mental health organizations, and schools (Clark and Unruh 2010; Leone, Quinn, and Osher 2002). Known as wraparound services, one agency serves as a lead coordinator for a youth requiring the services of multiple health, mental health, educational, and other organizations. The juvenile justice agent performs case management duties to ensure proper appointments with service agencies and that the service providers give feedback about the youth to the juvenile justice agent or case manager.

Completing formal education and achieving employment lie at the centre of transitioning to adulthood in most contemporary societies. In addition to the risk factors complicating employment prospects of many youths transitioning out of juvenile justice systems, employer concerns about justice-involved youth or state statutes barring employment for those convicted of felony render finding a job even more difficult (Ameen and Lee 2012). Hagner and colleagues (2008) suggest focusing on five dimensions of re-entry planning for positive reengagement with education or employment post-release. The transition model emphasizes rehabilitation programming, personal empowerment, natural supports, and work to assist youth in building prosocial skills and attachments that can facilitate a positive transition to community life after juvenile incarceration. This model uses a group-centred approach to identifying the juvenile's needs and includes the youth's immediate family and others in their social circle as stakeholders in the transition plan. Along with the details of transition planning, the juvenile and their significant others voice their concerns about the upcoming changes, provide encouragement and support for the juvenile, and critique the feasibility of the transition plan set forth by juvenile justice personnel and caseworkers in the non-profit sector (ibid.).

Although based on a small sample size, 81 percent of the RENEW youth who re-entered the community were either enrolled in high school or studying for their GED, and 74 percent of the re-entering youth were employed at the end of the three-year study period (Hagner et al. 2008). The model recommends that person-centred planning be recreated as a longitudinal process, over common current practices involving a few short-term meetings inside detention facilities. A longer-term re-entry planning process would allow the juvenile and their support team to make modifications as needed to the dynamic process of rejoining the outside world.

Similarly, in Oregon, the longitudinal research project Transition Research on Adjudicated Youth in Community Settings allowed researchers to evaluate the efficacy of youth transitions to their communities. Project SUPPORT (Service Utilization to Promote Positive Outcomes in Rehabilitation and Transition) provided youth incarcerated in Oregon Youth Authority facilities with a documented disability or mental health condition with transition planning and services (Unruh, Gau, and Waintrup 2009). Research targeted two areas: transition support (Clark and Unruh 2010; Unruh and Bullis 2005), and transition outcomes among youth (Bullis, Yovanoff, and Havel 2004; Unruh, Gau, and Waintrup 2009).

Both youth and community stakeholders identified family support as critical for re-entry, with youth ranking it as their most important attribute for a successful transition to the community (Unruh and Bullis 2005). All study participants identified education as the second greatest support need but also the most significant barrier to success, an issue that is not unique to this group of youth. In a jurisdiction neighbouring the SUPPORT program, one public education stakeholder working with students reenrolling in public school after a juvenile custody sentence stated, "I see a lot of fear in these kids. They have a lot of fear that they don't fit in. Small schools do better – it is easier to have good face-to-face contact with people in a smaller school ... but the large high schools – the kids [transitioning back] have a harder time because there are just so many people in them" (interview conducted by Laurie Drapela on February 13, 2017). To maximize a youth's potential for success in the community upon transition, Project SUPPORT's research staff recommended the following: 1) a single transition specialist responsible for coordinating the needs and services of the juvenile, these activities starting before the youth leaves the correctional facility; 2) continued counselling support; 3) flexible education opportunities, including training for education personnel receiving the youth; 4) social skills training targeted toward the youth's multiple environments; and (5) strengthening family and social network development (Clark and Unruh 2010).

Another intervention program located in Ohio focused on integrating mental health services with juvenile justice practice at every stage of the juvenile justice system. Specifically, Stark County, Ohio, integrated mental health care with justice practice at the justice agency administrative level, service delivery to youth at the system level, financing processes, and in justice personnel training. These integrated levels of care are implemented in the juvenile justice system under the administrative authority of the Stark County Family Council (Foster, Qaseem, and Conner 2004). The council includes juvenile justice officials on its board of trustees, and mental health staff are embedded within county juvenile justice facilities. When compared with juvenile justice outcomes to a matched control county, youth in Stark County experienced a 57 percent drop in serious crime compared with youth without mental health services while under juvenile justice authority (ibid.).

Holistic Approaches: Whole Child, Whole Services, Whole Communities

Despite the success of local programs, juvenile justice jurisdictions have not extensively focused on youth with disabilities and disabled youth in their re-entry curriculums (Leone, Quinn, and Osher 2002; Stenehjem 2005). The growing prevalence of autism, coupled with the significant gap in disability prevalence between general population youth and justice-involved youth underscore the critical need for disability-related services to be included in transition case planning for youth leaving custody facilities for their communities.

Two rehabilitation models popular in contemporary juvenile justice systems that could reasonably incorporate disability are restorative justice

(Bazemore and Schiff 2015) and wraparound services (Stenehjem 2005). Restorative justice reconceptualizes crime as harm against the community. In restorative justice practices, the person who harmed the community through law-violating behaviour becomes reintegrated into society by performing actions intended to repair the harm. The victim and the community are central stakeholders in this process, serving to voice the impact of the harm as well as determine alongside the person who committed the offence an appropriate set of tasks to repair the harm (Bazemore and Schiff 2015). Restorative justice frameworks draw heavily from received practices of some First Nations. Wraparound services approaches involve juvenile justice practitioners coordinating with community providers and support agencies providing services for people in transition. Example services include occupational therapy, yoga, social learning curriculums, physical conditioning, and empathy support protocols assisting the youth to (re)join community life. While not explicitly excluded, wraparound services do not necessarily include attempts to repair harm associated with criminal activities that brought the person in question into the justice system.

Assuming proper attention to the politics and practices of neurodiversity, wraparound services delivered under a restorative justice framework could provide youth with autism and autistic youth with opportunities to repair the harm caused to the community while treating the whole youth with an ethic of care. For example, if an autistic youth or youth with autism receives a vandalism disposition by the juvenile court, the youth could work with a local community accountability board to repair the property damage (or similar damage in the community generally) while also enhancing their self-care through yoga classes or occupational therapy. Such approaches reduce youths' risk of recidivism (Bergseth and Bouffard 2013). They also reciprocally tend to enhance community learning about and knowledge of autism. Both factors improve capacity for more successful practices of neurodiversity reducing the overall likelihood of crimes connected to legacies of ableism.

Successful Transition to the Community: The Role of Family

The importance of family involvement in transitional planning cannot easily be overemphasized (Hillian and Reitsma-Street 2003). Families of youth in custody of the juvenile justice systems represent a critical source of social support and are foundational to the youths' successful re-entry into the community. After all, once the court order has expired and jurisdiction of the juvenile system ceases, the family usually regains primary responsibility for seeing to the youth's life progress. For professionals working in juvenile justice systems, building a transition plan routinely means working with families who retain little hope for the youth or resist services for other reasons, ranging from their own compromised legal statuses, to exhaustion resulting from intensive and expensive efforts that unsuccessfully kept the youth from trouble, to other competing life demands (and beyond). Unfortunately, many youths in the juvenile system never had or have lost family support and a stable, structured family life. Family instability can serve as cause and consequence of youth delinquency, heightening re-entry challenges for both the youth under supervision and juvenile justice system personnel (Peterson-Badali and Broeking 2010). In the context of autism and juvenile justice, instability, exhaustion, compassion, or fatigue may also have resulted in the family long before justice system involvement, owing to increased strain too often associated with raising a child with a neurological difference in a world biased toward the so-called neurotypical experience (Baker and Drapela 2010; Silberman 2016, Pitney 2015).

Studies on interactions of justice system practitioners and parents or guardians of juveniles involved with juvenile justice systems speak to the complexity and fragility of stakeholder dynamics. Research involving juvenile probation officers describes practitioners unfairly judging parental engagement by having a biased interpretation of the quality of parenting observed, thus complicating a positive rapport between these stakeholders in the child's life (Schwalbe and Maschi 2010; Maschi, Schwalbe, and Ristow 2013). In this institutional-centric view of parents or guardians, perceived lack of care and participation undermines youth attempting to successfully employ new lessons and skills learned while in custody (Paik 2017). Furthermore, in some cases, parents or guardians of youth in the system become so overwhelmed that by the time the court becomes involved and they meet with a juvenile justice practitioner, parents or guardians are desperately ready to turn over some of the responsibilities for the child to the court. Parents or guardians feeling overwhelmed, whose past efforts have proven futile, or who observe professionals casually applying an incomplete understanding of the youth's history inspire their reluctance to participation in services.

On the other hand, parents or guardians actively attempting to satisfy the desires of the court and meet various practitioner expectations may feel discouraged and disrespected if the court does not communicate their expectations proactively and consistently. Many parents and guardians experience feelings of stress, despair, and non-support from the state agency exercising legal authority over their children and, as a result, participate unevenly in court processes (Peterson-Badali and Broeking 2009; Varma 2007). For example, interviews of Canadian parents with justice-involved sons found that study participants felt they made good-faith efforts to comply with court directives but perceived their efforts as being undermined by the court's recurrent contradictory expectations regarding their son's care (Hillian and Reitsma-Street 2003). Dislocation from juvenile justice systems can begin quite early in the experience of parents and guardians. Because many parents and guardians are not familiar with the legal bureaucratic procedures that are part and parcel of juvenile justice processing, they may feel powerless during court proceedings (Varma 2007). Furthermore, those with restricted leave from work, health concerns, or other responsibilities may have to budget the amount of time spent in court processes, further compromising the capacity to stay engaged and involved from the start of their family's experiences of the juvenile justice system.

Alienation may intensify if the sensory aspects of the proceedings further complicate an individual's ability to comprehend and process legal proceedings. Importantly, autism appears to have some genetic components, meaning that parents of youth with autism and autistic youth may be more likely to have their own neuroatypicalities. Courts struggle to practice the positive politics of neurodiversity. For example, in Clark County, Washington, the juvenile court provides a guide on how youth can successfully engage the judge and other courtroom personnel. One of the suggestions made is that youth make direct eye contact with the judge, ostensibly to show that the judge has their full attention (and respect) (Clark County Juvenile Court, n.d.). While such tips may be helpful in the immediate sense to youth who might otherwise unintentionally communicate disrespect, the message of preference for neurotypical behaviours is clear. The suggestion also ignores the fact that autistics have communicated enhanced difficulty in concentrating when making eye contact as a result of the pain associated with the effort to do so.

Finally, some parents and guardians do not care adequately for their children. Any threats to whole-hearted participation make transition planning more difficult. However, most problematically, some parents actively oppose assistance and court authority by resisting services and condoning undesirable behaviour. Some parents may experience the court as a threat to their own safety. There are also parents who minimize, excuse, or blame others for the behaviour of their child. Even if the youth accesses all the services offered and is rehabilitated from a criminogenic perspective, chance of long-term success is reduced if a home environment rejects prosocial efforts of the youth. This is especially problematic for youth with disabilities and disabled youth who have not been diagnosed or if parents deny the diagnosis, reject the process, and refuse the services that follow. Recognizing the signs and symptoms of potential illnesses, disorders, and disabilities is integral to holistically approaching rehabilitation through services. Some families become offended, are in denial, or do not understand why the recommendation exists. Juvenile justice practitioners must delicately address these issues and work to collaborate with family therapists or psychologists to help families see the benefits of engagement while also making any necessary follow-ups with child protective services and simultaneously avoiding descent into ableist and discriminatory practices of the past.

The Delinquency Paradox and Evidence-Based Practice for Youth

As mentioned, the majority of juveniles involved with the juvenile justice system do not experience incarceration as adults (Sampson and Laub 2003). Nevertheless, cohort research in both Canada and the United States demonstrates that juvenile incarceration increases the risk of future police contact and justice system involvement (Gilman, Hill, and Hawkins 2015). Inadequate or incomplete transition services further hinder young people from accessing services and mentors for assistance with making better life choices (Abrams, Shannon, and Sangalang 2008).

It is also important to remember that despite the popular myth asserting ongoing decline, people who commit crimes do not necessarily go on to commit more and more egregious offences over time. Continuity in offending is far more common than offence variability (Farrington 2003; Piquero, Farrington, and Blumstein 2003). Ideas of path dependency dominate much popular thinking about crime and those who commit it, especially people who get in legal trouble at a young age (Kalef 2000). While there are a relatively small proportion of individuals in any population who consistently commit ever more serious crimes, most individuals are criminally active while young and then desist into adulthood (DeLisi and Vaughn 2008). Narratives linking evidence of early offences as predictive of a lifetime of involvement in criminal activity hold popularity and appeal far surpassing any evidence of such connections.

One source of this confusion involves the miscomprehension of the difference between patterns observed looking at the histories of people known to have a particular outcome and patterns extant in the experiences of the general population. Finding that a large proportion of people who commit crimes as adults interacted with the juvenile justice system as youth is not the opposite of finding that a large proportion of the people who interact with the juvenile justice system never commit crimes as adults. It is, instead, the expected reality of simultaneous analysis of a small proportion of the population (those who commit crimes as adults) in the context of the population at large (those who avoid criminal activity as adults). Understanding how to differentiate between these two groups over time takes some comprehension of the logic of formal research methods, particularly quantitative techniques (Van Montfort, Oud, and Satorra 2010). The complexity of this activity proves somewhat elusive in multiple public contexts, especially those generally tolerant of innumeracy.

In addition, making predictions regarding individual transitions away from involvement with criminal activities involves contemplating population level percentages. Because rates can simultaneously involve both positive and negative numbers, analyses reported as multiple percentages can produce misleading impressions of the unfolding circumstances (Ellenberg 2015). Misunderstandings of percentages in such circumstances underlie extremely wrong interpretation of events while also increasing the potential for overreaction to random outcomes. For example, if one district happens to have a 15 percent decrease in successful transitions while a neighbouring district has a 20 percent increase in such transitions, interpreting this outcome as, on average, a 5 percent increase in successful transitions does not accurately reflect circumstances when the sizes of the communities differ. Furthermore, making any differential policy or programmatic choices based on this single point of data incurs the risk of wrongness, especially in the context of relatively small populations where percentages can reflect only a few people. Neither source of complications of analysis should inspire avoidance of examination of transitions data at the aggregate level. Instead, existing training in research methods and statistics should be enhanced for juvenile justice practitioners (and the population at large).

Thinking about transitions involves making predictions about individuals using population data. Such contemplation involves balancing the interests of stakeholders concerned about public safety given an individual's behaviour with the knowledge that both the tendency to engage in criminal activities and the neurological capacity to comprehend long-term consequences change dramatically as individuals leave young adulthood. On top of this complexity, juvenile justice practitioners are tasked with designing highly individualized transition plans for youth with often limited time and resources. Some juveniles will not return to custody again, whereas some return multiple times over the course of their lives (Jennings et al. 2015). Determining which juveniles need which services in the community to maximize their chances of success (attending school or seeking employment while remaining crime-free) requires the use of assessment tools identifying necessary supports. It also unavoidably involves taking chances and gambling with the lives of both youth and their communities. Humans typically have less capacity for contemplating probabilities and for tolerating failures than they imagine. Developing habits and practices associated with debriefing failures without relying on unfair blame helps improve transition services. Protocols for such practices may be adapted from those extant in both military and medical contexts.

Using Research to Inform Practice: The Promise of Cognitive Behavioural Therapy

Evidence-based interventions gained popularity in both Canada and the United States in recent decades. Effective interventions for youth in the juvenile justice system have been studied for nearly thirty years (Henggeler and Schoenwald 2011). Positive change following interventions may be reductions in recidivism, enhanced engagement in school, improvements in relationships with family members, reductions in associations with delinquent peers, or all of the above. As discussed in Chapter 4, risk assessments serve to predict the probability that a juvenile will engage in future law-violating behaviour. Given that juveniles' liberty restrictions and programming needs are assigned by the judge and other practitioners based in part on this risk assessment score, it is imperative that juvenile courts use accurate tools. Meta-analyses suggest that the results of mental health screening tools can vary widely by gender, race, ethnicity, social class, and culture (Castro, Barrera, and Holleran Steiker 2010; Vincent et al. 2008). Even so, successful interventions share the following characteristics: they are delivered proportionate to risk, they target risk factors for offending, they are tailored to the youth's personal strengths, and they are behavioural in nature (Andrews and Bonta 2010).

For some youth with autism and autistic youth, behavioural approaches may need to be delivered in an adapted manner. As described in Chapter 5, behavioural-based therapeutic curriculums for youth in confinement (or in the community) presume relative neurotypicality, potentially undermining the efficacy of these approaches among youth with neurological differences. Nonetheless, particular approaches with youth in confinement show promise. Landenberger and Lipsey (2005) found that with the CBT (cognitive behavioural therapy) programs implemented with fidelity and evaluated with rigorous methodological designs (e.g., random assignment, matched groups, and longitudinal designs), the average effect size for a one-year reduction in recidivism was 0.40, or 25 percent less than comparison subjects that did not receive CBT. Aspects of CBT significantly related to effect size were individualized attention, anger control therapies, and cognitive restructuring therapies. No single brand name (e.g., Thinking for a Change, Moral Reconation Therapy) significantly affected the measured efficacy of the program. Rather, it was the elements of curriculum delivery in addition to non-CBT services such as vocational training and education, mental health services, and educational programs that contributed to success (ibid.). Services for youth with autism such as emotional regulation, sensory integration therapies, and counselling can be worked into the CBT approach. When combined with transition services enhancing employment and education prospects, recidivism and returns to custody decrease (Clark and Unruh 2010). While additional research is necessary to confirm and fully understand the promise of CBT protocols, research suggests that incorporating these approaches could potentially improve transition services for youth with autism and autistic youth involved with juvenile justice systems in Canada and the United States.

Conclusion

Enhancing the capacity of practitioners to work successfully with autistics and persons with autism is not limited to individuals working with this population inside juvenile custody facilities. Many youth are not in juvenile custody for very long periods. In Canada, implementing the YCJA drastically reduced youths' length of stay in juvenile prisons. In the United States, a steep decline in juvenile crime rates after 1995 coupled with jurisdictions' participating in the Juvenile Detention Alternatives Initiative substantively reduced reliance on detention (Maggard 2015). As such, community practitioners working with youth are critical players in rehabilitation, community reintegration, and social support for youth with autism and autistic youth transitioning from custody to the community.

Youth with autism and autistic youth in the juvenile justice system need coordinated services delivered to them as soon as they re-enter their communities to maintain continuity of care, thereby enhancing the odds of a successful life outside custody. These services encompass therapies enhancing autistic youths' adaptations to the social, sensory, and stressor aspects of adjusting to life on the outside of juvenile facilities. Coordination of these services between community providers and schools by transition specialists in the juvenile justice system further enhances the probabilities of success for youth with autism and autistic youth as they rejoin civilian life. Receiving care in the community after juvenile custody is essential for youth looking to capitalize on education and therapies delivered while incarcerated. When consistently provided with programmatic fidelity and input from families and schools, the costs of managing complexities of continuing services for youth with autism and autistic youth pale in comparison to the potential gains for youth, their families, and for communities at large.

Chapter 7 summary

1. **Why consider autism in the context of juvenile justice?**
   - Youth with developmental disabilities have greater odds of being placed in juvenile confinement than do neurotypical youth. Services delivered to youth with autism and autistic youth within residential placements must meet non-criminogenic as well as criminogenic needs.
   - Successful community transitions for youth with autism and autistic youth require a *continuity of care* to build on gains achieved while in custody. Supports rendered to these youth must continue as soon as re-entry into the community occurs.

2. **How does the juvenile justice system particularly affect youth with autism and autistic youth?**
   - Scant availability of disability-specific services undermines rehabilitative potential while in custody.
   - Weak coordination between the juvenile justice system and community providers of autism-related services form a barrier to effective transitions among youth with autism and autistic youth and their families.

3. **How can circumstances be improved for youth with autism, autistic youth, and the personnel who interact with them in juvenile justice settings?**
   - Increase the amount of training for juvenile justice practitioners related to autism, autism-related conditions, and neurological differences in general.
   - Include transition specialists knowledgeable about autism to case manage for juveniles while in custody and in the community *for the entirety of their sentences.*
   - Community and justice personnel should empower the youth with autism and autistic youth and their families through consistent support, education, and feedback.

4. **What does rights-based disability policy look like in the context of rehabilitation of children with autism and autistic children who have become involved with the juvenile justice system?**
   - Youth with autism and autistic youth who are justice-involved have higher criminal and mental health risks than do such youth who are not justice involved. Conceptualizing health services and supports as positive rights for youth with autism and autistic youth provides legal impetus for the continuity of services between juvenile custody and the community.
   - Education is a critical part of successful community re-entry for justice-involved youth with autism and autistic youth. Developmental theories help articulate which services will maximize their adaptation to community life.

Figure 6 Chapter 7 summary

Looking Forward
Conclusions, Recommendations, and Next Steps

Public programs work for, with, and across all elements of diversity in society. Throughout the postcolonial history of North America, belief in this basic fact and the work that diversity of diversities entails to justly accomplish goals repeatedly waffled. Progress toward justice never ceased. However, the conception of an ideal way for being – that is male, of at least typical capacities, wealthy, Christian, and of European descent – rested at the core of public policy and the administering of public programs in North America for far too much of its history as a collection of Western democracies. Even as awareness of diversity and rights grew and continues to grow, regression to bias and prejudice too often clouds the thinking of even progressive stakeholders. Ableism, in particular, passes unnoticed or goes unchallenged even in self-consciously inclusive settings.

In recent years, especially in the United States, effects of ongoing injustices associated with the criminal justice system included death, pain, confusion, and widespread protest and counter-protest. Understandings of these events range from the belief that they illuminate the tip of the iceberg of a thoroughly corrupt system to the belief in an inherently unfair portrayal of the vast majority of dedicated professionals engaged in the criminal justice systems. Solving challenges related to the administration of justice in diverse societies requires a commitment to maintaining pace with the unfolding understandings of the diversity of diversities. Both mistakes and unanticipated gains will occur. Autism in the context of the juvenile justice systems in Canada and the United States presents no exception to this general rule. In seeking to make progress in incorporating neurodiversity into the practice of juvenile justice, blame-seeking serves progress far less well than does attention to maintaining and expanding successes, especially by learning from mistakes, shortfalls, and tragedies.

As has been discussed throughout this book, learning about the intersections of autism and juvenile justice system continues. Much remains unknown about the connections between crime and autism, the future of policing, neurodiversity, and the neuroethics of public policy given unfolding advances in neuroscience. Furthermore, as time goes on, individuals with autism and autistic individuals should increasingly join the various ranks of stakeholders in juvenile justice systems. This book focuses primarily on circumstances in which the individual with autism or autistic individual is the juvenile in custody. However, especially as inclusion and disability policy progress, there is an increasing likelihood that all stakeholders – among them, judges, lawyers, probation counsellors, detention officers, teachers, and parents – will include in their ranks people who are autistic or have autism. Future contemplation of this aspect of neurodiversity will shape conversations about juvenile justice systems and autism beyond this book.

Lessons from this book spring from both historical experiences and contemporary challenges. Resulting recommendations include short-, medium-, and long-term suggestions. Recommendations rarely prove final and, ideally, many of those that follow will soon become outdated. Some recommendations, such as working through histories of ableism, require more long-term effort with no foreseeable completion point. Finally, a caution to avoid repeating errors of past good intentions supersedes and infuses all else in this book. One key to this involves avoiding the proliferation of separated facilities for people with autism and autistic people (or on the basis of disability more generally). While separation might prove expedient in the event of certain medical emergencies, curtailing this approach as much as possible remains key to enhancing the social justice of our systems and to the effective practice of neurodiversity in our societies. Furthermore, movement away from the use of solitary confinement (another well-intentioned practice of the past demonstrated tragically unsuitable) should continue until the eclipse of the practice. Whereas myths about autism and misinterpretations of neurodiverse behaviours tend to minimize the implications of solitude for those perceived as unsocial or antisocial, human companionship remains as necessary for the autistic and people with autism as for any human being. The following recommendations should be considered in conjunction with these baseline elements.

Short-Term Recommendations

Little in the public sector changes quickly. Providing (and receiving) short-term recommendations involves many implied asterisks and comes with many grains of salt. For the purposes of this text, the working definition of "short term" encompasses changes to existing programs achievable in a year or less. In multilevel democratic systems, this time frame typically restricts options to those involving local changes in employee approaches or management protocols and, potentially, administrative policy. Versions of the following short-term recommendations have been attempted in some jurisdictions in either Canada or the United States (or both). Expanding their use beyond sparse implementation while incorporating lessons learned in policy experimented serves to enhance the practice of neurodiversity in juvenile justice with regard to autism and other neurological differences.

Improve Chances for Comprehension of Justice Processes among Youth and Families

Justice presumes comprehension of process. Historical expectations of this comprehension employed the neurotypical point of view, at least as the baseline and too often as an unapologetically ableist norm. These expectations also are surprisingly frequently neglected to fully account for the effects of trauma, stress, and paucity of time and other resources on comprehension capacities. In the short term, broad expansion of instructional materials for youth and their families as they proceed through juvenile justice system processes should take place. Thinking beyond the stereotypical trifold pamphlet and website FAQs rests at the core of this effort. For example, a plethora of YouTube videos regarding the juvenile justice process currently exists. Assisting in the selection and curation of such videos could assist youth and families, including those already viewing the materials. Similarly, youth and families could be given an opportunity to play a reality-based game illustrating the process prior to actual involvement, to help in the social coaching of autistic youth and youth with autism, many of whom have existing familiarity with such educational strategies.

Inviting iterative feedback on proposed strategies from youth, families, and autistic adults increases the probability of success and the proximity to fully realized neurodiversity. Activism and advocacy-oriented groups such as the Autistic Self Advocacy Network and the Juvenile Justice Information

Exchange stand to make meaningful contributions to this area. The largely untapped resource of aged-out youth and their families as potential contributors to process-clarification efforts exists and grows daily. As Sarah Cusworth Walker (2016, n.p.) writes in "Juvenile Justice System Should Morph into Surrogate Grandparent, Not Parent," for the Juvenile Justice Information Exchange, "the early marketing of the juvenile court idea as a 'child saving' endeavor has persisted in a process that provides no clear path for parental or community participation or input ... the impact of this is felt by thousands of parents, millions over the years, who are routinely stigmatized, terrified and ill-served by a system purporting to rehabilitate youth."

Acting as a second-degree stakeholder in the raising of children stands to serve justice, youth, families, and individuals with disabilities and disabled individuals much more effectively than does the presumption of deficit (or even absence) of parental or guardian attention. Even if such attention proves lacking, exclusion as default compromises potential. Finally, presuming role singularity limits discourse. For example, juvenile justice personnel include in their number those with direct or familial experiences as youth in the juvenile justice system. Broad recruitment of anyone willing and able to leverage and transcend anecdotal experiences by contributing to efforts to improve communication and comprehension of contemporary juvenile justice process involves effort and emotional labour but ultimately serves to improve the utility of services.

Initiating and Expanding Attention to Intersectionality

Complex societies repeatedly demonstrate the tendency to practice the *Breakfast Club* epithet of seeing one another in the simplest terms and convenient definitions. While such limited perceptions never appropriately described human beings, the twenty-first century is increasingly consciously diverse, heterogeneous, and divergent. In working with youth in contemporary juvenile justice systems, a baseline expectation of intersectionality serves to improve practices. Research continues to demonstrate differential experiences based on immutable characteristics. For example, as Rebecca Epstein, Jamilia J. Blake, and Thalia González (2017, 1, emphasis in original) explain, "in light of proven disparities in school discipline, we suggest that the perception that Black girls are less innocent may contribute to *harsher punishment* by educators and school resource officers ... furthermore, the view that Black girls need less nurturing, protection, and support and are more independent may translate into *fewer leadership and mentorship opportunities*." Working with the diversity of diversities requires an appreciation for multidimensional differences in human experiences that place exclusionary socially constructed infrastructure into sharp relief.

Autism itself involves both historical and ongoing limitations revolving around intersectionality. First, autism was once believed to primarily affect white middle- or upper-class families, leading many to expect the condition to be naturally concentrated in these populations, as opposed to more exclusively diagnosed in children coming from these backgrounds. Second, recorded incidence and prevalence of autism reveals a majority male population, leaving still open questions about whether this disparity accurately reflects gender distribution of the population or results of research more focused on expression of autistic behaviours in boys and men. Third, since the 1940s, both research and popular attention have more actively considered autism in children than in adults, reinforcing existing tendencies toward infantilization of people with disabilities and disabled people and a sense that an individual's best life prospects would be forever lost if individuals with autism and autistic individuals passed through childhood without successful assimilation into neurotypically dominated culture. Each of these elements of the history of autism specifically augments implications of intersectionality. In particular, it incurs responsibility on the part of all stakeholders to respect and seek to understand histories of harm in the construction of public policies and programs.

In the context of autism and juvenile justice, another intersectional history of harm still unfolding exists in the super-predator stereotype. This myth gained broad popularity in the early to mid-1990s, especially in the United States (Humes 2015). Promoted by authors such as John J. Dilulio, William J. Bennett, and John P. Walters, this theory predicted that juvenile crime was headed for a steep rise, leading to increasingly dangerous social conditions. The super-predator myth embraced (or at the least fostered) racist conceptions of, particularly, young black and First Nations men. Especially in the United States, social fear rose despite increased general safety, resulting in globally extraordinary rates of incarceration. Recorded instances of police violence distributed enthusiastically across social media and beyond at the beginning of the twenty-first century both highlighted and augmented stakeholder tensions. Similar, though arguably less pronounced or systematically brutal, instances occurred in Canada as well. Progress in all aspects of juvenile justice, including autism and juvenile justice, in the short term cannot avoid engaging the hurt feelings, stereotyping, and ongoing trauma associated with racially biased perceptions of youth in the guise of late twentieth-century social science.

Trauma in juvenile justice settings comes from many directions, each of which demands short-term attention on the part of the public sector while still recognizing solutions will be a long time coming (if ever possible). For example, parents and guardians frequently play the dual and impossibly conflicting roles of victims of the crime and advocate for the accused/perpetrator, all the while facing pervasive social judgment of their parenting, whether remotely warranted or not. Efforts to recast and reconsider relationships between professionals and the families of justice-involved youth are well underway in some jurisdictions. In certain instances, programs designed under the umbrella of wraparound services have included formal peer-support practices and create environments in which parents and professionals work together toward improving the life chances of youth. Ultimately, expansion of these practices requires additional resources (including professional time) and training. In the short term, however, a commitment to reframing first and blaming second (if ever) rests at the foundation of restorative justice.

Social construction of disability manifests poignantly in settings simultaneously designed to restrict and redirect in response to crime. Understanding diversity of prosocial identity, including as it relates to neurological differences such as autism, allows for a better focus on behaviours that are inherently antisocial, as opposed to simply reflections of majority or historical preferences. To the frustration of some, stipulations of prosocial behaviour continually shift. In the short term, scheduling and planning for the periodic review of screening tools and assessment for ableism, relevance, and purpose creates a mechanism by which organizations and institutions keep abreast of advancements in health care, neuroscience, and neurodiversity. Similarly, the examination of participation and behaviour expectations for unnecessary preferencing of neurotypicality can take place in the short term and develop into a long-term practice. As discussed in Chapter 6, probation services and other enrichment activities depending on social interaction insufficiently consider healthy differences in social strategies employed by those with neurological differences. For example, if a child or youth genuinely prefers to play alone during free time and is not being actively excluded from social activities by peers, efforts to force interaction resting on the assumption that interaction proves relaxing may adversely affect the individual preferring (or needing) moments of solitude.

In essence, short-term efforts involve initiating and expanding dynamic attention to inclusion and diversity. Progress will, of course, be uneven and reflective of the fact that some find more comfort in conditions of diversity whereas others crave a more separated existence along the lines of a selected immutable characteristic. Enhancing neuroinclusion in service of ongoing progress in juvenile justice involves management of identity politics and substantial goal displacement occurring throughout the continent. Enhancing awareness and incremental, proactive steps in the short term lays the foundation for the medium-term recommendations discussed next.

Medium-Term Recommendations

Much of the work in the public sector involves acting in the medium term, partly because this time frame fits the predominantly incremental approach to policy innovation, development, implementation, and evaluation common in democracies. In the democratic context of North America (especially in the United States, with its rigidly scheduled election cycles), a dominant medium-term focus also relates to the desire present in many elected officials to have reportable accomplishments to which they can point within a given election cycle. Medium-term recommendations tread an ever-fine line between urgent action and achievable goals.

The medium term allows for a period of policy design and adoption, followed by the implementation of the more immediate elements of the particular policy. In the context of administration and management, medium term is appealing in that it balances between too restricting a period, limiting the potential for action and change, and too long a period, rendering the actions contemplated less urgent or complete. For the purposes of this text, "medium term" encompasses approximately one to five years, with a relatively complete implementation at the end of that period. While medium-term recommendations might still be awaiting outcomes and definitive measures of success more generally, they do involve the expectation that time for preliminary process evaluation exists as well. Furthermore, medium-term recommendations could involve some coordination between agencies and levels of government.

In the medium term, arrest protocols require thorough attention. Widely reported botched interactions between particular justice system personnel and members of the public should open a window of opportunity for changes in policy and practice surrounding the questioning, arrest, and detention of individuals with suspected criminal involvement. Conversations about changes in professional training should include careful attention to the many non-criminal characteristics associated with autism, which have been particularly confounded with assuming an individual is under the influence of controlled substances or willfully ignoring official directions.

Overcoming implicit biases still associating differences with crime and explicit ableist discrimination depend on intensive and sustained consideration of protocols. In reconsidering interaction protocols, avoiding the soft bigotry of over-accommodation and lack of consideration of (real) threats to the safety of personnel and the general population complicate effective design. Talented and unbiased arbitrators with a solid understanding of both disability politics and the justice system will, in many cases, have to be cultivated alongside these ongoing conversations focused on the iterative development of policies and protocols. Adult autistics and others representing a broad spectrum of human neurodiversity must also participate in the process. Stakeholders may experience strain or bridle against requirements of saintly patience involved in this necessary work.

Questions of culpability intersect with disability activism. Different standards of responsibility do not sit well with some, while others consider these standards fundamental to human and civil rights, not to mention effective design of juvenile justice system. Finding complete balance of this paradox falls outside human capacities. Systems, especially systems within wicked policy areas incorporating statements about rights, can tend toward the absolute, creating conditions in which more individuals in more vulnerable circumstances stand a good chance of dying with their rights on. Absolute rights reflect the stated preferences of some people, especially in the United States, with its more negative, civil rights-oriented milieu of governance. However, in Canada, the preference for rights at all costs has historically manifested in competition for collective rights.

In the context of modern and contemporary disability rights, haunting histories and ongoing practices of exclusion, paternalism, infantilization, extermination, and discrimination reinforce the central position of articulation and protection of rights in disability activism. Disability advocates, on the other hand, tend to fall back on acquisition and expansion of services focused on either care or cure. As discussed in Chapter 2, the juvenile justice system exists in the modification of formal culpability in deference to assumed capacity. Human development proceeds at a much less predictable and linear pace than necessary for straightforward design of just policy treating individuals differently based on personal characteristics such as age. Added complications of neurological difference and intersectionalities tied to historical oppression will result in ongoing tensions and demands for change. Non-activist stakeholders, such as justice system professionals, are called to dynamically work out the philosophy of difference surrounding policies and protocols without turning back toward discrimination.

Responsible practice requires working directly with activists and advocates who, while working on ostensibly similar issues, are not on the same proverbial page when it comes to the fundamentals of disability. This takes time, investment, maturity, and a commitment to neurodiversity still in development in juvenile justice systems.

Such commitment requires consideration of the full sensory environment of neurological difference. Because each individual with autism and autistic individual differentially experiences sensory environments, full appreciation of the implications of sensory environments will likely take years to proximate and does not come to an end. In considering the sensory environment, the avoidance of over-accommodation also contributes to justice and genuine inclusion. Walking the line between attention to neurodiversity and over-accommodation presents particular challenges in juvenile justice systems, which, after all, include an element of correction of behaviour that has proven demonstrably inappropriate, harmful, or counterproductive. Excusing disability does not translate to diversity. However, the building of many environments favoured the neurologically typical. Sustaining the joint assumptions that reported experience is real and that behaviour is communication requires tireless commitment on the part of professionals working with youth. Dividends of attention to diversity exist and, once realized, can put all stakeholders in more comfortable positions. For example, if the lights or noise levels torture youth, the safest bet is that they will tend to pass along the misery in one way or another. Easy answers to environmental changes do not exist. Developing them requires engagement and professional energy, a resource almost always in constrained supply.

Finally, in the medium term, attention to the expansion of transition and onsite services is the key. Especially in the United States, ending profiteering and curtailing privatization rests at the core of expansion of such publicly provided services. Efficiency gains promised in the privatization of public goods rarely actualize. In the case of the juvenile justice system, profit taking reduces the potential to provide services standing a chance of reducing lifetime costs a challenging youth might impose on a society. In fact, the intent of such services involves increasing the potential for positive contribution to the tax base and to society at large. In the consideration of disability, institutionalizing services in central locations harkens back to ugly historical experiences. Remembering that much of the practice of juvenile justice already takes place in community-based settings is important in the attentive management of this concern. Furthermore, the potential for juvenile justice systems to minimize differential effects of family wealth and the socio-economic status of justice-involved youth depends on their capacity to provide state-of-the-art services to a population of young people obviously at substantial risk of long-term loss in earning potential and social productivity.

Long-Term Recommendations

As Harold Lasswell, an acclaimed twentieth-century political scientist, famously pointed out, policy is very rarely made once and for all. Malleability of public policy rests at the core of democracy. After all, in the absence of a realistic expectation that public policy could be changed, over time, a tyranny of the past develops. While societies typically benefit from stable pillars in policy subsystems, policy redesign from the root occasionally happens (Kingdon 2010; Lindblom 1979). A paucity of strengths in planned, long-term policy development exists in the North American democracies. Elections and a desire to prove results in a more limited time frame drive a desire to design public policies with outcomes in the shorter term. In addition, expanded assessment and employee evaluation practices of the last couple of decades worked to shorten the time horizon of workers in the public agencies, a part of the public sector still more well known for institutional memory and a longer-term focus than elected officials. These factors contributed to a decline investment in long-term work in the public sector, including public infrastructures at the beginning of the twenty-first century in both Canada and the United States. Even so, democracies are a going concern. Policy, or at least policy goals, with long-term horizons draws rightful attention from those engaged in large and influential policy subsystems, including juvenile justice.

For the purposes of this book, long-term recommendations involve a period of active development and implementation of more than five years. Importantly, these elements of public policy may either take this long to complete, to produce measurable results, or both. Those striving in the creation and implementation of these efforts require internal motivation generated from true belief or extrinsic motivation, located outside the public sector per se. In other words, these will be addressed only through inspired commitment and personal dedication.

Expanding access to services, including especially health care, education, and social support, has been woven into the fabric of juvenile justice systems since their inception. Investing in juvenile justice specifically proclaims a belief in the potential of youth and the capacity of a given society to reclaim and reshape the lives of children unfortunate enough to have found themselves accused of having committed crimes before the age of majority. The construction of juvenile justice systems perpetually involves careful management of the human propensity for vengeance – especially given heinous crimes. In the long term, reducing now deeply embedded, widespread, and often rather casually reinforced fear of youth (especially youth from minority groups) presents the only responsible and mature path to success in the context of autism and juvenile justice. Contemporary social acceptance of disparagement of young people runs high. Unfortunately, such generational bashing includes more than a little acceptance of more focused bashing of youth with disabilities, disabled youth, and other minority characteristics. Most recently, tolerance for abuse of "othered" youth among many in power has been devastatingly demonstrated by the horrific conditions in which migrant children detained at the United States' southern border have been held. Reawakening generalized adult responsibility for children, youth, and even young adults includes rejecting age-based fear. Transition from fear to responsibility and, in some instances, even accountability takes time.

One aspect of accountability especially relevant to autism and juvenile justice in Canada and the United States exists in the availability of health interventions and social services specific to individuals with autism, autistic individuals, and those with other neurological differences. Of course, a substantial portion of the challenges surrounding access to appropriate care and services owes to the fact that the needed interventions and protocols have yet to be invented. Dedication of substantial time and effort exists in primary research, program development, and program evaluation in both nations. Many such efforts have been extraordinarily productive, commendable, and life-saving.

Current efforts are not, however, enough. Efforts can be constrained, underfunded, and too focused on a fragmented part of the population during a specific time of development. Ongoing and broad support for research that contextualizes autism and respects the diversity inherent in any form of neurodiversity is necessary. As Ami Tint and Jonathan A. Weiss (2016, 262) put it: "Families play an important role in supporting individuals with autism spectrum disorder across the lifespan." As Tint and Weiss go on to discuss, clinical approaches to autism and other differences handled in medical contexts tend to focus on the individual as the sole (or at least primary) unit of analysis. In the context of juvenile justice in Canada and the United States, more consideration of the family and environment exists. However, these assumptions are generally built on both intersectional bias and neurotypical preferences. Furthermore, involvement of medical personnel in the administration and management of autism and juvenile justice tends to turn attention back to the individual and their essential experience of autism. Real headway in the long term depends on more sociological approaches to interventions that are themselves better embedded in the complicated institutional contexts in which real-life programs exist.

Finally, long-term success depends on focus on success. Positive emotions differ from the simple absence of negative emotions or irritating stimuli (Seligman 2004). Even so, studies of well-being tend to focus more on the absence of the negative than on the presence of the positive (Tint and Weiss 2016). Owing in large part to the absence of metrics with consensus in the positive case, scholars and practitioners remaining largely stuck attempting to understand flourishing through the lens of an absence of perceptible failure. As Tint and Weiss put it: "The field of well-being in families of individuals with ADS is ripe for further theoretical and methodological development and stands to inform policy and practice" (ibid., 271). The key to success in this development involves better protocols and practices for managing complexity surrounding modern identity politics at the individual, family, professional, and other levels. In the context of neurodiversity, one long-term aspect of this work involves creating mechanisms that effectively and respectfully manage tensions between cure and identity. Zolyomi and Tennis (2017, 139) explain: "Within the broad neurodiverse community, there are people at different stages of being out." Complete understandings of success depend on supporting this diversity of identification, even between moments of time or across settings in which one individual exists.

Insufficient understanding of positive experiences thwarts the creation of effective public policy and programs, especially when it comes to intractable problems such as those existing in the context of autism and juvenile justice. In the long run, developing and diffusing measurements of success rests at the core of progress. Involvement with the juvenile justice system begins with a tragedy of some kind or another. Movement through the juvenile justice system occurs best in the measurement of sustainable success. Intensive work will be necessary in the reframing of measurement, especially in the context of juvenile justice. While progress-oriented efforts are already underway and with deep roots in juvenile justice systems, reversion to the negative in the name of motivations ranging from efficiency to vengeance to discrimination to ignorance threatens the long-term focus on positive outcomes. In the long term, expanding focus on positive psychology will promote success in complex organizations and wicked policy problems. An openness to learning across all kinds of borders – up to and including international – creates bold potential to enhance institutional neurodiversity and the ever more just practice of juvenile justice.

Glossary

ableism: Preference or privilege for capacities understood as at least typical. These preferences include attitudes, environments, beliefs, and practices that devalue and limit people with disabilities and the disabled.

ableness: An individual's capacity or ability to do something.

accommodation(s): Changes made to render a non-universally designed environment or practice accessible. This book primarily uses the term in two ways: accommodations in education, and accommodations to public places and resources. Educational accommodations are required by law in both Canada and the United States and provide students with disabilities support and services in obtaining general education requirements – for example, a proctor reading an examination aloud, or allowing a student more time to complete an exam. Accommodations to public places and resources refer to modifying the environment or process in order to provide a person with disability or disabled person access to a place or service – for example, providing sign language at court hearings to those with a hearing impairment.

adolescent: The developmental stage of physical and neurological transformation from child to adult, usually marked as from puberty through maturity, ending at the age of majority.

arraignment: An initial hearing where the juvenile is notified of the charges against them and enters an initial plea. At this stage, a not-guilty plea is almost always entered.

autism spectrum disorder (ASD): Spectrum of conditions and capacities understood as being related to autism. The DSM-5 identifies the following types of ASD: Asperger's syndrome, childhood disintegrative disorder, and pervasive developmental disorders not otherwise specified.

autistic: A person engaging their autism as a positive element of identity.

best practices: Evidence-based strategies or activities demonstrated to have a desired outcome in empirical research.

capacity hearing: A mandatory for any juveniles charged with a crime. Age requirements for hearing vary. The hearing must demonstrate that the juvenile understands their actions were wrong. This hearing occurs before arraignment.

children: In the legal sense of the word, refers to a person under the age of eighteen. Specifically, the term "children" is used in civil court or dependency court where children are involved not as a fault of their own (in both Canada and the United States).

comparative policy analysis: Using policies from various government, cultures, histories, or networks to examine relative outcomes and impacts of policy.

community-based services: Programs provided in the community in an effort to rehabilitate the offender and restore the harm done to the community. They can be in lieu of being detained or required after the fact as part of the transition back into the community.

comorbid: Having one or more disability or disorder that co-occur with a primary condition. For example, a youth with autism may also have depression.

competency hearing: A hearing to determine whether the juvenile is mentally able to stand trial. The court must determine whether the juvenile has the ability to consult with their attorney and has a rational understanding of what is going on, including a factual understanding of the case. A competency evaluation is completed by a medical doctor and a referral provided to the court of whether there is competency.

culpability: The responsibility for a person to take blame for an action or behaviour. One of the three elements in determining mens rea, or criminal intent.

custody: The legal state in which a person is being held by another responsible for the safety and well-being of that person. Mostly refers to being incarcerated and, therefore, in the custody of juvenile courts.

delinquency: Actions committed by juveniles who violate criminal laws (Mayes 2003) or an observed tendency to commit such actions.

delinquency case: An offence for which the juvenile could be charged in criminal court (Sickmund and Puzzanchera 2014). This does not include status offences, which are laws that apply only to juveniles based on their age – for example, minor in possession, truancy, or runaway.

detention: A secure facility that is responsible for short-term or temporary custody of juvenile offenders.

Diagnostic and Statistical Manual (DSM): The standard classification of mental disorders used by mental health professionals in the United States and Canada, published by the American Psychiatric Association (American Psychiatric Publishing). It is intended to be used in all clinical settings by clinicians of different theoretical orientations. It can be used by mental health and other health professionals, including psychiatrists and other physicians, psychologists, social workers, nurses, occupational and rehabilitation therapists, and counsellors.

disability-first language (or identity-first language): An approach to communicating where the person's disability is the primary and positive element of identity – for example, "autistic person."

disposition: A juvenile sentencing hearing where, in most cases, a disposition order is entered that requires specific rules and conditions the juvenile must follow and complete within a certain time. A case could also be dismissed at disposition.

diversion: A program available for first-time offenders or non-serious offences to be handled outside of the formal court process. The number of diversions offered varies between counties in the United States and provinces and territories in Canada.

doli incapax: A common law presumption that a child is incapable of crime because they do not have understanding between right and wrong. Also known as "culpability."

empathy: The ability to understand what another person is feeling. Empathy involves the imagining of feelings connected to the position or circumstance occupied by another.

ethnocentrism: The perception that the group that one belongs to is superior than other perceived groups.

fact-finding: Also known as an "adjudicatory hearing," in which the judge makes a decision regarding guilt. Fact-findings are equivalent to an adult trial.

free and appropriate public education (FAPE): In the United States, a right protected by IDEA that requires schools to provide a free and appropriate education for all students with disabilities.

intersections and intersectionalities: Combinations of characteristics associated with historical and ongoing oppression, such as race, gender, class, sexual orientation, neurotribe, and other characteristics.

issue definition or problem definition: Perception that an element of a condition needs a solution. For example, gun violence at school is a condition. An issue or problem definition for gun violence at school could be attributing the cause to increased access to guns and, therefore, the policy solution would be to decrease public access to firearms.

issue framing: A tool used to present a public problem so that it appears especially relevant to the intended audience.

jurisdiction: Refers to the authority and extent of the power of a court to make a legal decision or judgment. In this book, "jurisdiction" refers primarily to geographical jurisdiction, such as county, province, or state. Jurisdiction also relates to age and transfers to adult court.

juvenile: A young person under the age of seventeen, often specific to a child of this age who is involved with the justice system. In Canada, the juvenile court has jurisdiction for youth between the ages of twelve and seventeen; any youth under the age of twelve cannot be held criminally responsible (Allen et al. 2014). In the United States, the minimum age is dependent on the state. In every state, juvenile jurisdiction ends at the youth's eighteenth birthday unless jurisdiction is extended through a court order.

least restrictive environment (LRE): Refers to Part B of the 1975 Individuals with Disabilities Education Act. Compliance with LRE includes the requirement that school districts attempt to provide education for students with disabilities in the regular classroom with the appropriate services first. If possible, each student with disabilities receives specific aids and supports to facilitate their classroom placement before a more restrictive placement is used.

meta-analysis: A methodological technique synthesizing the results of studies on a particular intervention. Researchers calculate a quantitative statistic across studies expressing the efficacy of the intervention on the desired outcome. The pooled estimate – often referred to as an effect size – measures the magnitude of the differences between groups that receive the intervention relative to those that do not.

negative rights: Where governments proscribe behaviours that deny basic civil rights to people of a given nation and affirm protection of their exercise for that group.

neurodivergent: Involving a difference in brain function or type from a standard neurology.

neurodiversity: A natural condition of variation in the neurology of a population.

neurodiversity movement: A social movement that promotes positive interpretations of neurological differences of human beings.

neuroethics: Consideration of the interactions between neurology, policy, ethics, and human behaviour.

neurological difference: Involves the individual experience of being neurodivergent. This is an individual's private relationship with their own neurocognitive functioning.

offence: A crime typically refers to the law that was broken. An offence is the behaviour that led to the law being broken.

parens patriae: Meaning state as the parent. Places on the government the responsibility of the parent to protect juveniles from harm and also hold them accountable for breaking the law (Vito and Kunselman 2011).

parole: The release of a juvenile from a residential care facility back into the community. In other words, the community supervision that takes place for a court-ordered period after the youth is released from juvenile prison.

people- or person-first language: A language form recognizing that individuals are not defined primarily by their functional differences. Failure to implement person-first language has historically been interpreted as being discriminatory or derogatory.

positive rights: Rights dependent on the effort of others to provide resources, opportunities, or circumstances for exercise.

probation: Court order to follow a specific set of rules listed in a court order. During the probation period, juveniles are monitored by a probation officer for compliance of those rules.

proportionality: Requires that the culpability of the offender must be taken into consideration in order to uphold a fair and just process.

punctuated equilibrium theory: According to Baumgartner and Jones (1991), punctuated equilibrium theory is the idea that change is usually slow and occurs in incremental steps but is punctuated, or defined, by large fundamental changes to the policy or political system.

rational choice theory or rationality: According to Kraft and Furlong (2012, 531), rational choice theory assumes that people are hedonistic and make decisions to maximize their own self-interest. The theory is used to help predict how a person will behave based on how the outcome will affect their individual livelihood.

recidivism: Likelihood that a person will reoffend.

regime theory: How state actors and non-governmental stakeholders collectively identify problems, design, and implement policy solutions to those problems (Wijen and Ansari 2007). Regimes are defined as "social institutions consisting of agreed-on principles, norms, rules, decision-making procedures, and programs around which actors' expectations converge in specific issue areas" (ibid., 1083).

residential placement: A juvenile sentenced to a long-term correctional facility or residential training centre. Examples include camps, farms, ranches, and schools with various levels of security.

restorative justice: An approach to carrying out sentencing that balances community safety with accountability for offenders through practices that increase responsibility and competency.

restraint: According to Gagnon, Mattingly, and Connelly (2017, 66), it is "a practice that uses physical or mechanical means to restrict freedom of motion."

seclusion: According to Gagnon, Mattingly, and Connelly (2017, 66) it is "a practice that involves the involuntary isolation of a student."

sentencing: A hearing after a juvenile is found guilty. This hearing is when they will be ordered a punishment for their crime. The type of punishment can be as punitive or restorative as the judge would like. A sentence can include but is not limited to probation, community service, fines, fees, and restitution.

special needs or special educational needs: Refers to the educational accommodations and programs available to students with disabilities. Examples include specific classrooms for youth with sensory impairment, or proctors reading an assignment aloud to students with dyslexia.

stakeholder: An individual or group of individuals who have an interest in or will be directly affected by a policy or policy outcome.

transition: Change from one setting or circumstances to another. In this text, transition often refers to the period after which a youth is released from long-term residential placement and back into the community. Probation officers connect the youth with community resources, and parents initiate enrolling their youth in a school program.

violation: When a juvenile does not follow a condition of their disposition order.

youth: An often informal reference to individuals under the age of eighteen.

Caselaw and Legislation

Caselaw
Alexander S. v Boyd, 113 F.3d 1373 (4th Cir. 1997)
Auton v British Columbia, [2004] 3 SCR 657
Board of Education of Hendrick Hudson Central School District v Rowley. 458 U.S. 176 (1982)
Breed v Jones, 421 U.S. 519 (1975)
Daniel R.R. v State Board of Education, 874 F.2d 1036 (5th Circuit, 1989).
Deal v Hamilton County Board of Education No. 03–5396, 6th Circuit (2004)
Eaton v Brant County Board of Education, [1997] 1 S.C.R. 24
Graham v Florida. 560 U.S. 48 (2010)
Hartmann v Loudoun County Board of Education, 113 F.3d 996 (1997).
In re Gault, 387 U.S. 1 (1967)
In re Winship, 397 U.S. 358 (1970)
Johnson v Upchurch, No. 86–195, District Court of Arizona (2000)
Kent v United States, 383 U.S. 541 (1966)
McKeiver v Pennsylvania, 403 U.S. 528 (1971)
Miller v Alabama, 567 U.S. 460 (2012)
Moore v British Columbia, [2012] S.C.C. 61
Olmstead v LC, 257, US 581 (1999)
Pate v Robinson, 383 U.S. 375 (1966)
Roper v Simmons, 543 U.S. 551 (2005)
Sacramento City Unified School District v Rachel H., 14 F.3d 1398 (9th Circuit, 1994)

Legislation

Affordable Care Act. 2013. 45 CFR 156.115. https://www.law.cornell.edu/cfr/text/45/156.115.

Americans with Disabilities Act of 1990. 1990. Public Law 101–336. 108th Congress, 2nd session. July 26.

Canadian Charter of Rights and Freedoms, Part I of the Constitution Act, 1982, being Schedule B to the Canada Act 1982 (UK), 1982, c. 11.

Corrections and Conditional Release Act: PART 1 Institutional and Community Corrections Health Care. 2016. (SC 1992, c. 20). http://laws-lois.justice.gc.ca/eng/acts/C-44.6/.

Family Educational Rights and Privacy Act of 1974. 20 U.S.C. § 1232g. February 21, 1974.

Health Insurance Portability and Accountability Act of 1996. Public Law 104–191. 104th Congress (August 21, 1996).

"Nondiscrimination under Federal Grants and Programs" 29 U.S. Code §794.

Patient Protection and the Affordable Care Act, 45 CFR 156.115 (2010).

Rehabilitation Act of 1973, Public Law 93–112, *U.S. Statutes at Large* 87 (1973): 355–94. *United States Constitution.* 1787. National Constitution Center. https://constitutioncenter.org/media/files/constitution.pdf.

United States Code: Juvenile Delinquency, 18 U.S.C. §§ 5031–37 (Suppl. 2 1946).

United States Constitution. 1787. National Constitution Center. https://constitutioncenter.org/media/files/constitution.pdf.

Youth Criminal Justice Act. SC 2002. C. 1. http://laws-lois.justice.gc.ca/eng/acts/Y-1.5/page-1.html.

References

Abrams, Laura S., Sarah K.S. Shannon, and Cindy Sangalang. 2008. "Transition Services for Incarcerated Youth: A Mixed Methods Evaluation Study." *Children and Youth Services Review* 30, 5: 522–35.

Acoca, Leslie, Jessica Stephens, and Amanda van Vleet. 2014. "Health Coverage and Care for Youth in the Juvenile Justice System: The Role of Medicaid and CHIP." Menlo Park, CA: Kaiser Commission on Medicaid and the Uninsured.

Adams, Guy B., and Danny L. Balfour. 2009. "Ethical Failings, Incompetence, and Administrative Evil: Lessons from Katrina and Iraq." In *Ethics and Integrity in Public Administration: Concepts and Cases,* edited by Raymond W. Cox III, 40–64. Armonk, NY: M.E. Sharpe.

Alexander, Michelle. 2012. *The New Jim Crow: Mass Incarceration in the Age of Colorblindness.* New York: The New Press.

Alimahomed, Sabrina. 2010. "Thinking Outside the Rainbow: Women of Color Redefining Queer Politics and Identity." *Social Identities* 16, 2: 151–68.

Allen, Mary K., and Tamy Superle. 2016. "Youth Crime in Canada, 2014." *Juristat: Canadian Centre for Justice Statistics:* 1. http://www.statcan.gc.ca/pub/85-002-x/2016001/article/14309-eng.htm.

Almquist, Lauren, and Elizabeth Dodd. 2009. *Mental Health Courts: A Guide to Research-Informed Policy and Practice.* New York: Council of State Governments, Justice Center.

Altschuler, David M., and Rachel Brash. 2004. "Adolescent and Teenage Offenders Confronting the Challenges and Opportunities of Reentry." *Youth Violence and Juvenile Justice* 2, 1: 72–87.

Ameen, Edward J., and Debbiesiu L. Lee. 2012. "Vocational Training in Juvenile Detention: A Call for Action." *Career Development Quarterly* 60, 2: 98–108.

American Probation and Parole Association. https://www.appa-net.org/eweb.

Amstutz, Lorraine Stutzman. 2015. *The Little Book of Restorative Discipline for Schools: Teaching Responsibility; Creating Caring Climates*. New York: Skyhorse.

Anand, Sanjeev S. 1999. "Catalyst for Change: The History of Canadian Juvenile Justice Reform." *Queen's Law Journal* 24: 515.

Andrews, Don A., James Bonta, and J. Stephen Wormith. 2006. "The Recent Past and Near Future of Risk and/or Need Assessment." *Crime and Delinquency* 52, 1: 7–27.

Andrews, Donald Arthur, and James Bonta. 2010. *The Psychology of Criminal Conduct*. New York: Routledge.

Annamma, Subini Ancy. 2014. "Disabling Juvenile Justice: Engaging the Stories of Incarcerated Young Women of Color with Disabilities." *Remedial and Special Education* 35, 5: 313–24.

Ansell, Nicola. 2016. *Children, Youth and Development*. New York: Routledge.

Appleby, Julie, and Mary Agnes. 2017. "6 Lesser-Known Obamacare Provisions That Could Evaporate." *National Public Radio*. January 11. http://www.npr.org/sections/health-shots/2017/01/11/509310734/6-obamacare-provisions-that-could-evaporate.

Armstrong, Thomas. 2011. *The Power of Neurodiversity: Unleashing the Advantages of Your Differently Wired Brain*. Cambridge, MA: Da Capo Lifelong Books.

Asthana, Sheena, and Joyce Halliday. 2006. "Developing an Evidence Base for Policies and Interventions to Address Health Inequalities: The Analysis of "Public Health Regimes." *Milbank Quarterly* 84, 3: 577–603.

Austin, Lisa M. 2006. "Reviewing PIPEDA: Control, Privacy and the Limits of Fair Information Practices." *Canadian Business Law Journal* 44: 21–53.

Autism Speaks. n.d.(a). "Affordable Health Care Act and Autism." Accessed on January 14, 2017. https://www.autismspeaks.org/sites/default/files/docs/gr/aca_community_f.pdf.

–. "DSM-5 Diagnosis Criteria." n.d.(b). https://www.autismspeaks.org/dsm-5-criteria.

Baglivio, Michael T., Nathan Epps, Kimberly Swartz, Mona Sayedul Huq, Amy Sheer, and Nancy S. Hardt. 2014. "The Prevalence of Adverse Childhood Experiences (ACE) in the Lives of Juvenile Offenders." *Journal of Juvenile Justice* 3, 2: 1.

Bahena, Sofía, North Cooc, Rachel Currie-Rubin, Paul Kuttner, and Monica Ng. 2012. *Disrupting the School-to-Prison Pipeline*. Cambridge, MA: Harvard Education Press.

Baker, Dana Lee. 2004. "Public Policy and the Shaping of Disability: Incidence Growth in Educational Autism." *Education Policy Analysis Archives* 12: 11.

–. 2011. *The Politics of Neurodiversity: Why Public Policy Matters*. Boulder, CO: Lynne Rienner.

Baker, Dana Lee, and Brandon Leonard. 2017. *Neuroethics in Higher Education Policy*. New York; Springer.

Baker, Dana Lee, and Laurie A. Drapela. 2010. "Mostly the Mother: Concentration of Adverse Employment Effects on Mothers of Children with Autism." *The Social Science Journal* 47, 3: 578–92.

Baker, Dana Lee, and Shannon Stokes. 2007. "Brain Politics: Aspects of Administration in the Comparative Issue Definition of Autism-Related Policy." *Public Administration Review* 67, 4: 757–67.

Baker, Dana Lee, and Trudy Steuernagel. 2009. "Comparative Policy Entrepreneurship: The Case of Autism-Related Policy in North America." *Journal of Comparative Policy Analysis* 11, 2: 233–48.

Bala, Nicholas. 2004. "Canada's Juvenile Justice Law and Children's Rights." Paper presented at Making Children's Rights Work: National and International Perspectives, International Bureau for Children's Rights, Montreal, November 19.

–. 2007. "Responding to Young Offenders: Diversion, Detention and Sentencing under Canada's YCJA." *Queens University Legal Studies Research Paper* No. 07-10. https://papers.ssrn.com/sol3/papers.cfm?abstract_id=1023893.

Bala, Nicholas, and Julian V. Roberts. 2006. "Canada's Juvenile Justice System: Promoting Community-Based Responses to Youth Crime." *International Handbook of Juvenile Justice*. Dordrecht, Netherlands: Springer: 37-63.

Bala, Nicholas, Peter J. Carrington, and Julian V. Roberts. 2009. "Evaluating the Youth Criminal Justice Act after Five Years: A Qualified Success." *Canadian Journal of Criminology and Criminal Justice* 51, 2: 131-67.

Bambra, Clare. 2007. "Going Beyond the Three Worlds of Welfare Capitalism: Regime Theory and Public Health Research." *Journal of Epidemiology and Community Health* 61, 12: 1098-102.

Barker, Brittany, Gerald Taiaiake Alfred, Kim Fleming, Paul Nguyen, Evan Wood, Thomas Kerr, and Kora DeBeck. 2015. "Aboriginal Street-Involved Youth Experience Elevated Risk of Incarceration." *Public Health* 129, 12: 1662-68.

Barman, Samir, and Alejandra E. Canizares. 2015. "A Survey of Mass Customization in Practice." *International Journal of Supply Chain Management* 4, 1: 65-72.

Barnert, Elizabeth S., Raymond Perry, and Robert E. Morris. 2016. "Juvenile Incarceration and Health." *Academic pediatrics* 16, 2: 99-109.

Baron-Cohen, Simon. 2002. "The Extreme Male Brain Theory of Autism." *Trends in Cognitive Sciences* 6, 6: 248-54.

Baumgartner, Frank R., and Bryan D. Jones. "Agenda Dynamics and Policy Subsystems." 1991. *The Journal of Politics* 53, 4: 1044-74.

–. 2010. *Agendas and Instability in American Politics*. Chicago: University of Chicago Press.

Bazemore, Gordon, and Mara Schiff. 2015. *Restorative Community Justice: Repairing Harm and Transforming Communities*. New York: Routledge.

Beal, Catherine. 2014. "Insider Accounts of the Move to the Outside: Two Young People Talk about Their Transitions from Secure Institutions." *Youth Justice* 14, 1: 63-76.

Bellini, Scott, Jessica K. Peters, Lauren Benner, and Andrea Hopf. 2007. "A Meta-Analysis of School-Based Social Skills Interventions for Children with Autism Spectrum Disorders." *Remedial and Special Education* 28, 3: 153-62.

Ben-Moshe, Liat. 2011. "The Contested Meaning of 'Community' in Discourses of Deinstitutionalization and Community Living in the Field of Developmental Disability." In *Disability and Community*, edited by Allison C. Carey and Richard K. Scotch, 241-64. West Yorkshire, England: Emerald Group.

Ben-Moshe, Liat, and Sandy Magaña. 2014. "An Introduction to Race, Gender, and Disability: Intersectionality, Disability Studies, and Families of Color." *Women, Gender, and Families of Color* 2, 2: 105-14.

Berger, Ronald J. 2013. *Introducing Disability Studies*. Boulder, CO: Lynne Rienner.

Bergseth, Kathleen J., and Jeffrey A. Bouffard. 2013. "Examining the Effectiveness of a Restorative Justice Program for Various Types of Juvenile Offenders." *International Journal of Offender Therapy and Comparative Criminology* 57, 9: 1054-75.

Berman, Greg, and Aubrey Fox. 2009. *Lessons from the Battle over D.A.R.E.: The Complicated Relationship between Research and Practice*. Center for Court Innovation.

Bhattacharjee, Ken. 2003. "The Ontario Safe Schools Act: School Discipline and Discrimination." Ontario Human Rights Commission. July 8. http://www.ohrc.on.ca/sites/default/files/attachments/The_Ontario_Safe_Schools_Act%3A_School_discipline_and_discrimination.pdf.

Blevins, Kristie R., Francis T. Cullen, and Jody L. Sundt. 2007. "The Correctional Orientation of 'Child Savers': Support for Rehabilitation and Custody among Juvenile Correctional Workers." *Journal of Offender Rehabilitation* 45, 3–4: 47–83.

Bonta, James, and Donald Arthur Andrews. 2016. *The Psychology of Criminal Conduct*. New York: Routledge Taylor and Francis.

Booth, Jamar, Maggie K.J. Butler, Taryn V. Richardson, Ahmad R. Washington, and Malik S. Henfield. 2016. "School-Family-Community Collaboration for African American Males with Disabilities." *Journal of African American Males in Education* 7: 87–97.

Borum, Randy. 2003. "Managing At-Risk Juvenile Offenders in the Community: Putting Evidence-Based Principles into Practice." *Journal of Contemporary Criminal Justice* 19, 1: 114–37.

Bouffard, Leana Allen, and Nicole Leeper Piquero. 2010. "Defiance Theory and Life Course Explanations of Persistent Offending." *Crime and Delinquency* 56, 2: 227–52.

Boyle, Teresa. 2003. "Discipline Policy Draws Criticism." *Toronto Star*, July 4. http://www.mapinc.org/drugnews/v03/n1004/a06.html?4259.

Branson, Christopher Edward, Carly Lyn Baetz, Sarah McCue Horwitz, and Kimberly Eaton Hoagwood. 2017. "Trauma-Informed Juvenile Justice Systems: A Systematic Review of Definitions and Core Components." *Psychological Trauma: Theory, Research, Practice, and Policy*. February 6.

Brewer, Neil, and Robyn Louis Young. 2015. *Crime and Autism Disorder: Myths and Mechanisms*. London: Jessica Kingsley.

Brown, Jerrod, Bethany Hastings, Laura Cooney-Koss, Deb Huntley, and Dawn Brasch. 2016. "Autism Spectrum Disorder in the Criminal Justice System: A Review for Caregivers and Professionals." *Journal of Law Enforcement* 5, 5: 1–13.

Brown, Lydia. n.d. "Identity-First Language." Autistic Self Advocacy Network. http://autisticadvocacy.org/home/about-asan/identity-first-language/.

Bullis, Michael, Paul Yovanoff, and Emily Havel. 2004. "The Importance of Getting Started Right: Further Examination of the Facility-to-Community Transition of Formerly Incarcerated Youth." *Journal of Special Education* 38, 2: 80–94.

Bullis, Michael, Paul Yovanoff, Gina Mueller, and Emily Havel. 2002. "Life on the 'Outs' – Examination of the Facility-to-Community Transition of Incarcerated Youth." *Exceptional Children* 69, 1: 7–22.

Bunge, Valerie Pottie, Holly Johnson, and Thierno A. Baldé. 2005. *Exploring Crime Patterns in Canada*. Ottawa: Canadian Centre for Justice Statistics and Time Series Research and Analysis Centre, Statistics Canada.

Burke, W. Warner. 2014. *Organization Change: Theory and Practice*. Los Angeles: Sage Publications.

Burnett, John. 2016. "Justice Department Will Phase Out Its Use of Private Prisons." National Public Radio. August 18.

Campbell, Kathryn M. 2016. "The Youth Criminal Justice System in Ontario." In *Implementing and Working with the Youth Criminal Justice Act across Canada*, edited by Marc Alain, Raymond R. Corrado, and Susan Reid, 248–70. Toronto: University of Toronto Press.

Campie, Patricia E., Allyson Pakstis, Kalen Flynn, and Kathleen McDermott. 2015. "Developing a Coherent Approach to Youth Well-Being in the Fields of Child Welfare, Juvenile Justice, Education, and Health: A Systematic Literature Review." *Families in Society: The Journal of Contemporary Social Services* 96, 3: 175–84.

Canadian Paediatric Society. 2005. *Are We Doing Enough? A Status Report on Canadian Public Policy and Child and Youth Health (2005 Edition)*. Ottawa: Canadian Pediatric Society.

Castro, Felipe González, Manuel Barrera Jr., and Lori K. Holleran Steiker. 2010. "Issues and Challenges in the Design of Culturally Adapted Evidence-Based Interventions." *Annual Review of Clinical Psychology* 6: 213–39.

CATIE. n.d. "Healthy Living." http://www.catie.ca/en/healthy-living.

CBS Miami. 2017. "Autistic Man's Family Sues over Florida Police Shooting." Aired June 5. http://miami.cbslocal.com/2017/06/05/autistic-mans-family-sues-police-shooting/.

Centre for Addiction and Mental Health. 2013. *Mental Health and Criminal Justice Policy Framework*. https://www.camh.ca/-/media/files/pdfs---public-policy-submissions/mh_criminal_justice_policy_framework-pdf.pdf.

Cha, Ariana Eunjung. 2015. "Autism Cases in US Jump to 1 in 45: Who Gets Diagnosis, in 8 Simple Charts." *Washington Post*. November 13. https://www.washingtonpost.com/news/to-your-health/wp/2015/11/13/autism-cases-in-u-0s-rise-to-1-in-45-a-look-at-who-gets-the-diagnosis-in-8-simple-charts/.

Challet, Anna. 2017. "Court Schools: Educating Juveniles in Lockup." *Compton Herald*. Accessed in Spring 2016. http://comptonherald.com/court-schools-educating-juveniles-lockup/.

Charette, Yanick, Anne G. Crocker, Michael C. Seto, Leila Salem, Tonia L. Nicholls, and Malijai Caulet. 2015. "The National Trajectory Project of Individuals Found Not Criminally Responsible on Account of Mental Disorder in Canada. Part 4: Criminal Recidivism." *Canadian Journal of Psychiatry* 60, 3: 127–34.

Charlton, James I. 1998. *Nothing about Us without Us: Disability Oppression and Empowerment*. Berkley: University of California Press.

Cheely, Catherine A., Laura A. Carpenter, Elizabeth J. Letourneau, Joyce S. Nicholas, Jane Charles, and Lydia B. King. 2012. "The Prevalence of Youth with Autism Spectrum Disorders in the Criminal Justice System." *Journal of Autism and Developmental Disorders* 42, 9: 1856–62.

Chesney-Lind, Meda, Merry Morash, and Tia Stevens. 2008. "Girls Troubles, Girls' Delinquency, and Gender Responsive Programming: A Review." *Australian and New Zealand Journal of Criminology* 41, 1: 162–89.

Chester, Alisa, and Elizabeth W. Burak. 2016. "Fact Sheet: Medicaid's Role for Young Children." *Georgetown University Health Policy Institute*. December 13. https://ccf.georgetown.edu/2016/12/13/fact-sheet-medicaids-role-for-young-children/.

Christensen, Deborah L. 2016. "Prevalence and Characteristics of Autism Spectrum Disorder Among Children Aged 8 Years – Autism and Developmental Disabilities Monitoring Network." *Morbidity and Mortality Weekly Report* 65: 1–23.

Christle, Christine A., Kristine Jolivette, and C. Michael Nelson. 2005. "Breaking the School to Prison Pipeline: Identifying School Risk and Protective Factors for Youth Delinquency." *Exceptionality* 13, 2: 69–88.

City of Coral Gables. n.d. "The Wallet Card." Accessed on December 12, 2017. http://card-usf.fmhi.usf.edu/docs/wallet%20card%20brochure.pdf.

Clark, Heather Griller, and Deanne Unruh. 2010. "Transition Practices for Adjudicated Youth with E/BDs and Related Disabilities." *Behavioral Disorders* 36(1): 43–51.

Clark, Michael D. 2005. "Motivational Interviewing for Probation Staff: Increasing the Readiness to Change (Part I)." *Federal Probation* 69: 22–28.

Clark County Juvenile Court. "First Time in Court?" Accessed on December 18, 2019 from https://www.clark.wa.gov/sites/default/files/dept/files/juvenile-court/Web%20CT%20Brochure%20ENGLISH.pdf.

Clibbon, Jennifer. 2015. "Seclusion Rooms in Schools Do More Harm Than Good, Experts Say." *CBC News*, October 12. https://www.cbc.ca/news/health/seclusion-rooms-1.3264834.

Compton, Michael T., Roger Bakeman, Beth Broussard, Dana Hankerson-Dyson, Letheshia Husbands, Shaily Krishan, Tarianna Stewart-Hutto, Barbara M. D'Orio, Janet R. Oliva, Nancy J. Thompson, and Amy C. Watson. 2014. "The Police-Based Crisis Intervention Team (CIT) Model: II. Effects on Level of Force and Resolution, Referral, and Arrest." *Psychiatric Services* 65, 4: 523–29.

Conference Board of Canada. "Life Expectancy." 2019. https://www.conferenceboard.ca/hcp/provincial/health/life.aspx.

–. n.d. "Life Expectancy, Provinces, Territories, and International Peers, 2011." http://www.conferenceboard.ca/hcp/provincial/health/life.aspx.

Corrado, Raymond R., Alan Markwart, Karla Gronsdahl, and Anne Kimmitt. 2016. "The YCJA in British Columbia." *Implementing and Working with the Youth Criminal Justice Act across Canada:* 64.

Corrado, Raymond R., Karla Gronsdahl, David MacAlister, and Irwin M. Cohen. 2010. "Youth Justice in Canada: Theoretical Perspectives of Youth Probation Officers." *Canadian Journal of Criminology and Criminal Justice* 52, 4: 397–426. https://muse.jhu.edu/article/383956.

Corrado, Raymond R., Sarah Kuehn, and Irina Margaritescu. 2014. "Policy Issues Regarding the Overrepresentation of Incarcerated Aboriginal Young Offenders in a Canadian Context." *Youth Justice* 14, 1: 40–62.

Correctional Service Canada. 2012a. "The Safe Streets and Communities Act." June 13. http://www.csc-scc.gc.ca/acts-and-regulations/005006-1000-eng.shtml.

–. 2012b. "About Us." http://www.csc-scc.gc.ca/about-us/index-eng.shtml.

Cowan, Richard J., Leah Abel, and Lindsay Candel. 2017. "A Meta-Analysis of Single-Subject Research on Behavioral Momentum to Enhance Success in Students with Autism." *Journal of Autism and Developmental Disorders:* 1–14.

Crais, Elizabeth R., Cara S. McComish, Betsy P. Humphreys, Linda R. Watson, Grace T. Baranek, J. Steven Reznick, Rob B. Christian, and Marian Earls. 2014. "Pediatric Healthcare Professionals' Views on Autism Spectrum Disorder Screening at 12–18 Months." *Journal of Autism and Developmental Disorders* 44, 9: 2311–28.

Cramer, Elizabeth D., Liana Gonzalez, and Cynthia Pellegrini-Lafont. 2014. "From Classmates to Inmates: An Integrated Approach to Break the School-to-Prison Pipeline." *Equity and Excellence in Education* 47, 4: 461–75.

Crawford, Neta C. 2014. "Institutionalizing Passion in World Politics: Fear and Empathy." *International Theory* 6, 3: 535–57.

Cullen, Francis T., Bonnie S. Fisher, and Brandon K. Applegate. 2000. "Public Opinion about Punishment and Corrections." *Crime and Justice* 27: 1–79. https://www.ncjrs.gov/pdffiles1/Digitization/142440NCJRS.pdf.

Curry, Keith L., Mark P. Posluszny and Sundra L. Kraska. 1993. "Training Criminal Justice Personnel to Recognize Offenders with Disabilities." *OSERS News in Print* 5, 3: 4–8. Daniel, Yvette, and Karla Bondy. 2008. "Safe Schools and Zero Tolerance: Policy, Program and Practice in Ontario." *Canadian Journal of Educational Administration and Policy* 70: 1–20.

Daniels, Amy M., and David S. Mandell. 2014. "Explaining Differences in Age at Autism Spectrum Disorder Diagnosis: A Critical Review." *Autism* 18, 5: 583–97.

Davidson, Joyce, and Michael Orsini, eds. 2013. *Worlds of Autism: Across the Spectrum of Neurological Difference*. Minnesota: University of Minnesota Press.

Davis, Jaya, and Jon R. Sorensen. 2013. "Disproportionate Minority Confinement of Juveniles: A National Examination of Black–White Disparity in Placements, 1997–2006." *Crime and Delinquency* 59, 1: 115–39.

Davis, Krista M., Michele Peterson-Badali, Brian Weagant, and Tracey A. Skilling. 2015. "A Process Evaluation of Toronto's First Youth Mental Health Court." *Canadian Journal of Criminology and Criminal Justice* 57, 2: 159–88.

Davis, Krista M., Michele Peterson-Badali, and Tracey A. Skilling. 2016. "A Theoretical Evaluation of a Youth Mental Health Court Program Model." *International Journal of Law and Psychiatry* 45): 17–24.

Day, David M., Jason D. Nielsen, Ashley K. Ward, Ye Sun, Jeffrey S. Rosenthal, Thierry Duchesne, Irene Bevc, and Lianne Rossman. 2012. "Long-Term Follow-Up of Criminal Activity with Adjudicated Youth in Ontario: Identifying Offence Trajectories and Predictors/Correlates of Trajectory Group Membership." *Canadian Journal of Criminology and Criminal Justice* 54, 4: 377–413.

Debbaudt, Dennis. 2001. *Autism, Advocates, and Law Enforcement Professionals: Recognizing and Reducing Risk Situations for People with Autism Spectrum Disorders*. Philadelphia: Jessica Kingsley.

Debbaudt, Dennis, and Darla Rothman. 2001. "Contact with Individuals with Autism: Effective Resolutions." Federal Bureau of Investigations. April. http://www.poac.net/download/resources/le-ContactwithIndividualswithAutism-EffectiveResolutions.pdf.

DeLisi, Matt, and Michael G. Vaughn. 2008. "The Gottfredson-Hirschi Critiques Revisited: Reconciling Self-Control Theory, Criminal Careers, and Career Criminals." *International Journal of Offender Therapy and Comparative Criminology* 52, 5: 520–37.

Department of Justice Canada. 2004. "The Evolution of Juvenile Justice in Canada." Department of Justice Canada. http://publications.gc.ca/collections/Collection/J2-248-2004E.pdf.

–. 2013. "The Youth Criminal Justice Act: Summary and Background." https://www.justice.gc.ca/eng/cj-jp/yj-jj/tools-outils/pdf/back-hist.pdf.

Des Roches Rosa, Shannon. 2017. "What Happens to Autistic People in Prison?" Posted April 24, 2017 on the "Thinking Person's Guide to Autism." http://www.thinkingautismguide.com/2017/04/what-happens-to-autistic-people-in.html.

Desai, Rani A., Joseph L. Goulet, Judith Robbins, John F. Chapman, Scott J. Migdole, and Michael A. Hoge. 2006. "Mental Health Care in Juvenile Detention Facilities: A Review." *Journal of the American Academy of Psychiatry and the Law* 34, 2: 204–14.

Development Services Group. 2017. "Youths with Intellectual and Developmental Disabilities in the Juvenile Justice System." *Literature Review*. Washington, DC: Office of Juvenile Justice and Delinquency Prevention. https://www.ojjdp.gov/mpg/litreviews/Intellectual-Developmental-Disabilities.pdf.

Dicker, Sheryl, and Robert Marion. 2012. "Judicial Spectrum Primer: What Judges Need to Know about Children with Autism Spectrum Disorders." *Juvenile and Family Court Journal* 63, 2: 1–19.

Dilulio, John, Jr. 1995. "The Coming of the Super-Predators." *Weekly Standard* 1, 11: 23–30.

Disability Independence Group. n.d. "The Wallet Card Application." http://www.justdigit.org/wallet-cards/.

Doepke, Matthias, and Fabrizio Zilibotti. 2005. "The Macroeconomics of Child Labor Regulation." *American Economic Review* 95, 5: 1492–524.

Dolmage, Jay Timothy. 2014. *Disability Rhetoric*. New York: Syracuse University Press.

Donvan, John Joseph, and Caren Brenda Zucker. 2016. *In a Different Key: The Story of Autism*. New York: Broadway Books.

Dowden, Craig, and Don A. Andrews. 1999. "What Works in Young Offender Treatment: A Meta-Analysis." *Forum on Corrections Research*. 11: 21–24.

–. 2004. "The Importance of Staff Practice in Delivering Effective Correctional Treatment: A Meta-Analytic Review of Core Correctional Practice." *International Journal of Offender Therapy and Comparative Criminology* 48, 2: 203–14.

Drapela, Laurie A., and Dana Lee Baker. 2014. "Policy Awareness, Financial Hardship, and Work Impact: Correlates of Negative Experiences with Health Care Providers and Health Care Insurers among Caregivers of Children with Autism Spectrum Disorder." *SAGE Open* 4, 3: 1–13.

Eaves, Linda C., and Helena H. Ho. 1997. "School Placement and Academic Achievement in Children with Autistic Spectrum Disorders." *Journal of Developmental and Physical Disabilities* 9, 4: 277–91.

Ecenbarger, William. 2012. *Kids for Cash: Two Judges, Thousands of Children, and a $2.8 Million Kickback Scheme*. New York: The New Press.

Edmonton Police Service. n.d. "School Resource Officers (SROs)." http://www.edmontonpolice.ca/CommunityPolicing/FamilyProtection/SchoolResourceOfficers.aspx.

Eggleston, A. 2007. "Perceptual Punishment: The Consequences of Adult Convictions for Youth." *Policy Brief: Adultification Series* 4: 1–18.

Elkin, William F. 1982. "Rethinking Bill 82: A Critical Examination of Mandatory Special Education Legislation in Ontario." *Ottawa Law Review* 14: 314–39.

Ellenberg, Jordan. 2015. *How Not to Be Wrong: The Power of Mathematical Thinking*. New York: Penguin Books.

Elliott, April S., and Debra K. Katzman. 2011. "Youth Justice and Health: An Argument against Proposed Changes to the Youth Criminal Justice Act." *Paediatrics and Child Health* 16, 7: 414.

Epstein, Rebecca, Jamilia J. Blake, and Thalia González. 2017. "Girlhood Interrupted: The Erasure of Black Girls' Childhood." *Georgetown Law Center on Poverty and Inequality:* 1–19.

Erickson, W., C. Lee, and S. von Schrader. 2014. "Disability Statistics from the 2012 American Community Survey." Ithaca, NY: Cornell University Employment and Disability Institute.

Erikson, Erik H. 1993. *Childhood and Society.* New York: W.W. Norton.

Espinoza, Reginaldo Chase, and Debra Warner. 2015. "The Potential for Change in Rehabilitation and Reentry for Behaviorally and Mentally Disordered Offenders in the Post-Affordable Care Act and Second Chance Act Health Care Climate." *Journal of Economics and Banking* 2.

Family Support Institute of BC. 2013. "Stop Hurting Kids: Restraint and Seclusion in British Columbia Schools – Survey Results and Recommendations." November.

Farrington, David P. 2003. "Developmental and Life Course Criminology: Key Theoretical and Empirical Issues." *Criminology* 41, 2: 221–25.

Federal Bureau of Prisons. n.d. "About Our Agency." https://www.bop.gov/about/agency/.

Feld, Barry C. 2003. "The Politics of Race and Juvenile Justice: The 'Due Process Revolution' and the Conservative Reaction." *Justice Quarterly* 20, 4: 765–800.

Feldman, Heidi, Buysse Christina, Hubner Lauren, Huffman Lynne, and Loe Irene. 2015. "Patient Protection and Affordable Care Act of 2010 and Children and Youth with Special Health Care Needs." *Journal of Developmental and Behavioral Pediatrics* 36, 3: 207–17.

Feldstein, Sarah W., and Joel I.D. Ginsburg. 2007. "Sex, Drugs, and Rock 'n' Rolling with Resistance: Motivational Interviewing in Juvenile Justice Settings." In *Handbook of Forensic Mental Health with Victims and Offenders: Assessment, Treatment and Research.* New York; Springer, 247–71.

Flores, Glenn, Hua Lin, Candy Walker, Michael Lee, Janet M. Currie, Rick Allgeyer, Marco.

Fierro, Monica Henry, Alberto Portillo, and Kenneth Massey. 2016. "Parent Mentors and Insuring Uninsured Children: A Randomized Controlled Trial." *Pediatrics* 137, 4.

Foster, E. Michael, Amir Qaseem, and Tim Connor. 2004. "Can Better Mental Health Services Reduce the Risk of Juvenile Justice System Involvement?" *American Journal of Public Health* 94, 5: 859–65.

Foucault, Michel. *Madness and Civilization: A History of Insanity in the Age of Reason.* 1988. New York: Vintage.

Frase, Richard S. 2005. "Punishment Purposes." *Stanford Law Review* 58: 67–83.

Freckelton, Ian. 2013. "Autism Spectrum Disorder: Forensic Issues and Challenges for Mental Health Professionals and Courts." *Journal of Applied Research in Intellectual Disabilities* 26, 5: 420–34.

Fritz, Mike, and April Brown. 2012. "Juvenile Education: Inside a Confined World." PBS online. February 2. http://www.pbs.org/newshour/updates/american-graduate-jan-june12-richardross_02-02/.

Gaarder, Emily, Nancy Rodriguez, and Marjorie S. Zatz. 2004. "Criers, Liars, and Manipulators: Probation Officers' Views of Girls." *Justice Quarterly* 21, 3: 547–78.

Gagnon, Douglas J., Marybeth J. Mattingly, and Vincent J. Connelly. 2017. "The Restraint and Seclusion of Students with a Disability: Examining Trends in US School Districts and Their Policy Implications." *Journal of Disability Policy Studies* 28, 2: 66–76.

Galer, Dustin. 2015. Disability Rights Movement in Canada" *Historica Canada*. http://www.thecanadianencyclopedia.ca/en/article/disability-rights-movement/.

Gallagher, Tiffany L., and Sheila Bennett. 2015. "A Canadian Perspective on the Inclusion of Students with Intellectual Disabilities in High Schools." In *Inclusive Education for Students with Intellectual Disabilities*, edited by Rhonda G. Craven, Alexandre J.S. Morin, Danielle Tracey, and Hua Flora Zhong. Charlotte, NC: Information Age, 25–44.

Gergelis, Kristyn, Jonathan Kole, and Elizabeth A. Lowenhaupt. 2016. "Health Care Needs of Incarcerated Adolescents." *Rhode Island Medical Journal* 99, 9: 24–26.

Gilman, Amanda B., Karl G. Hill, and J. David Hawkins. 2015. "When Is a Youth's Debt to Society Paid? Examining the Long-Term Consequences of Juvenile Incarceration for Adult Functioning." *Journal of Developmental and Life-Course Criminology* 1, 1: 33–47.

Gilmour, Robert S., and Laura S. Jensen. 1998. "Reinventing Government Accountability: Public Functions, Privatization, and the Meaning of 'State Action.'" *Public Administration Review:* 247–58.

Gobbo, Ken, and Solvegi Shmulsky. 2016. "Autistic Identity Development and Postsecondary Education." *Disability Studies Quarterly* 36: 1–17.

Goldstein, Dana. 2016. "Who's a Kid?" The Marshall Project. October 27. https://www.themarshallproject.org/2016/10/27/who-s-a-kid#.nBeV3Zcde.

Goolsby, Wendy, Michael Worman, Kazim Jafri, and Madison Harden. (forthcoming). http://www.cistudentresearch.com/wp-content/uploads/2018/08/Summer-SURF-Celebration-Presentation-2018.pdf.

Gordon, Leslie A. 2016. "Autism Awareness Project Trains Pennsylvania's Juvenile Judges." *ABA Journal,* September 1. http://www.abajournal.com/magazine/article/autism_awareness_pennsylvania_juvenile_courts.

Gordon-Lipkin, Eliza, Jessica Foster, and Georgina Peacock. 2016. "Whittling Down the Wait Time: Exploring Models to Minimize the Delay from Initial Concern to Diagnosis and Treatment of Autism Spectrum Disorder." *Pediatric Clinics of North America* 63, 5: 851–59.

Government of Canada. 2017. "Health Care in Canada." July 11. http://www.cic.gc.ca/english/newcomers/after-health.asp.

–. 2018. "A Report of the National Autism Spectrum Disorder Surveillance System." April 9. https://www.canada.ca/en/public-health/services/publications/diseases-conditions/autism-spectrum-disorder-children-youth-canada-2018.html#a2-1.

Griffin, Patrick, Sean Addie, Benjamin Adams, and Kathy Firestine. 2011. *Trying Juveniles as Adults: An Analysis of State Transfer Laws and Reporting*. Washington, DC: US Department of Justice, Office of Justice Programs, Office of Juvenile Justice and Delinquency Prevention.

Grisso, Thomas, and Lee A. Underwood. 2004. *Screening and Assessing Mental Health and Substance Use Disorders among Youth in the Juvenile Justice System: A Resource Guide for Practitioners*. Washington, DC: United States Department of Justice.

Gupta, Samarth. 2015. "School Shootings: An American Problem?" *Harvard Political Review*. April 19. http://harvardpolitics.com/special_features/gun.html.

Gurney, Kyra. 2018. "Handcuffs and a Pysch Exam for a 7-Year-Old?" *Miami Herald*. February 2. https://www.miamiherald.com/news/local/education/article 197958454.html.

Hackney, Donald D., Daniel Friesner, and Erica H. Johnson. 2016. "What Is the Actual Prevalence of Medical Bankruptcies?" *International Journal of Social Economics* 43, 12: 1284–99.

Hagner, David, JoAnne M. Malloy, Melanie W. Mazzone, and Gail M. Cormier. 2008. "Youth with Disabilities in the Criminal Justice System Considerations for Transition and Rehabilitation Planning." *Journal of Emotional and Behavioral Disorders* 16, 4: 240–47.

Hall, Alicia V., Michele Godwin, Harry H. Wright, and Ruth K. Abramson. 2007. "Criminal Justice Issues and Autistic Disorder." In *Growing Up with Autism: Working with School Age Children and Adolescents*, edited by Robin L. Gabriels and Dina E. Hill, 272–92. New York: Guilford Press.

Hamilton-Wentworth Catholic District School Board. 2015. "Believing, Achieving, Serving: Transition Planning Handbook for Students with Special Education Needs." April. Accessed on February 21, 2020. http://www.edugains.ca/resourcesSpecEd/IEP&Transitions/BoardDevelopedResources/TransitionPlanning/SupportGuides/Transition_Planning_Handbook_Students_Special_Education_Needs_HReferencesDSB.pdf.

Hamilton-Wentworth District School Board. 2017. "HWDSB System Programs: Gateway Program." February 27. http://www.hwdsb.on.ca/altered/gateway-program/#non-academic.

Haqanee, Zohrah, Michele Peterson-Badali, and Tracey Skilling. 2015. "Making 'What Works' Work: Examining Probation Officers' Experiences Addressing the Criminogenic Needs of Juvenile Offenders." *Journal of Offender Rehabilitation* 54, 1: 37–59.

Harrell, Erica. 2015. "Crime against Persons with Disabilities." Bureau of Justice Statistics, Department of Justice. May. https://www.bjs.gov/content/pub/pdf/capd0913st.pdf.

Henggeler, Scott W., and Sonja K. Schoenwald. 2011. "Evidence-Based Interventions for Juvenile Offenders and Juvenile Justice Policies that Support Them." *Society for Research in Child Development: Social Policy Report* 25, 1.

Henry, Jessica S. 2009. "The Second Chance Act of 2007." *Criminal Law Bulletin* 45, 3: 3–19.

Raymond R. Corrado, and Susan Reid, 41. Toronto: University of Toronto Press.

Hillian, Doug, and Marge Reitsma-Street. 2003. "Parents and Youth Justice." *Canadian Journal of Criminology and Criminal Justice* 45, 1: 19–41.

Hillmer, Norman, and Richard Foot. 2015. "Statute of Westminster." Historica Canada. http://www.thecanadianencyclopedia.ca/en/article/statute-of-westminster/.

Hincks, Crystal, and John Winterdyk. 2016. "The Youth Justice System: An Alberta Overview." In *Implementing and Working with the Youth Criminal Justice Act across Canada*, edited by Marc Alain,

Historica Canada. 2013. "Constitution Act of 1982." http://www.thecanadianencyclopedia.ca/en/article/constitution-act-1982-document/.

Hockenberry, Sarah. 2016. *Juveniles in Residential Placement, 2013*. Washington, DC: US Department of Justice, Office of Justice Programs, Office of Juvenile Justice and Delinquency Prevention.

Hockenberry, Sarah, and Puzzanchera, Charles. 2015. Juvenile Court Statistics 2013. Pittsburgh, PA: National Center for Juvenile Justice.

Hogan, Kathleen A., Lyndal M. Bullock, and Eric J. Fritsch. 2010. "Meeting the Transition Needs of Incarcerated Youth with Disabilities." *Journal of Correctional Education* 61, 2: 133–47.

Hoge, Robert. 2008. "Introduction to the Canadian Juvenile Justice System." 139th International Training Course for United Nations Asia and Far East Institute for the Prevention of Crime and the Treatment of Offenders. Resource Material Series no. 78. https://www.unafei.or.jp/publications/pdf/RS_No78/No78_00All.pdf.

Hollimon, Sandra E. 2015. "Third Gender." In *The International Encyclopedia of Human Sexuality*. New York: John Wiley and Sons: 1355–1404.

hooks, bell. 1981. *Ain't I a Woman: Black Women and Feminism*. Boston: South End Press.

Hovbrender, Axel, and Silvia Ursula Raschke. 2009. *Identification of Potential Risk Factors for Injury to Police Officers in Using New Technologies*. Richmond, BC: WorkSafeBC.

Hulett, Kurt. 2009. *Legal Aspects of Special Education*. Upper Saddle River, NJ: Pearson Education.

Humes, Edward. 2015. *No Matter How Loud I Shout: A Year in the Life of Juvenile Court*. New York: Simon and Schuster.

Irvine, Angela. 2010. "We've Had Three of Them: Addressing the Invisibility of Lesbian, Gay, Bisexual, and Gender Nonconforming Youths in the Juvenile Justice System." *Columbia Journal of Gender and Law* 19: 675.

James, Chrissy, Geert Jan JM Stams, Jessica J. Asscher, Anne Katrien De Roo, and Peter H. van der Laan. 2013. "Aftercare Programs for Reducing Recidivism among Juvenile and Young Adult Offenders: A Meta-Analytic Review." *Clinical Psychology Review* 33, 2: 263–74.

Jennings, Wesley G., Rolf Loeber, Dustin A. Pardini, Alex R. Piquero, and David P. Farrington. 2015. *Offending from Childhood to Young Adulthood: Recent Results from the Pittsburgh Youth Study*. New York: Springer.

Johnston, Emily E., Bianca R. Argueza, Caroline Graham, Janine S. Bruce, Lisa J. Chamberlain, and Arash Anoshiravani. 2016. "In Their Own Voices: The Reproductive Health Care Experiences of Detained Adolescent Girls." *Women's Health Issues* 26, 1: 48–54.

Jones, Kyle B., Kristina Cottle, Amanda Bakian, Megan Farley, Deborah Bilder, Hilary Coon, and William M. McMahon. 2016. "A Description of Medical Conditions in Adults with Autism Spectrum Disorder: A Follow-Up of the 1980s Utah/UCLA Autism Epidemiologic Study." *Autism* 20, 5: 551–61.

Jongbloed, Lyn. 2003. "Disability Policy in Canada: An Overview." *Journal of Disability Policy Studies* 13, 4: 203–9.

Justice Institute of British Columbia. "Program Guide." https://www.jibc.ca/.

Kalef, Sandy. 2000. "Hard Times for Youth Crime." *Alberta Views*. September 1. https://albertaviews.ca/hard-times-youth-crime/.

Kamenetz, Anya, and Cory Turner. 2017. "The Supreme Court Rules in Favor of Special Education Student." National Public Radio. March 22. http://www.npr.org/sections/ed/2017/03/22/521094752/the-supreme-court-rules-in-favor-of-a-special-education-student.

Kempf-Leonard, Kimberly. 2007. "Minority Youths and Juvenile Justice: Disproportionate Minority Contact after Nearly 20 Years of Reform Efforts." *Youth Violence and Juvenile Justice* 5, 1: 71–87.

Khan, Yasmeen. 2016. "Getting Students with Autism through High School, to College and Beyond." National Public Radio. December 18. http://www.wnyc.org/story/getting-students-with-autism-through-high-school-to-college-and-beyond/.

King, Claire, and Glynis H. Murphy. 2014. "A Systematic Review of People with Autism Spectrum Disorder and the Criminal Justice System." *Journal of Autism and Developmental Disorders* 44, 11: 2717–33.

Kingdon, John. 2010. *Agendas, Alternatives, and Public Policites: Updated Edition with an Epilogue on Health Care.* New York: Pearson.

Kirchner, Lauren. 2014. "The Cost of Juvenile Incarceration." Justice Policy Institute, December 11. http://www.justicepolicy.org/news/8570.

Kong, Rebecca. 2009. "Youth Custody and Community Services in Canada, 2007/2008." *Juristat* 29, 2: 4–25.

Kovacs Burns, Katharina, and Gary L. Gordon. 2010. "Analyzing the Impact of Disability Legislation in Canada and the United States." *Journal of Disability Policy* 20, 4: 205–18.

Knupfer, Anne Meis. 2001. *Reform and Resistance: Gender, Delinquency, and America's First Juvenile Court.* London: Routledge.

Kraft, Michael E., and Scott R. Furlong. 2012. *Public Policy: Politics, Analysis, and Alternatives.* CQ Press.

Kretschmar, Jeff M., Fredrick Butcher, Daniel J. Flannery, and Mark I. Singer. 2016. "Diverting Juvenile Justice-Involved Youth with Behavioral Health Issues from Detention: Preliminary Findings from Ohio's Behavioral Health Juvenile Justice (BHJJ) Initiative." *Criminal Justice Policy Review* 27, 3: 302–25.

Kretschmar, Jeff M., Krystel Tossone, Fredrick Butcher, and Daniel J. Flannery. 2017. "Patterns of Poly-Victimization in a Sample of At-Risk Youth." *Journal of Child and Adolescent Trauma* 10, 4: 363–75.

Kulis, Stephen, Tanya Nieri, Scott Yabiku, Layne K. Stromwall, and Flavio Francisco Marsiglia. 2007. "Promoting Reduced and Discontinued Substance Use among Adolescent Substance Users: Effectiveness of a Universal Prevention Program." *Prevention Science* 8, 1: 35–49.

Kurzer, Paulette, and Alice Cooper. 2007. "Consumer Activism, EU Institutions and Global Markets: The Struggle over Biotech Foods." *Journal of Public Policy* 27, 2: 103–28.

Kvarfordt, Connie L., Patricia Purcell, and Patrick Shannon. 2005. "Youth with Learning Disabilities in the Juvenile Justice system: A Training Needs Assessment of Detention and Court Services Personnel." *Child and Youth Care Forum* 34, 1: 27–42.

Lai, Meng-Chuan, Michael V. Lombardo, Bonnie Auyeung, Bhismadev Chakrabarti, and Simon Baron-Cohen. 2015. "Sex/Gender Differences and Autism: Setting the Scene for Future Research." *Journal of the American Academy of Child and Adolescent Psychiatry* 54, 1: 11–24.

Lamoureux, Mack. 2015. "Canada's Courts Are Failing Offenders with Mental Illness." Vice Media, May 1. http://www.vice.com/read/how-the-canadian.

Landenberger, Nana A., and Mark W. Lipsey. 2005. "The Positive Effects of Cognitive-Behavioral Programs for Offenders: A Meta-Analysis of Factors Associated with Effective Treatment." *Journal of Experimental Criminology* 1, 4: 451–76.

Laub, John H., and Robert J. Sampson. 2003. *Shared Beginnings, Divergent Lives: Delinquent Boys to Age 70*. Cambridge, MA: Harvard University Press.

Laub, John H., Robert J. Sampson, and Gary A. Sweeten. 2006. "Assessing Sampson and Laub's Life-Course Theory of Crime." In *Taking Stock: The Status of Criminological Theory*, edited by Francis T. Cullen, John Paul Wright, and Kristie R. Blevins, 313–31. New Brunswick, NJ: Transaction.

Lawrence, Richard. 2006. *School Crime and Juvenile Justice*, 2nd ed. New York: Oxford University Press.

Leiber, Michael, Donna Bishop, and Mitchell B. Chamlin. 2011. "Juvenile Justice Decision Making Before and After the Implementation of the Disproportionate Minority Contact (DMC) Mandate." *Justice Quarterly* 28, 3: 460–92.

Leiber, Michael J., and Kristin Y. Mack. 2003. "The Individual and Joint Effects of Race, Gender, and Family Status on Juvenile Justice Decision-Making." *Journal of Research in Crime and Delinquency* 40, 1: 34–70.

Leiter, Valerie. 2004. "Parental Activism, Professional Dominance, and Early Childhood Disability." *Disability Studies Quarterly* 24, 2.

Leone, Peter, Mary Magee Quinn, and David M. Osher. 2002. "Collaboration in the Juvenile Justice System and Youth Serving Agencies: Improving Prevention, Providing More Efficient Services, and Reducing Recidivism for Youth with Disabilities." *Monograph Series on Education, Disability and Juvenile Justice*.

Leone, Peter E., and Sheri Meisel. 1997. "Improving Education Services for Students in Detention and Confinement Facilities." *Child Legal Rights Journal* 17: 2.

Leone, Peter E., Sherri Meisel, and Will Drakeford. 2003. "Special Education Programs for Youth with Disabilities in Juvenile Corrections." *Journal of Juvenile Court, Community, and Alternative School* 16: 31–37.

Lerner, Matthew D., Omar Sultan Haque, Eli C. Northrup, Lindsay Lawer, and Harold J. Bursztajn. 2012. "Emerging Perspectives on Adolescents and Young Adults with High-Functioning Autism Spectrum Disorders, Violence, and Criminal Law." *Journal of the American Academy of Psychiatry and the Law Online* 40, 2: 177–90.

Lewis, Alexandra, Robert Pritchett, Clare Hughes, and Kim Turner. 2015. "Development and Implementation of Autism Standards for Prisons." *Journal of Intellectual Disabilities and Offending Behaviour* 6, 2: 68–80.

Liebenberg, Linda, and Michael Ungar. 2014. "A Comparison of Service Use Among Youth Involved with Juvenile Justice and Mental Health." *Children and Youth Services Review* 39: 117–22.

Lim, Chong Ming. 2015. "Accommodating Autistics and Treating Autism: Can We Have Both?" *Bioethics* 29, 8: 564–72.

Lindblom, Charles E. 1979. "Still Muddling, Not Yet Through." *Public Administration Review* 39, 6: 517–26.

Lipsey, Mark W., and Francis T. Cullen. 2007. "The Effectiveness of Correctional Rehabilitation: A Review of Systematic Reviews." *Annual Review of Law and Social Science* 3: 297–320.

Lleras-Muney, Adriana. 2002. "Were Compulsory Attendance and Child Labor Laws Effective? An Analysis from 1915 to 1939." *Journal of Law and Economics* 45, 2: 401–35.

Lo, Bee H., Felicity Klopper, Elizabeth H. Barnes, and Katrina Williams. 2017. "Agreement between Concern about Autism Spectrum Disorder at the Time of

Referral and Diagnosis, and Factors Associated with Agreement." *Journal of Paediatrics and Child Health* 53, 8: 742–48.

Loughran, Thomas A., Alex R. Piquero, Jeffrey Fagan, and Edward P. Mulvey. 2012. "Differential Deterrence: Studying Heterogeneity and Changes in Perceptual Deterrence among Serious Youthful Offenders." *Crime and Delinquency* 58, 1: 3–27.

Lubell, Mark. 2013. "Governing Institutional Complexity: The Ecology of Games Framework." *Policy Studies Journal* 41, 3: 537–59.

Mack, Julian W. 1909. "The Juvenile Court." *Harvard Law Review:* 107.

Macomber, Donna, Thomas Skiba, Jaime Blackmon, Elisa Esposito, Lesley Hart, Elisa Mambrino, Thompson Richie, and Elena L. Grigorenko. 2010. "Education in Juvenile Detention Facilities in the State of Connecticut: A Glance at the System." *Journal of Correctional Education* 61, 3: 223–61.

Madden, Jeanne M., Matthew D. Lakoma, Frances L. Lynch, Donna Rusinak, Ashli A. Owen-Smith, Karen J. Coleman, Virginia P. Quinn, Vincent M. Yau, Yinge X. Qian, and Lisa A. Croen. 2017. "Psychotropic Medication Use among Insured Children with Autism Spectrum Disorder." *Journal of Autism and Developmental Disorders* 47, 1: 144–54.

Maden, Monique O. 2015. "Coral Gables Police Department Introduces Tool for Autistic Residents." *Miami Herald.* January 28. http://www.miamiherald.com/news/local/community/miami-dade/coral-gables/article8523989.html.

Maggard, Scott R. 2015. "Assessing the Impact of the Juvenile Detention Alternatives Initiative (JDAI): Predictors of Secure Detention and Length of Stay Before and After JDAI." *Justice Quarterly* 32, 4: 571–97.

Malakieh, Jamil. 2017. "Youth correctional statistics in Canada, 2015/2016." *Juristat: Canadian Centre for Justice Statistics:* 3–15.

Malatesta, Deanna, and Julia L. Carboni. 2015. "The Public–Private Distinction: Insights for Public Administration from the State Action Doctrine." *Public Administration Review* 75, 1: 63–74.

Mallett, Christopher A. 2011. "Seven Things Juvenile Courts Should Know about Learning Disabilities." *National Council of Juvenile and Family Court Judges.* Reno, NV: 1–20.

–. 2012. "Youth with Learning Disabilities: Seven Things Juvenile Courts Should Know." *Juvenile and Family Court Journal* 63, 3: 55–71.

–. 2013. *Linking Disorders to Delinquency: Treating High-Risk Youth in the Juvenile Justice System.* Boulder, Colorado: First Forum Press.

–. 2014. "Youthful Offending and Delinquency: The Comorbid Impact of Maltreatment, Mental Health Problems, and Learning Disabilities." *Child and Adolescent Social Work Journal* 31, 4: 369–92.

–. 2015. *The School-to-Prison Pipeline: A Comprehensive Assessment.* New York: Springer.

Mann, Ruth, 2014. "Canada's Amended Youth Criminal Justice Act and the Problem of Serious Persistent Youth Offenders: Deterrence and the Globalization of Juvenile Justice," *Journal of the Institute of Justice and International Studies* 14: 59–72.

Manna, Paul. 2011. *Collision Course: Federal Education Policy Meets State and Local Realities.* Washington, DC: CQ Press.

Marx, Teri A., and Joshua N. Baker. 2017. "Analysis of Restraint and Seclusion Legislation and Policy Across States: Adherence to Recommended Principles." *Journal of Disability Policy Studies* 28, 1: 23–31.

Maschi, Tina, Craig Schwalbe, and Jennifer Ristow. 2013. "In Pursuit of the Ideal Parent in Juvenile Justice: A Qualitative Investigation of Probation Officers' Experiences with Parents of Juvenile Offenders." *Journal of Offender Rehabilitation* 52, 7: 470–92.

Maschi, Tina, Schnavia Smith Hatcher, Craig S. Schwalbe, and Nancy Scotto Rosato. 2008. "Mapping the Social Service Pathways of Youth to and Through the Juvenile Justice System: A Comprehensive Review." *Children and Youth Services Review* 30, 12: 1376–85.

Matsueda, Ross L., Derek A. Kreager, and David Huizinga. 2006. "Deterring Delinquents: A Rational Choice Model of Theft and Violence." *American Sociological Review* 71, 1: 95–122.

Mayes, Thomas. 2003. "Persons with Autism and Criminal Justice: Core Concepts and Leading Cases." *Journal of Positive Behavior Interventions* 5: 92–100.

Mays, G. Larry, and L. Thomas Winfree, Jr. 2006. *Juvenile Justice*. 2nd ed. Long Grove, IL: Waveland Press.

McCauley, Erin J. 2017. "The Cumulative Probability of Arrest by Age 28 Years in the United States by Disability Status, Race/Ethnicity, and Gender." *American Journal of Public Health* 107, 12: 1977–81.

McCormick, Sarah, Michele Peterson-Badali, and Tracey A. Skilling. 2017. "The Role of Mental Health and Specific Responsivity in Juvenile Justice Rehabilitation." *Law and Human Behavior* 41, 1: 55.

McCrimmon, Adam W. 2015. "Inclusive Education in Canada: Issues in Teacher Preparation." *Intervention in School and Clinic* 50, 4: 234–37.

McFarland, Joel, Patrick Stark, and Jiashan Cui. 2016. "Trends in High School Dropout and Completion Rates in the United States: 2013. Compendium Report. NCES 2016-17." Washington, DC: National Center for Education Statistics.

McLeod, Jane D., and Timothy J. Owens. 2004. "Psychological Well-Being in the Early Life Course: Variations by Socioeconomic Status, Gender, and Race/Ethnicity." *Social Psychology Quarterly* 67, 3: 257–78.

Meagher-Stewart, Donna, Shirley M. Solberg, Grace Warner, Jo-Ann MacDonald, Charmaine McPherson, and Patricia Seaman. 2012. "Understanding the Role of Communities of Practice in Evidence-Informed Decision Making in Public Health." *Qualitative Health Research* 22, 6: 723–39.

Mears, Daniel P., and Laudan Y. Aron. 2003. "Addressing the Needs of Youth with Disabilities in the Juvenile Justice System: The Current State of Knowledge." Urban Institute, Justice Policy Center. http://webarchive.urban.org/UploadedPDF/410885_youth_with_disabilities.pdf.

Medicaid and CHIP. n.d. "The Children's Health Insurance Program (CHIP)." https://www.healthcare.gov/medicaid-chip/childrens-health-insurance-program/.

Mercer, Stewart W., Maria Higgins, Annemieke M. Bikker, Bridie Fitzpatrick, Alex McConnachie, Suzanne M. Lloyd, Paul Little, and Graham C.M. Watt. 2016. "General Practitioners' Empathy and Health Outcomes: A Prospective Observational Study of Consultations in Areas of High and Low Deprivation." *Annals of Family Medicine* 14, 2: 117–24.

Michalowski, Raymond J. 2016. "What Is Crime?" *Critical Criminology* 24, 2: 181–99.

Miladinovic, Zoran. 2016. "Youth Court Statistics in Canada, 2014/2015." *Juristat: Canadian Centre for Justice Statistics*: 3.

Mishra, Sandeep, and Martin Lalumière. 2009. "Is the Crime Drop of the 1990s in Canada and the USA Associated with a General Decline in Risky and Health-Related Behavior?" *Social Science and Medicine* 68, 1: 39–48.

Moreno, Sylvia. 2007. "In Texas, Scandals Rock Juvenile Justice System." *Washington Post*. April 5. Accessed on February 21, 2020. http://www.washingtonpost.com/wpdyn/content/article/2007/04/04/AR2007040402400.html.

Morris, Anne, and Malin Enstrom. 2016. "The Implementation of the *Youth Criminal Justice Act* in Newfoundland and Labrador: No Problem?" In *Implementing and Working with the Youth Criminal Justice Act across Canada*, edited by Marc Alain, Raymond R. Corrado, and Susan Reid, 159–98. Toronto: University of Toronto Press.

Motiuk, Laurence L. 2012. "The Effectiveness, Efficiency and Relevancy of Correctional Programs: A System's Perspective." *Res. Mater. Ser* 88: 14–21. https://www.unafei.or.jp/publications/pdf/RS_No88/No88_07VE_Motiuk_Effectiveness.pdf.

Nader, Anne-Marie, Valérie Courchesne, Michelle Dawson, and Isabelle Soulières. 2016. "Does WISC-IV Underestimate the Intelligence of Autistic Children?" *Journal of Autism and Developmental Disorders* 46, 5: 1582–89.

Nasser, Shanifa. 2017. "TDSB Decision to Scrap Officers in Schools Program Not 'Anti-Police,' Says Chair." *CBC News*. November 23. http://www.cbc.ca/news/canada/toronto/school-resource-officers-toronto-board-police-1.4415064.

National Center on Education, Disability and Juvenile Justice. n.d. *The Care for Quality Education in Juvenile Corrections Facilities*. http://www.edjj.org/focus/education/.

National Juvenile Justice Network. 2016. *Improving Educational Outcomes for Youth in the Juvenile Justice System*. March. www.njjn.org/our-work/improving-education-for-youth-in-juvenile-justice-snapshot.

Nelsen, Anne M. 2014. "Admission and Intake." *National Institute of Corrections' Desktop Guide to Quality Practice for Working with Youth in Confinement*. National Partnership for Juvenile Services and Office of Juvenile Justice and Delinquency Prevention.

Neufeldt, Aldred H. 2003. "Growth and Evolution of Disability Advocacy in Canada." In *Making Equality: History of Advocacy and Persons with Disability in Canada*, edited by Deborah Stienstra and Aileen Wight-Felske, 10–32. Concord, ON: Captus Press.

Noble, Ronald D. 1970. "The Struggle to Make the Accused Competent in England and in Canada." *Osgoode Hall Law Journal* 8: 249–75.

Obama, Barack. 2016. "United States Health Care Reform: Progress to Date and Next Steps." *Journal of the American Medical Association* 316, 5: 525–32.

O'Connor, Christopher D. 2017. "The Police on Twitter: Image Management, Community Building, and Implications for Policing in Canada." *Policing and Society* 27, 8: 899–912.

O'Donovan, Maeve M. 2010. "Cognitive Diversity in the Global Academy: Why the Voices of Persons with Cognitive Disabilities Are Vital to Intellectual Diversity." *Journal of Academic Ethics* 8, 3: 171–85.

Office for Civil Rights, US Department of Education. 2016. "Securing Equal Educational Opportunity: Report to the President and Secretary of Education." http://www2.ed.gov/about/reports/annual/ocr/report-to-president-and-secretary-of-education-2016.pdf.

Office of Special Education and Rehabilitative Services (OSERS). 2017. "Supporting Youth with Disabilities in Juvenile Corrections." *United State Department of Education.* May 23. https://sites.ed.gov/osers/2017/05/supporting-youth-with-disabilities-in-juvenile-corrections/.

—. "Supporting Youth with Disabilities in Juvenile Corrections." *United State Department of Education.* Accessed on December 16, 2019. https://www2.ed.gov/about/offices/list/osers/index.html.

Ohio State Bar Foundation. n.d. "O.P.E.N. Court Lets Youth with Exceptional Needs Learn about Court Proceedings." Accessed on February 21, 2020. http://www.courtnewsohio.gov/happening/2013/openCourt_100213.asp#.XfwvHWRKjIU.

OJJDP (Office of Juvenile Justice and Delinquency Prevention). 2013. "Juvenile Arrests 2011." *Juvenile Offenders and Victims: National Report Series Bulletin.* December. https://www.ojjdp.gov/pubs/244476.pdf.

—. 2015a. "Juvenile Arrest Rate Trends." *Statistical Briefing Book.* December 13. http://www.ojjdp.gov/ojstatbb/crime/JAR_Display.asp?ID=qa05200.

—. 2019. "Time in Placement." *Statistical Briefing Book.* February 23. https://www.ojjdp.gov/ojstatbb/corrections/qa08401.asp?qaDate=2017.

—. n.d. "Juveniles in Corrections: Overview." Accessed December 21, 2019. https://www.ojjdp.gov/ojstatbb/corrections/overview.html.

Oliver, M.E., K.C. Stockdale, and S.C. Wong. 2012. "Short and Long-Term Prediction of Recidivism Using the Youth Level of Service/Case Management Inventory in a Sample of Serious Young Offenders." *Law and Human Behavior* 36, 4: 331–44.

Omura, John D., Evan Wood, Paul Nguyen, Thomas Kerr, and Kora DeBeck. 2014. "Incarceration among Street-Involved Youth in a Canadian Study: Implications for Health and Policy Interventions." *International Journal of Drug Policy* 25, 2: 291–96.

Ontario Justice Education Network. 2009. "The Top Five – 2005." http://ojen.ca/wp-content/uploads/Auton-v-AG-of-British-columbia-Aug-2009.pdf.

Ontario Ministry of Children and Youth Services. 2015. *Supporting Effective Transitions for Ontario Youth: A Reintegration Resource.* Ontario Ministry of Children and Youth Services, February. http://www.children.gov.on.ca/htdocs/English/documents/youthandthelaw/ReintegrationResource.pdf.

—. 2016a. "About the Ministry." July 7. http://www.children.gov.on.ca/htdocs/English/about/index.aspx.

—. 2016b. "Youth Justice: Secure and Open Custody/Detention." http://www.children.gov.on.ca/htdocs/English/professionals/childwelfare/residential/residential-review-panel-report/youthjustice.aspx.

—. 2016c. "Guidelines: Bridging Children from Intensive Behavioral Intervention Services to the New Ontario Autism Program." *Ministry of Children and Youth Services.* July. Accessed on February 21, 2020. http://www.children.gov.on.ca/htdocs/English/documents/specialneeds/autism/TransitioningIBIGuidelines2016.pdf.

—. n.d. "Ontario Autism Program." http://www.children.gov.on.ca/htdocs/English/specialneeds/autism/ontario-autism-program.aspx.

Ontario Ministry of Education. 2010. *Caring and Safe Schools in Ontario: Supporting Students with Special Education Needs through Progressive Discipline, Kindergarten to Grade 12.* Toronto: Queen's Printer for Ontario.

Orsini, Michael, and Miriam Smith. 2010. "Social Movements, Knowledge and Public Policy: The Case of Autism Activism in Canada and the US." *Critical Policy Studies* 4, 1: 38–57.

Osborne, Allan G. Jr., and Charles J. Russo. 2014. *Special Education and the Law: A Guide for Practitioners*. Thousand Oaks, CA: Corwin Press.

O'Sullivan, Owen P. 2017. "Autism Spectrum Disorder and Criminal Responsibility: Historical Perspectives, Clinical Challenges and Broader Considerations within the Criminal Justice System." *Irish Journal of Psychological Medicine*: 1–7.

Paik, Leslie. 2017. "Good Parents, Bad Parents: Rethinking Family Involvement in Juvenile Justice." *Theoretical Criminology* 21, 3: 307–23.

Palmer, Karen. 1999. "A Brief History: Universal Health Care Efforts in the US." Presented at the 1999 Physicians for a National Health Program." http://www.pnhp.org/facts/a-brief-history-universal-health-care-efforts-in-the-us.

Pasha, Shaheen. 2017. "The U.S. Justice System Has an Autism Problem." *Dallas Morning News*. August 15. https://www.dallasnews.com/opinion/commentary/2017/08/15/us-justice-system-autism-problem.

Paternoster, Raymond. 2010. "How Much Do We Really Know about Criminal Deterrence?" *Journal of Criminal Law and Criminology* 100, 3: 765–24.

Paterson, Philip. 2007. "How Well Do Young Offenders with Asperger Syndrome Cope in Custody?" *British Journal of Learning Disabilities* 36: 54–58.

Payette, Glenn. 2015. "RNC Officer in Dane Spurrell Autism Case Criticized Again." *CBC News*, 17 March. https://www.cbc.ca/news/canada/newfoundland-labrador/rnc-officer-in-dane-spurrell-autism-case-criticized-again-1.2997947.

Peel District School Board. n.d. "Peel Alternative School." http://schools.peelschools.org/sec/pas/academic/programs/Freshstart/Pages/default.aspx.

Penner, Melanie. 2016. "Policy Analysis and Evaluation of National Clinician-Reported Practices for the Diagnosis of Autism Spectrum Disorder." PhD diss., University of Toronto.

Perlin, Michael L., and Alison J. Lynch. 2017. "'She's Nobody's Child/the Law Can't Touch Her at All': Seeking to Bring Dignity to Legal Proceedings Involving Juveniles." *New York Law School Legal Studies Research Paper* no. 2912499. February 7. https://papers.ssrn.com/sol3/papers.cfm?abstract_id=2912499##.

Perry, Raymond C.W., and Robert E. Morris. 2014. "Health Care for Youth Involved with the Correctional System." *Primary Care: Clinics in Office Practice* 41: 691–705.

Pesco, Diane, Andrea A. MacLeod, Elizabeth Kay-Raining Bird, Patricia Cleave, Natacha Trudeau, Julia Scherba de Valenzuela, Kate Cain, Stefka H. Mannova-Todd, Paola Colozzo, Hillary Stahl, Eliane Segers, and Ludo Verhoeven. 2016. "A Multi-Site Review of Policies Affecting Opportunities for Children with Developmental Disabilities to Become Bilingual." *Journal of Communication Disorders* 63: 15–31.

Peterson-Badali, Michele, and Julia Broeking. 2009. "Parents' Involvement in the Youth Justice System: A View from the Trenches." *Canadian Journal of Criminology and Criminal Justice* 51, 1: 255–70.

–. 2010. "Parents' Involvement in the Youth Justice System: Rhetoric and Reality." *Canadian Journal of Criminology and Criminal Justice* 52, 1: 1–27.

Petrosino, Anthony, Carolyn Turpin-Petrosino, and James O. Finckenauer. 2000. "Well-Meaning Programs Can Have Harmful Effects! Lessons from Experiments of Programs Such as Scared Straight." *Crime and Delinquency* 46, 3: 354–79.

Philpott, D.F., and C.A.M. Fiedorowicz. 2012. *The Supreme Court of Canada Ruling on Learning Disabilities*. Ottawa: Learning Disabilities Association of Canada.

Piaget, Jean. 1951. *The Child's Conception of the World*. New York: Rowman and Littlefield.
Pielke, Roger A., Jr. 2007. *The Honest Broker: Making Sense of Science in Policy and Politics*. Cambridge: Cambridge University Press.
Pieper, Kevin. 2012. "Smart911 Being Adopted by a Growing Number of Communities." *USA Today*. July 12. http://usatoday30.usatoday.com/news/nation/story/2012-07-12/smart911-database/56285514/1.
Pinker, Steven. 2012. *The Better Angels of Our Nature: Why Violence Has Declined*. New York: Penguin Books.
"PIPEDA in Brief." 2019. *Office of the Privacy Commissioner of Canada*. https://www.priv.gc.ca/en/privacy-topics/privacy-laws-in-canada/the-personal-information-protection-and-electronic-documents-act-pipeda/pipeda_brief/.
Piquero, Alex R., David P. Farrington, and Alfred Blumstein. 2003. "The Criminal Career Paradigm." *Crime and Justice: A Review of Research* 30: 359–506.
Pitney, John J., Jr. 2015. *The Politics of Autism: Navigating the Contested Spectrum*. New York: Rowman and Littlefield.
Platt, Anthony M. 2009. *The Child Savers: The Invention of Delinquency*. New Jersey: Rutgers University Press.
Poteat, V. Paul, Jillian R. Scheer, and Eddie S.K. Chong. 2016. "Sexual Orientation-Based Disparities in School and Juvenile Justice Discipline: A Multiple Group Comparison of Contributing Factors." *Journal of Educational Psychology* 108, 2: 229–41.
Prince, Michael J. 2002. "Designing Disability Policy in Canada: The Nature and Impact of Federalism on Policy Development." In *Federalism, Democracy, and Disability Policy in Canada*, edited by Alan Puttee, 29–77. Kingston, ON: McGill-Queen's University Press.
–. 2009. *Absent Citizens: Disability Politics and Policy in Canada*. Toronto: University of Toronto Press.
Prizant, Barry M. 2016. *Uniquely Human: A Different Way of Seeing Autism*. New York: Simon and Schuster.
Public Health Agency of Canada. 2018. "Autism Spectrum Disorder among Children and Youth in Canada 2018." March 29. https://www.canada.ca/en/public-health.
Pullmann, Michael D., Jodi Kerbs, Nancy Koroloff, Ernie Veach-White, Rita Gaylor, and Dede Sieler. 2006. "Juvenile Offenders with Mental Health Needs: Reducing Recidivism Using Wraparound." *Crime and Delinquency* 52, 3: 375–97.
Puritz, Patricia, and Mary Ann Scali. 1998. *Beyond the Walls: Improving Conditions of Confinement for Youth in Custody*. Rockville, MD: Juvenile Justice Clearinghouse/NCJRS. http://files.eric.ed.gov/fulltext/ED419201.pdf.
Puzzanchera, Charles, and Steven Hockenberry. 2017. "National Disproportionate Minority Contact Databook." National Center for Juvenile Justice and the Office of Juvenile Justice and Delinquency Prevention. August. http://www.ojjdp.gov/ojstatbb/dmcdb/.
Quinn, Mary Magee, Robert Rutherford, Peter Leone, David Osher, and Jeffery Poirier. 2005. "Youth with Disabilities in Juvenile Corrections: A National Survey." *Exceptional Children* 71, 3: 339–45.
Raby, Rebecca. 2005. "Polite, Well-Dressed and on Time: Secondary School Conduct Codes and the Production of Docile Citizens." *Canadian Review of Sociology* 42, 1: 71–91.

Rand, Erin J. 2014. *Reclaiming Queer: Activist and Academic Rhetorics of Resistance.* Tuscaloosa, Alabama: University of Alabama Press.

Rankin, Jim, Kristin Rushowy, and Louise Brown. 2013. "Toronto School Suspension Rates Highest for Black and Aboriginal Students." *Toronto Star.* March 22. https://www.thestar.com/news/gta/2013/03/22/toronto_school_suspension_rates_highest_for_black_and_aboriginal_students.html.

Raphael, Dennis, Ann Curry-Stevens, and Toba Bryant. 2008. "Barriers to Addressing the Social Determinants of Health: Insights from the Canadian Experience." *Health Policy* 88, 2: 222–35.

Rava, Julianna, Paul Shattuck, Jessica Rast, and Anne Roux. 2017. "The Prevalence and Correlates of Involvement in the Criminal Justice System among Youth on the Autism Spectrum." *Journal of Autism and Developmental Disorders* 47, 2: 340–46.

Redlich, Allison D., Henry J. Steadman, John Monahan, Pamela Clark Robbins, and John Petrila. 2006. "Patterns of Practice in Mental Health Courts: A National Survey." *Law and Human Behavior* 30, 3: 347–62.

Reid, Shannon. 2017. "Policies of Disability: From Ugly Ordinances to the Disability Rights Movement." In *Disability and U.S. Politics – Participation, Policy, and Controversy.* Volume 1 of *Disability and Political Participation,* edited by Dana Lee Baker, 37–61. Santa Barbara, CA: Praeger Press.

Reid, T.R. 2010. *The Healing of America: A Global Quest for Better, Cheaper and Fairer Health Care.* New York: Penguin Press.

Reiner, Dan. 2017. "New Rochelle Police Get Creative for Autism Awareness." March 13. http://www.lohud.com/story/news/local/westchester/new-rochelle/2017/03/13/new-rochelle-police-autism-awareness/98583384/#&utm_campaign=fbboost.

Reitano, Julie. 2004. "Youth Custody and Community Services in Canada, 2002/2003." *Juristat* 24, 9: 1–20.

Riggs, Fred W. 1980. "The Ecology and Context of Public Administration: A Comparative Perspective." *Public Administration Review* 40, 2: 107–15.

Rios, Victor M. 2011. *Punished: Policing the Lives of Black and Latino Boys.* New York: New York University Press.

Rioux, Marcia, and Anne Carbert. 2003. "Human Rights and Disability: The International Context." *Journal on Developmental Disabilities* 10, 2: 1–13.

Rioux, Marcia, and Michael J. Prince. 2002. "The Canadian Political Landscape of Disability: Policy Perspectives, Social Status, Interest Groups, and the Rights Movement." In *Federalism, Democracy, and Disability Policy in Canada,* edited by Alan Puttee, 11–28. Kingston, ON: McGill-Queen's University Press.

Ritzer, George. 2004. *Handbook of Social Problems: A Comparative International Perspective.* Thousand Oaks, CA: Sage.

Roberge, Marie-Élène. 2013. "A Multi-Level Conceptualization of Empathy to Explain How Diversity Increases Group Performance." *International Journal of Business and Management* 8, 3: 122–33.

Roberts, Dorothy, and Sujatha Jesudason. 2013." Movement Intersectionality: The Case of Race, Gender, Disability, and Genetic Technologies." *Du Bois Review: Social Science Research on Race* 10, 2: 313–28.

Roberts, Julian V. 2004. "Public Opinion and Youth Justice." *Crime and Justice* 31: 495–542.

Robinson, Louise, Michael D. Spencer, Lindsay D.G. Thomson, Andrew C. Stanfield, David G.C. Owens, Jeremy Hall, and Eve C. Johnstone. 2012. "Evaluation of a

Screening Instrument for Autism Spectrum Disorders in Prisoners." *PLoS ONE* 7: e36078. https://doi.org/10.1371/journal.pone.0036078.

Robinson, Rowand T., and Mary Jane K. Rapport. 1999. "Providing Special Education in the Juvenile Justice System." *Remedial and Special Education* 20, 1: 19–35.

Rossman, Shelli B., Janeen Buck Willison, Kamala Mallik-Kane, KiDeuik Kim, Sara Debus-Sherrill, and D. Mitchell Downey. 2012. "Criminal Justice Interventions for Offenders with Mental Illness: An Evaluation of Mental Health Courts in Bronx and Brooklyn, New York." National Institute of Justice. https://www.ncjrs.gov/pdffiles1/nij/grants/238264.pdf.

Roth, Alisa. 2018. "A Worried Mom Wanted the Police to Take Mentally Ill Son to Hospital." *The Big Idea*, May 30. https://www.vox.com/the-big-idea/2018/5/30/17406900/police-shootings-mental-illness-book-vidal-vassey-mental-health.

Rothman, David J. 1980. *Conscience and Convenience: The Asylum and Its Alternatives in Progressive America*. New York: Aldine de Gruyter.

Ruck, Martin D., and Scot Wortley. 2002. "Racial and Ethnic Minority High School Students' Perceptions of School Disciplinary Practices: A Look at Some Canadian Findings." *Journal of Youth and Adolescence* 31, 3: 185–95.

Ruiz-Casares, Mónica, Nico Trocmé, and Barbara Fallon. 2012. "Supervisory Neglect and Risk of Harm. Evidence from the Canadian Child Welfare System." *Child Abuse and Neglect* 36, 6: 471–80.

Rutherford, R. B., Michael Bullis, Cindy W. Anderson, and Heather M. Griller-Clark. 2002. *Youth with Disabilities in the Correctional System: Prevalence Rates and Identification Issues*. Washington, DC: Office of Juvenile Justice and Delinquency Prevention.

Salem-Keizer System. 2017. "Student Threat Assessment." http://www.studentthreatassessment.org/home.

Salseda, Lindsay M., Dennis R. Dixon, Tracy Fass, Deborah Miora, and Robert A. Leark. 2011. "An Evaluation of *Miranda* Rights and Interrogation in Autism Spectrum Disorders." *Research in Autism Spectrum Disorders* 5, 1: 79–85.

Sampson, Robert J., and John H. Laub. 2003. "Life Course Desisters? Trajectories of Crime among Delinquent Boys Followed to Age 70." *Criminology* 41, 3: 555–92.

—. 2016. "Turning Points and the Future of Life-Course Criminology: Reflections on the 1986 Criminal Careers Report." *Journal of Research in Crime and Delinquency* 53, 3: 321–35.

Sampson, Robert J., Stephen W. Raudenbush, and Felton Earls. 1997. "Neighborhoods and Violent Crime: A Multilevel Study of Collective Efficacy." *Science* 277, 5328: 918–24.

Sattler, Ann L. 2017. "Treating Youths in the Juvenile Justice System." *Pediatric Clinics of North America* 64, 2: 451–62.

Schneider, Anne. 2012. *Deterrence and Juvenile Crime: Results from a National Policy Experiment*. New York: Springer-Verlag.

Schoen, Cathy, David C. Radley, Pamela Riley, Jacob Lippa, Julia Berenson, Cara Dermody, and Anthony Shih. 2013. "Health Care in the Two Americas: Findings from the Scorecard on State Health System Performance for Low-Income Populations, 2013." September 13. New York: Commonwealth Fund.

Schuknecht, Cat. 2018. "School Where Student with Autism Died Violated State Regulations." *National Public Radio*, December 9, https://www.npr.org/2018/12/09/675145052/school-where-student-with-autism-died-violated-state-regulations-officials-say.

Schwalbe, Craig S. 2007. "Risk Assessment for Juvenile Justice: A Meta-Analysis." *Law and Human Behavior* 31, 5: 449–62.
—. 2008. "A Meta-Analysis of Juvenile Justice Risk Assessment Instruments Predictive Validity by Gender." *Criminal Justice and Behavior* 35, 11: 1367–81.
Schwalbe, Craig S., and Tina Maschi. 2010. "Patterns of Contact and Cooperation between Juvenile Probation Officers and Parents of Youthful Offenders." *Journal of Offender Rehabilitation* 49, 6: 398–416.
Scotch, Richard K. 1984. *From Good Will to Civil Rights: Transforming Federal Disability Policy.* Temple University Press: Philadelphia, PA.
—. 2001. "American Disability Policy in the Twentieth Century." In *The New Disability History: American Perspectives,* edited by Paul K. Longmore and Lauri Umansky, 375–92. New York: New York University Press.
Scott, Elizabeth S., and Laurence Steinberg. 2008. "Adolescent Development and the Regulation of Youth Crime," *The Future of Children* 8: 15–33.
Scully, Brian, and Judy Finlay. 2015. *Cross-Over Youth: Care to Custody.* Toronto: Cross-Over Youth Committee. March. https://docplayer.net/64549375-Cross-over-youth-care-to-custody.html.
Seligman, Martin E.P. 2004. *Authentic Happiness: Using the New Positive Psychology to Realize Your Potential for Lasting Fullfillment.* New York: Atria Books.
Shapiro, Joseph. 1994. *No Pity: People with Disabilities Forging a New Civil Rights Movement.* New York: Broadway Books.
Sharpe, Deanna L., and Dana L. Baker. 2011. "The Financial Side of Autism: Private and Public Costs." In A Comprehensive Book on Autism Spectrum Disorders, edited by Mohammad-Reza Mohammadi, 275–96. InTech. Accessed on February 21, 2020. http://www.intechopen.com/books/a-comprehensive-book-on-autismspectrum-disorders/the-financial-side-of-autism-private-and-public-costs.
Shaver, Kelly. 2012. *The Attribution of Blame: Causality, Responsibility, and Blameworthiness.* New York: Springer-Verlag.
Shipps, Dorothy. 2008. "Urban Regime Theory and the Reform of Public Schools: Governance, Power, and Leadership." In *Handbook of Education Politics and Policy,* edited by Bruce S. Cooper, James G. Cibulka, and Lance D. Fusarelli, 89–108. New York: Taylor and Francis.
Shirk, Martha. 2009. "Unjust Medicine: Why Health Care in Juvenile Facilities is Often Atrocious, and What's Being Done about It." *Youth Today.* July 31. https://www.centerforhealthjournalism.org/fellowships/projects/health-care-juvenile-detention-centers.
Shulman, Elizabeth P., Laurence D. Steinberg, and Alex R. Piquero. 2013. "The Age–Crime Curve in Adolescence and Early Adulthood is not Due to Age Differences in Economic Status." *Journal of Youth and Adolescence* 42, 6: 848–60.
Sickmund, Melissa, and Charles Puzzanchera, eds. 2014. "Juvenile Offenders and Victims: 2014 National Report." National Center for Juvenile Justice. https://www.ojjdp.gov/ojstatbb/nr2014/downloads/NR2014.pdf.
Sickmund, Melissa, T.J. Sladky, and W. Kang. 2017. "Easy Access to Juvenile Court Statistics: 1985–2014." http://ojjdp.gov/ojstatbb/ezajcs/.
Silberman, Steve. 2016. *Neurotribes: The Legacy of Autism and the Future of Neurodiversity.* New York: Penguin Random House.
Sinclair, Mary F., Sandra L. Christenson, and Martha L. Thurlow. 2005. "Promoting School Completion of Urban Secondary Youth with Emotional or Behavioral Disabilities." *Exceptional Children* 71, 4: 465–82.

Skenazy, Lenore. 2010. *Free-Range Kids, How to Raise Safe, Self-Reliant Children (without Going Nuts with Worry)*. San Francisco: Jossey-Bass.

Skowyra, Kathleen R., and Joseph J. Cocozza. 2007. *Blueprint for Change: A Comprehensive Model for the Identification and Treatment of Youth with Mental Health Needs in Contact with the Juvenile Justice System*. Delmar, NY: National Center for Mental Health and Juvenile Justice Policy Research Associates.

Smart911. 2018. "How It Works." Accessed on February 21, 2020. https://safety.smart911.com/#smart911.

Smith, Phil. 2005. "'There Is No Treatment Here': Disability and Health Needs in a State Prison System." *Disability Studies Quarterly* 25, 3: 1–18.

Sneed, Tierney. 2015. "School Resource Officer: Safety Priority or Part of the Problem?" *US News*, January 30. https://www.usnews.com/news/articles/2015/01/30/are-school-resource-officers-part-of-the-school-to-prison-pipeline-problem.

Société Canadienne de Pédiatrie. 2005. "Les Normes de Santé pour les Jeunes en Éstablissement de Detention." *Paediatric Child Health* 10, 5: 290–92.

Sommers, Benjamin D., and C. David Naylor. 2017. "Medicaid Block Grants and Federalism: Lessons from Canada." *Journal of the American Medical Association* 317, 16: 1619–20.

Sommers, Benjamin D., Munira Z. Gunja, Kenneth Finegold, and Thomas Musco. 2015. "Changes in Self-Reported Insurance Coverage, Access to Care, and Health under the Affordable Care Act." *Journal of the American Medical Association* 314, 4: 366–74.

Sprague, Joey, and Diane Kobrynowicz. 2006. "A Feminist Epistemology." In *Handbook of the Sociology of Gender*, edited by Janet Saltzman Chafetz, 25–43. New York: Springer.

Stafford, Mark C. 1995. "Children's Legal Rights in the US." *Marriage and Family Review* 21, 3–4: 121–40.

Statistics Canada, Correctional Services Program. 2016. "Youth Correctional Statistics in Canada, 2014/2015." *Juristat: Canadian Centre for Justice Statistics*: 4–15. https://www.statcan.gc.ca/pub/85-002-x/2016001/article/14317-eng.htm.

Stearns, Linda Brewster, and Paul D. Almeida. 2004. "The Formation of State Actor-Social Movement Coalitions and Favorable Policy Outcomes." *Social Problems* 51, 4: 478–504.

Steele, Eurídice Martínez, Larissa Galastri Baraldi, Maria Laura da Costa Louzada, Jean-Claude Moubarac, Dariush Mozaffarian, and Carlos Augusto Monteiro. 2016. "Ultra-Processed Foods and Added Sugars in the US Diet: Evidence from a Nationally Representative Cross-Sectional Study." *BMJ Open* 6, 3: 1–8.

Steinberg, Laurence. 2008. "Introducing the Issue." *The Future of Children* 8: 3–14.

Steinberg, Laurence, He Len Chung, and Michelle Little. 2004. "Reentry of Young Offenders from the Justice System: A Developmental Perspective." *Youth Violence and Juvenile Justice* 2, 1: 21–38.

Stenehjem, Pam. 2005. "Youth with Disabilities in the Juvenile Justice System: Prevention and Intervention Strategies." *Examining Current Challenges in Secondary Education and Transition: Issue Brief* 4: 1–5.

Stienstra, Deborah. 2003. "Listen, Really Listen, to Us." In *Making Equality: History of Advocacy and Persons with Disabilities in Canada*, edited by Deborah Stienstra and Aileen Wight-Felske, 33–47. Concord, Ontario: Captus Press.

Stone, Clarence N. 1998. "Regime Analysis and the Study of Urban Politics, a Rejoinder." *Journal of Urban Affairs* 20, 3: 249–60.

Strand, Lauren Rose. 2017. "Charting Relations between Intersectionality Theory and the Neurodiversity Paradigm." *Disability Studies Quarterly* 37, 2: 1–23.

Suarez, Lanette. 2016. "Restraints, Seclusion, and the Disabled Student: The Blurred Lines between Safety and Physical Punishment." *University of Miami Law Review* 71: 859–94.

Sugie, Naomi F., and Kristin Turney. 2017. "Beyond Incarceration: Criminal Justice Contact and Mental Health." *American Sociological Review* 82, 4: 719–43.

Suitts, Steve. 2014. *Just Learning: The Imperative to Transform the Juvenile Justice Systems into an Effective Educational Systems*. Atlanta: Southern Education Foundation.

Sutter, John D. 2009. "Columbine Massacre Changed School Security." *CNN*. April 20. http://www.cnn.com/2009/LIVING/04/20/columbine.school.safety/index.html?iref=24hours.

Taylor, Luke E., Amy L. Swerdfeger, and Guy D. Eslick. 2014. "Vaccines Are Not Associated with Autism: An Evidence-Based Meta-Analysis of Case-Control and Cohort Studies." *Vaccine* 32, 29: 3623–29.

Taylor, Melanie, Scott H. Decker, and Charles Katz. 2013. "Consent Decrees and Juvenile Corrections in Arizona: What Happens When Oversight Ends?" *JRSA Forum* 31: 1–5.

Teplin, Linda A., Karen M. Abram, Gary M. McClelland, Jason J. Washburn, and Ann K. Pikus. 2005. "Detecting Mental Disorder in Juvenile Detainees: Who Receives Services." *American Journal of Public Health* 95, 10: 1773–80.

Theriot, Matthew T. 2009. "School Resource Officers and the Criminalization of Student Behavior." *Journal of Criminal Justice* 37, 3: 280–87.

Thinking Person's Guide to Autism. 2017. "What Happens to Autistic People in Prison?" http://www.thinkingautismguide.com/search?q=Feltham.

Thompson, Carleen, and Anna Stewart. 2006. *Review of Empirically-Based Risk/Needs Assessment Tools for Youth Justice: Amended Report for Public Release*. Southport, Queensland, Australia: Griffith University Press. https://www.researchgate.net/profile/Carleen_Thompson/publication/311768274_Review_of_empirically_based_riskneeds_assessment_tools_for_youth_justice_Amended_report_for_public_release/links/5859c42908ae3852d2559cc8.pdf.

Thompson, Kristin C., and Richard J. Morris. 2016. *Juvenile Delinquency and Disability*. Advancing Responsible Adolescent Development Series, edited by Roger J.R. Levesque. Switzerland: Springer International.

Tint, Ami, Anna M. Palucka, Elspeth Bradley, Jonathan A. Weiss, and Yona Lunsky. 2017. "Correlates of Police Involvement among Adolescents and Adults with Autism Spectrum Disorder." *Journal of Autism and Developmental Disorders* 47, 9: 2639–47.

Tint, Ami, and Jonathan A. Weiss. 2016. "Family Wellbeing of Individuals with Autism Spectrum Disorder: A Scoping Review." *Autism* 20, 3: 262–75.

Towle, Helena. 2015. *Disability and Inclusion in Canadian Education: Policy, Procedure, and Practice*. Canadian Centre for Policy Alternatives. June.

Trent, James W. 2016. *Inventing the Feeble Mind: A History of Intellectual Disability in the United States*. Oxford: Oxford University Press.

Tulman, Joseph B. 2003. "Disability and Delinquency: How Failures to Identify, Accommodate, and Serve Youth with Education-Related Disabilities Lead to Their Disproportionate Representation in the Delinquency System." *Whittier Journal of Children and Family Advocacy* 3: 3–76.

Twomey, Katherine. 2008. "The Right to Education in Juvenile Detention under State Constitutions." *Virginia Law Review* 94, 3: 766–801.

Tyler, Tracey." 2008. Parents Vow to Keep Up Autism Fight: Families Plan Next Steps in Battle for Better Services after Supreme Court Refuses to Hear Their Appeal." *Toronto Star*. December 5. https://www.thestar.com/news/canada/2008/12/05/parents_vow_to_keep_up_autism_fight.html.

United Nations General Assembly. 1949. "Universal Declaration of Human Rights." Adopted 10 December 1948. http://www.jus.uio.no/lm/un.universal.declaration.of.human.rights.1948/portrait.a4.pdf.

United States Department of Education. n.d. "About ED: What We Do." https://www2.ed.gov/about/what-we-do.html.

United States Department of Justice. 2016. "Guide to Procurements under DOJ Grants and Cooperative Agreements." *Office of Justice Programs*. https://www.ojp.gov/funding/Implement/Resources/GuideToProcurementProcedures.pdf.

United States Departments of Education and Justice. 2014. *Guiding Principles for Providing High-Quality Education in Juvenile Justice Secure Care Settings*. Washington, DC: US Government Printing Office.

United States Government Accountability Office. 2018. *Discipline Disparities for Black Students, Boys, and Students with Disabilities*. March. https://www.gao.gov/assets/700/690828.pdf.

University of British Columbia. n.d. "What is Applied Behaviour Analysis (ABA)." https://ecps.educ.ubc.ca/special-education/behaviour-analyst-certification/.

Unruh, Deanne K., Jeff M. Gau, and Miriam G. Waintrup. 2009. "An Exploration of Factors Reducing Recidivism Rates of Formerly Incarcerated Youth with Disabilities Participating in a Re-entry Intervention." *Journal of Child and Family Studies* 18, 3: 284–93.

Unruh, Deanne, and Michael Bullis. 2005. "Facility-to-Community Transition Needs for Adjudicated Youth with Disabilities." *Career Development for Exceptional Individuals* 28, 2: 67–79.

Van Dreal, John. 2011. *Assessing Student Threats: A Handbook for Implementing the Salem-Keizer System*. Blue Ridge Summit, PA: Rowan and Littlefield Education.

Van Montfort, Kees Van, Johan H.L. Oud, and Albert Satorra, eds. 2010. *Longitudinal Research with Latent Variables*. New York: Springer Science and Business Media.

Van Ness, Daniel, Gabrielle Maxwell, and Allison Morris. 2003. "Introducing Restorative Justice." In *Restorative Justice for Juveniles Conferencing, Mediation and Circles*, edited by Gabrielle Maxwell and Allison Morris, 3–16. London: Hart.

Vance, J. D. *Hillbilly Elegy: A Memoir of a Family and Culture in Crisis*. London: William Collins, 2016.

Varma, Kimberly N. 2007. "Parental Involvement in Youth Court." *Canadian Journal of Criminology and Criminal Justice* 49, 2: 231–60.

Vieira, Tracey A., Tracey A. Skilling, and Michele Peterson-Badali. 2009. "Matching Court-Ordered Services with Treatment Needs: Predicting Treatment Success with Young Offenders." *Criminal Justice and Behavior* 36, 4: 385–401.

Vincent, Gina M., Thomas Grisso, Anna Terry, and Steven Banks. 2008. "Sex and Race Differences in Mental Health Symptoms in Juvenile Justice: The MAYSI-2 National Meta-Analysis." *Journal of the American Academy of Child and Adolescent Psychiatry* 47, 3: 282–90.

Vito, Gennaro F., and Julie Kunselman. 2011. *Juvenile Justice Today*. New York: Pearson.

Vitopoulos, Nina A., Michele Peterson-Badali, and Tracey A. Skilling. 2012. "The Relationship between Matching Service to Criminogenic Need and Recidivism in Male and Female Youth Examining the RNR Principles in Practice." *Criminal Justice and Behavior* 39, 8: 1025–41.

Wagner, Peter, and Bernadette Rabuy. 2017. "Mass Incarceration: The Whole Pie 2017." *Prison Policy Initiative*, March 14. Accessed on February 21, 2020. http://www.antoniocasella.e/nume/Wagner_Rabuy_14mar17.pdf.

Wald, Johanna, and Daniel J. Losen. 2003. "Defining and Redirecting a School to Prison Pipeline." *New Directions for Student Leadership 2003*, 99: 9–15.

Walker, Sarah Cusworth. 2016. "Juvenile Justice System Should Morph into Surrogate Grandparent, Not Parent." *Juvenile Justice Information Exchange*. July 27. http://jjie.org/2016/07/27/juvenile-justice-system-should-morph-into-surrogate-grandparent-not-parent/.

Walker, Sarah Cusworth, Ann Muno, and Cheryl Sullivan-Colglazier. 2015. "Principles in Practice: A Multistate Study of Gender-Responsive Reforms in the Juvenile Justice System." *Crime and Delinquency* 61, 5: 742–66.

Walker, Sarah Cusworth, Asia Sarah Bishop, Karen Trayler, Ron Jaeger, Steve Gustaveson, and Anne C. Guthrie. 2015. "Impact of Peer Partner Support on Self-Efficacy for Justice-Involved Parents: A Controlled Study of Juvenile Justice 101." *Journal of Child and Family Studies* 24, 5: 443–54.

Warner, Leah R. 2008. "A Best Practices Guide to Intersectional Approaches in Psychological Research." *Sex Roles* 59, 5–6: 454–63.

Warr, Mark. 2002. *Companions in Crime: The Social Aspects of Criminal Conduct*. New York: Cambridge University Press.

Washington Initiative for Supported Employment. "Autism and Employment." 2015. Webinar, Oakville, WA, September 23.

Washington State Criminal Justice Training Comission. "Juvenile Corrections Personnel Academy-Detention." On December 16, 2019. https://www.cjtc.wa.gov/training-education/juvenile-corrections-personnel-academy.

Waslander, Sietske. 2007. "Mass Customization in Schools: Strategies Dutch Secondary Schools Pursue to Cope with the Diversity-Efficiency Dilemma." *Journal of Education Policy* 22, 4: 363–82.

Wasserman, Gail A., Kate Keenan, Richard E. Tremblay, John D. Cole, Todd I. Herrenkohl, Rolf Loeber, and David Petechuk. 2003. "Risk and Protective Factors of Child Delinquency." *Child Delinquency Bulletin Series*, April: 1–14. Accessed on February 21, 2020. https://cops.usdoj.gov/html/cd_rom/sro/FinalCDPubs/RiskFactorsChildDelinq.pdf.

Webster, Cheryl Marie, and Anthony N. Doob. 2007. "Punitive Trends and Stable Imprisonment Rates in Canada." *Crime and Justice* 36, 1: 297–369.

Weiler, Spencer C., and Martha Cray. 2011. "Police at School: A Brief History and Current Status of School Resource Officers." *The Clearing House: A Journal of Educational Strategies, Issues and Ideas* 84, 4: 160–63.

Weinrath, Michael, Gavin Donatelli, and Melanie J. Murchison. 2016. "Mentorship: A Missing Piece to Manage Juvenile Intensive Supervision Programs and Youth Gangs?" *Canadian Journal of Criminology and Criminal Justice* 58, 3: 291–321.

Wexler, David B. 2010. "Therapeutic Jurisprudence and Its Application to Criminal Justice Research and Development." *Irish Probation Journal* 7: 94–107.

Wiener, Richard L., and Eve M. Brank. 2015. *Problem Solving Courts*. New York: Springer.

Wijen, Frank, and Shahzad Ansari. 2007. "Overcoming Inaction through Collective Institutional Entrepreneurship: Insights from Regime Theory." *Organization Studies* 28, 7: 1079–100.

Winn, Maisha T., and Nadia Behizadeh. 2011. "The Right to Be Literate: Literacy, Education, and the School-to-Prison Pipeline." *Review of Research in Education* 35, 1: 147–73.

Winter, Jerry Alan. 2003. "The Development of the Disability Rights Movement as a Social Problem Solver." *Disability Studies Quarterly* 23, 1: 1–28.

Wolbring, Gregor, and Kalie Mosig. 2017. "Autism in the News: Content Analysis of Autism Coverage in Canadian Newspapers." *Disability and US Politics: Participation, Policy, and Controversy:* 63–94.

Wordes, Madeline, Timothy S. Bynum, and Charles J. Corley. 1994. "Locking up Youth: The Impact of Race on Detention Decisions." *Journal of Research in Crime and Delinquency* 31, 2: 149–65.

World Health Organization. 2017. *World Health Statistics 2017: Monitoring Health for the SDGs Sustainable Development Goals*. New York: World Health Organization.

Woshinsky, Oliver H. 2008. *Explaining Politics: Culture, Institutions, and Political Behavior*. New York: Routledge.

Younhee, Kim, and Byron E. Price. 2012. "Revisiting Prison Privatization: An Examination of the Magnitude of Prison Privatization." *Administration and Society* 46, 3: 255–75.

Zhang, Dalun, Hsien-Yuan Hsu, Antonis Katsiyannis, David E. Barrett, and Song Ju. 2011. "Adolescents with Disabilities in the Juvenile Justice System: Patterns of Recidivism." *Exceptional Children* 77, 3: 283–98.

Zheng, Samuel, and Stefanie DeJesus. 2017. *Expulsion Decision-Making Process and Expelled Students' Transition Experience in the Toronto District School Board's Care and Safe School Program and Their Graduation Outcomes (Research Report No. 16/17–15)*. Toronto: Toronto District School Board.

Zitomer, Michelle Ruth. 2016. "Creating Inclusive Elementary School Dance Education Environments." PhD diss., University of Alberta.

Zolyomi, Annuska, and Joseph T. Tennis. 2017. "Autism Prism: A Domain Analysis Examining Neurodiversity." *NASKO* 6, 1: 139–72.

Index

ableism, 4–6, 43, 48–49, 54, 59, 71–72, 100, 104, 131–32, 167, 176–77, 181
Aboriginal populations (Canada), 19, 114, 139–40
Abrams, Marcus, 56
Accessibility for Ontarians with Disabilities Act, 67
actus reus, 28–29
Alexander S. v Boyd, 122
American Medical Association, 80
Americans with Disabilities Act of 1990, 37, 145
Andre H. v Sobol, 125
Andrew (case study), 29–30
arraignment. *See* juvenile court, client flow
arrest, 49–52
ASD Nest, 106
assessments, 88–92; evidence-based practice (RNR) model, 90–91, 147–48, 170–73
attorney: defense, 65; prosecution, 52–53
Autism Nova Scotia, 58
Autism Spectrum Disorder (autism) (ASD), 4, 29–30, 38, 41, 47, 48–49, 54, 64, 75, 96, 110, 128, 130–31, 149, 163, 173; Applied Behavioral Analysis (ABA), 39, 163; comorbidity, 84–85; court processing, 46–47, 64–65; diagnosis, 9–12; first responder training, 69–70; history, 9–12; identity language, 5–9; medical model, 156–57; risk of police contact, 52–53; Tourette's Syndrome, 117
Auton v British Columbia, 38, 41, 78

Baker Act, 111. *See also* juvenile detention
Becker, Howard, 26
Black Lives Matter, 139. *See also* police
Breakfast Club, 179
Breed v Jones, 23
Breivik, Anders, 48
Bryant, Martin, 48

Caltagirone, Tom, 97
Canada Elections Act, 36
Canada Health Act, 78

Canada Pension Plan Disability, 77
Canadian Association for Community Living (CACL), 34
capacity hearing, 29–30
Caring and Safe Schools Policy, 114, 116–17
Charter of Rights and Freedoms, 19, 24, 36, 37, 39, 54–55, 78, 105, 145
Children's Health Insurance Program (CHIP), 79, 82
civil rights movement, 43
Civil War, 22
Clark County, Washington, Juvenile Court, 94
Columbine High School, 102
Constitution Act of 1867, 105
Corrections and Conditional Release Act, 87
Cottrell, William, 48
Council of Canadians with Disabilities (CCD), 34, 36
courts, 60–66; mental health caseloads, 92–94; therapeutic, 66–69
Crisis Intervention Team (CIT), 57

Dahmer, Jeffrey, 48
Daniel R.R. v State Board of Education, 40
Department of Justice Canada, 20–21, 31
Descartes, Rene, 85
Diagnostic and Statistical Manual of Mental Disorders (DSM), 9–10, 48
diminished capacity, 28–30
disability, 52–53, 59, 110; policy subsystems, 71–72, 155–56, 163; rights movement 32–37, 138–39 (*see* civil rights movement); social construction, 4–5, 11–12, 34–35, 142, 181 (*see Diagnostic and Statistical Manual of Mental Disorders* [DSM]); victimization risk, 98
diversion, 66–69, 111; mandatory, 66–67
doli incapax, 20, 30, 43
Drug Abuse Resistance Education (DARE), 103

due process, 23, 24–31; disability, 48–49; revolution, 43–44

Eaton v Brant County Board of Education, 38
education, 102–4; "each belongs" statement, 107; inclusion, 104–6; juvenile detention, 120–26; special, Canada, 106–8; special, United States, 108–12; special and restraint, 111–12, 123
Education for All Handicapped Children Act, 40. *See also* education
Education Amendment Act (Bill 82), 107
Elementary and Secondary Education Act of 1965, 109. *See also* education
empathy. *See* juvenile court
English Poor Laws, 33
essentialist. *See* ableism
Estelle v Gamble, 85
ethnocentrism, 49–55, 57, 59, 66, 69, 71, 73
evidence-based practice. *See* assessments

First Nations, 123, 180. *See also* Aboriginal populations (Canada)
fiscal federalism, 81–82
Free and Public Education (FAPE), 40, 109–10. *See also* Individuals with Disabilities in Education Act of 1990 (IDEA) (United States)
Fresh Start Program, 114

Galloway, Joseph, and whistleblower, 23
General Equivalency Degree (GED), 124–25, 165
Graham v Florida, 23

Harper, Stephen, 14, 28, 142
health care, 75–76; autism, 83; Canada, 76–79; empathy, 95–98; juvenile detention, 84–92; United States, 79–84; wait times, 77–79, 83, 163

In a Different Key, 9
In re Gault, 23, 25
In re Winship, 23
inclusion, 4, 34–99, 43, 53–54, 68, 79–80, 94, 107–8, 132, 138, 177, 181, 184; education (*see* education)
Individualized Education Plan (IEP), 40, 110, 122, 124–26
Individuals with Disabilities in Education Act of 1990 (IDEA) (United States), 40–43, 83, 105, 109–10, 125–26; Section 504, 53–54
intersectionality, 13–16, 53, 114–16, 128, 133, 180; juvenile detention (*see* juvenile detention); policy recommendations, 179–82; theory (*see* theory)

Johnson, Lyndon B., 109
Johnson v Upchurch, 125
juvenile, 12–13; age of majority, 51–52; crime rates, 49–51; delinquency paradox, 170–72; due process rights (*see* due process)
juvenile court, 26–32, 30, 31, 43; client flow, Canada and the United States, 54–69; empathy, 95–98; family stakeholders, 178–79; gender-responsive programming, 137; learning disabilities, 119; legal authority, 20, 22–23; parental involvement challenges, 64; processing, 26–27, 54–66; trials, 69–71
Juvenile Delinquents Act of 1908, 20–21
juvenile detention, 51, 59, 60–61, 75, 130–36, 139–40, 145–47, 151; community re-entry (*see* transitioning to community); costs, 135; crossover youth, 164; guidelines (*Juvenile Justice and Delinquency Prevention Act of 2002*), 134–35; intersectionality, 136–40, 154; neurodiversity, 138–40; proportionality, 143–44; residential placement, 132–36; services available, 145–50
Juvenile Detention Alternatives Initiative (JDAI), 24

Kaczynski, Ted, 48
Kent v United States, 23, 24
Kushniruk, Donald, 68

Lanza, Adam, 48
Latson, Reginald "Neli," 71
Least Restrictive Environment (LRE), 40, 65, 110. *See also* Individuals with Disabilities in Education Act of 1990 (IDEA) (United States)
LGBTIA+, 138

McKeiver v Pennsylvania, 26
Medicaid. *See* health care, United States
Medicare. *See* health care, Canada; health care, United States
mens rea, 27–30, 144
Miller v Alabama, 23
Moore v British Columbia, 38

Napper, Robert, 48
National Autistic Society (NAS), 149–50; Feltham Juvenile Prison, 150
National Council on Disability, 37
neurodiversity, 4, 11–12, 17, 54, 65, 69, 73, 75, 104, 108, 128, 131–32, 138, 167, 169, 177–78; first responders, 56–60; health care, 97–100; juvenile detention, 138–40; policy recommendations; 181–88; regime theory, 155–57; theory (*see* theory)
Neurotribes, 9
No Child Left Behind (NCLB), 109
not criminally responsible on account of mental disorder (NCRMD). *See* diminished capacity

Obama, Barack, 23, 81
Obamacare. *See* Patient Protection and Affordable Care Act (ACA)

Obstacles, 35, 106
Office of Special Education and Rehabilitative Services (OSERS). *See* police, autism training
Ohio State Bar Foundation, 66
Ozeki, Colin, 106

Painsley, Omar, 86
parens patriae, 22–23, 31, 43
Pate v Robinson, 28
Patient Protection and Affordable Care Act (ACA). *See* health care, United States
Personal Information Protection and Electronic Documents Act, 59
police, 48, 54–60; Autism Patch Challenge, 60; autism training, 69–70; Smart 911, 59; wallet card, 58
policy, and autism, and comparative analysis, 16–17, 83; disability policy subsystems (*see* disability); entrepreneurs, 49, 57; framework, 49; subsystems, 4, 19, 71, 98, 155, 185
Preventing Harmful Restraint and Seclusion in School Act, 112
Privacy Act, Canada, 59
Progressive Era, 20, 22–23, 33, 52, 80
proportionality, 30; juvenile detention (*see* juvenile detention); "just deserts" (*see* theory, retributive justice); punishment (*lex talionis*), 140

Reilly, Nicky, 48
Report of the Department of Justice Committee on Juvenile Delinquency, 31
research questions, 3–4
Rethink Discipline, 128
Riggs, Fred, 72
rights, disability 32–37; negative, 26; positive, 26, 76; Second World War, 33–34
risk assessments. *See* assessments
Roberts, John, 126

Roosevelt, Franklin, D., 80
Roosevelt, Theodore, 80
Roper v Simmons, 23, 27
Royal Mounted Canadian Police (RCMP), 57–58

Salem-Keizer Public School. *See* Student Threat Assessment Model
school-to-prison pipeline, 102–3, 111, 113–16, 120, 128; *Gun-Free Schools Act*, 117; zero-tolerance policy, 116–19
school resource officer (SRO), 51, 103–4, 117, 128, 179. *See also* school-to-prison pipeline
Smith v Wheaton, 126
Social Security Act of 1935, 80
Spurell, Dane, 56
Student Threat Assessment Model, 117–19
Supreme Court of the United States, 24

theory, 16–17; ableism (see ableism); attribution, 144–45; deterrence, 140–42; developmental, 157–58; differential treatment, 120; "just deserts," 143; intersectionality, 138–39; life course theory, 158–60; neurodiversity, 138; punctuated equilibrium, 49, 53–54; regime, 17, 77, 83–84, 154–57; restorative justice, 24, 31–32, 63, 114, 154, 167; retributive justice, 140, 143; school failure, 119; standpoint, 141–42; susceptibility, 119–20
transition from juvenile detention (re-entry), 120, 127, 153–54, 160–62, 171–74; in Canada, 162–64; Cognitive Behavioural Therapy (CBT), 172–73; family supports, 167–70; RENEW, 165; SUPPORT, 165–66; in United States, 164–66; wraparound services, 167
Trudeau, Justin, 14
Trump, Donald, 81

Index

United Nations, 31, 32–33, 39; Convention on the Rights of the Child, 39, 104; Convention on the Rights of Persons with Disabilities, 39; Declaration on the Rights of Disabled Persons, 32–33, 39; International Year of Disabled Persons, 33, 35; Special Committee on the Disabled and the Handicapped, 35; Universal Declaration of Human Rights, 31; World Programme of Action Considering Disabled Persons, 33

Young Offenders Act, 20–21, 31
Youth Criminal Justice Act (YCJA), Canada, 21, 62–64, 133–34, 139, 142, 173